THE
MISSION
STATEMENT
BOOK

"Mission statement work is the single most important work because the decisions made there affect all other decisions. In addition to giving 301 real company examples, this contains many excellent suggestions on the characteristics and processes of producing outstanding mission statements."

—DR. STEPHEN R. COVEY, author of
The 7 Habits of Highly Effective People

THE MISSION STATEMENT BOOK

REVISED

◆

301

Corporate Mission Statements from America's Top Companies

◆

Jeffrey Abrahams

Ten Speed Press
Berkeley, California

The inclusion of these mission statements is not intended to convey business information to be relied upon in generating business statements or in making business decisions. Ten Speed Press does not explicitly or implicitly offer any representation or warranty that these mission statements will be of use in forming a business conclusion. People read these at their own risk.

A Kirsty Melville Book

Ten Speed Press
PO Box 7123
Berkeley, CA 94707
www.tenspeed.com

Cover Design by Libby Oda
Interior Design by Margery Cantor
Design Implementation by Jeff Brandenburg/ImageComp

Distributed in Australia by Simon and Schuster Australia, in Canada by Ten Speed Press Canada, in New Zealand by Southern Publishing Group, in South Africa by Real Books, and in the United Kingdom and Europe by Airlift Books.

Library of Congress Cataloging-in-Publication Data

Abrahams, Jeffrey.
    The mission statement book : 301 corporate mission statements from America's top companies / Jeffrey Abrahams. — 2nd ed.
        p.   cm.
    ISBN 1-58008-132-0
    1. Mission statements—Authorship.   2. Mission statements—United States.
I. Title.   II. Title: 301 corporate mission statements from America's top companies.
III. Title: Three hundred and one corporate mission statements from America's top companies.
HD30.285.A27   1999
658.4'012—dc21   99-23607
                                                                                   CIP

Printed in Canada

4   5   6   7   8   9   10   —   07 06 05 04 03

To my mother,

Betty Jane Abrahams,

and my father,

Harris Sanders Abrahams—

great communicators.

And in memory of Sophie Spungen.

CONTENTS

The Companies and Their Statements, *continued*

The Companies and Their Statements, *continued*

The Companies and Their Statements, *continued*

The Companies and Their Statements, *continued*

The Companies and Their Statements, *continued*

The Companies and Their Statements, *continued*

The Companies and Their Statements, *continued*

The Companies and Their Statements, *continued*

The Companies and Their Statements, *continued*

The Companies and Their Statements, *continued*

ACKNOWLEDGMENTS

THIS BOOK COULD not have been written without the help of at least four hundred people.

Behind each of the more than 300 companies represented in these pages, there is at least one patient soul who responded to my letters, phone calls, and faxes over a period of three years. At some companies, I spoke or corresponded with as many as four and five different representatives in order to receive a copy of the latest mission statement and corporate data and to secure a legal release form. Listing all of these people would trivialize their importance to this project. But as you read through this book, you should know that although my name is on the cover, hundreds of other people have passed the information along to your hands.

I also had enormous help from friends and associates close to home—and computer.

First, my thanks to Phil Wood and Kirsty Melville at Ten Speed Press for embracing this project and welcoming me to their world. I'm enormously grateful to my editors Lorena Jones and Holly A. Taines, who ushered me through the process of turning an unwieldy manuscript into a book. And thanks to my agent Michael Katz for making the connection with Ten Speed Press.

For helping me with the mountain of details required to gather and assemble all the information presented here, I'm grateful to Chris Ackerman, Karen Zukor, Robin Wirthlin, Cecile Lozano, Cheryl and Jillian and Eric Olsen, Kim Pipkin, Kate Peterson, and Marc Greenberg.

Without the computer skills, generosity, and steady hand on the mouse provided by Richard Ackley, I simply could not have tackled the enormous task of assembling and massaging the database that gave birth to this manuscript.

For providing crucial support throughout the years of research and writing, I'm grateful to Bill McCoy, Elizabeth Peek, Mary Cooper, Peter Anastos and Claudia Falconet, Susan Page, Tana and Michael Powell, Denise Powell, and Susan Fassberg. Thanks also to my colleagues at

Ketchum Advertising, especially Christopher Jones, Leonard Pardoe, and Patrick Feely.

Research for this book was made possible with the help of the staff of the Alameda County Business Library, the Rockridge Branch of the Oakland Public Library, and the library at the Mechanics' Institute of San Francisco.

Finally, my thanks to all those people at companies all over the country, for doing the hard work of writing the following missions, visions, goals, objectives, creeds, philosophies, and other statements.

INTRODUCTION

"YOU KNOW, I get five or six people in here every week asking me for a book on that, and there's nothing written on the subject."

That's the response I got from the head librarian of the Alameda County Business Library in Oakland, California, in the summer of 1991, when I asked if he had any books on the topic of corporate mission statements. I was astonished by his reply and inspired—there and then—to write the very first book on the topic. I figured if the librarian was getting so many requests for information, there *must* be an audience.

Why was I doing this research in the first place? In May of 1991, I changed jobs. I left Ogilvy & Mather Advertising in San Francisco, where I was a senior copywriter, to accept a position with a competitor down the street, Ketchum Advertising.

On my first day of work, I noticed a copy of the company's mission statement posted in the lobby. I was intrigued by Ketchum's corporate mission statement because it seemed so dramatically different from Ogilvy & Mather's, even though both companies are in the same business: large communications companies with advertising and public relations divisions at offices across the country and around the world.

I started asking friends to send me copies of the mission statements for their companies. Some companies had them, some didn't. The more examples I saw, the more intrigued I became. So, I went to my local business library to conduct some research—and had that fateful conversation with the librarian.

Just to be sure the topic hadn't been covered in another medium, the librarian and I checked all the library's resources, including the *Guide to Periodic Literature,* microfilm, and computer files. We discovered there had been no articles written on mission statements either. No how-to-write-one pieces. Nothing in the business magazines. Or business newspapers. Nothing at all.

So I set out with even greater fervor to complete this book.

With more than fifteen years of experience in advertising, including eight years in direct marketing, as well as five years in newspaper journalism, marketing, and promotion, I knew how to put together a direct mail campaign to obtain the information I wanted. I wrote to 2,600 companies requesting a copy of their mission statement along with an annual report and anything else that would help me provide some background information on each company I profiled.

Of the 1,600 companies I queried first—comprised of the *Fortune* 1000, the *Forbes* 500, the companies listed in the book *The 100 Best Companies to Work for in America* by Robert Levering, Milton Moscowitz, and Michael Katz—I heard from about 875. Of those, 374 actually had mission statements. From General Motors to Ben and Jerry's, you'll find the mission statements from the top companies in America in the pages that follow.

I also wrote to 1,000 companies of the second tier of the *Fortune* 2000 to add more well-known and largely publicly held companies to the collection, companies like Wendy's International and Blockbuster Entertainment Group.

In the course of writing this book, I had an opportunity to speak and exchange letters with hundreds of people from a wide variety of companies. Through these conversations and interviews, I learned firsthand about their struggles with the writing and rewriting of mission statements. It can be a grueling, lengthy process—or an inspiring, motivational experience. The results can yield words that truly distinguish the company and ring true for more than a hundred years.

It is my intention for you to benefit from their experience—and mine.

NOTES ON THE NEW EDITION

THE BUSINESS CLIMATE in America changes so rapidly, it is only natural that a book like this needs to be updated periodically.

Since the first edition was published in 1995, there has been a significant number of company mergers and acquisitions, resulting in the loss of many familiar names from the marketplace and from the list of companies profiled here. Among them are Chrysler, purchased by Daimler-Benz in 1998 and thus regrettably removed from this edition, and Mobil, which merged with Exxon in 1998, so you'll find Exxon as a new listing here to replace Mobil.

Also, many companies that didn't have mission statements in the early 1990s have since produced one, making them eligible for consideration.

To prepare this new edition, I contacted the original 301 companies plus another 850 from the *Fortune* 1000.

Although I've kept the total number of companies in this edition at 301, there are 40 new profiles here, including some of the best-known brand names in the world, such as

American Express	Merrill Lynch & Co., Inc.
AMGEN	New York Life
Apple Computer	Office Depot
Avis Rent A Car	OfficeMax, Inc.
Bethlehem Steel	Pfizer
John Deere	Saturn Corporation
Exxon	Sprint
Ford Motor Company	Staples
Honeywell	Tandy Corporation (RadioShack)
Johnson & Johnson	Texas Instruments
Kmart	Time Warner Inc.
Lockheed Martin	TravelSmith
Lucent Technologies	

It is my judgment that mission statements have not only grown in popularity as a business tool, but in many cases they have also been refined, shortened, and enlivened. So I have included sixty-seven revised and updated statements from companies in the first edition. Even the Internal Revenue Service has written a new mission statement. I've included it toward the end of the book.

Between the new company profiles and the updated versions, one-third of the statements in this edition are new.

The fact that many companies don't change their mission, vision, credo, or beliefs is significant. Northwestern Mutual Life still embraces the original company statement written in 1888. It is part of the company's heritage and an indelible part of its positioning today. And I'm delighted to include it here again.

A company can change its name without abandoning its mission. When TRINOVA became Aeroquip-Vickers, the new company kept most of the language of the original mission statement.

Then again, some companies changed both their names and their company statements, such as FDX, formerly Federal Express.

A company can also expand its mission once it reaches certain goals. For instance, Dana Corporation's old statement was "Dana 2000," which focused on its objectives as the new millennium approached. Its updated statement is entitled, appropriately, "Beyond 2000, Our Commitment to Growth."

The titles of the statements changed for many companies. Some changed from a mission to a vision, a vision to a strategy, or a principles statement to a mission. Most statements are shorter.

Some companies extended their statements to include a series to reflect the company's mission, vision, values, and ethics, instead of simply a mission statement alone. Perini changed from a Mission Statement to a "Statement of Beliefs." CUNA Mutual Insurance Group changed from a Mission and Operating Principles to a set of statements that include a Mission, Vision, Corporate Objectives, and Team Shared Commitments.

However, a great many of the company *descriptions* have changed. After all, many companies have evolved, broadening or narrowing their focus, selling off divisions, acquiring new companies and their markets, and growing within the U.S. and around the world.

The introductory chapter offers new interviews with corporate executives explaining how their companies produced or revised their mission statements, new examples of the ways companies use their statements in the workplace, and an updated tally of the frequency with which certain key words and phrases are used.

I have also incorporated suggestions from readers, university professors who have used this book in their classes, journalists, librarians, and businesspeople who have contacted me from all over the world.

It is the hope of this author and the book's publisher that by updating this edition, you will profit from a book that's more revealing, helpful, and instructive—whether you're trying to write a statement for your company or seeking insight into the companies profiled here.

PART I

THE MISSION OF THIS BOOK

To HELP BUSINESS people, executives, managers, employees, investors, students, and consumers achieve a greater understanding of corporate mission statements.

To achieve this mission, this book endeavors to explain the following:

♦ What a mission statement is
♦ What a mission statement is used for
♦ Why it is important for every company and organization to have a mission statement, vision, goal, or purpose
♦ Which elements comprise a mission statement
♦ How mission statements differ from one another
♦ How to write a mission statement
♦ And how 301 of America's biggest companies define their own mission statements, visions, values, principles, objectives, goals, strategies, aspirations, ethics, pledges, promises, and creeds

If this book succeeds in educating, guiding, inspiring, and motivating the reader, then it will have achieved its mission.

HOW TO USE THIS RESOURCE

THIS BOOK HAS been designed to help you understand the nature, structure, style, and language of mission statements. It is also intended to provide a how-to guide to help you write or rewrite your organization's statement, whether you work for a large corporation, small company, a nonprofit organization, government agency, municipality, or university. Moreover, I've structured the book so it is easy to use and refer to.

Part I is an introduction to the world of mission statements. In the next three chapters you'll find short, substantive sections that address the following topics:

- The history of the mission statement
- Its purpose
- Definition of terms
- Ways that companies compose, present, and distribute their mission statements
- Target audience, length, tone, and format
- Titles, key words, and phrases
- Presentation
- How a mission can evolve and change with the company

The last chapter in Part I, entitled "How to Write a Mission Statement (Or Mission *Not* Impossible)," may prove to be a very valuable chapter for you. I wrote it to be brief and instructive, rather than pedantic, respecting both your unique organizational structure and application. So although it may seem broad, it is by no means simplistic.

As you know, writing can be hard work. And when something as important and visible as a mission statement is being created, there may be many editors who have a hand at shaping the final words. Therefore, the guidelines I have provided are intended to help facilitate the process, not automatically formulate the results.

Part II is a compendium of 301 mission statements collected from among America's largest companies selected from the *Fortune* 2000, *Forbes* 200, and other sources.

Each mission statement is accompanied by a profile of the company. The profile is comprised of the company's address, a corporate description (usually in the company's own words as found in its annual report), and industry category. This data was compiled in order to create Part III.

Part III is comprised of two indexes that list and arrange the companies by industry and state. The indexes will help you target companies that are similar to yours (by industry or geographic region) so you can see how they've handled the challenge of creating their mission statements.

GUIDELINES

Here are some additional guidelines for using this book:

1. If you're trying to write a mission statement from scratch:
   - Read the chapters in Part I.
   - Scan the collection of mission statements in Part II.
   - Refer to the indexes in Part III for companies similar to yours. Make a list of those companies. Look them up one-by-one in Part II and study each company's approach, use of language, tone, and overall message.
   - Look closely at the word list (pages 25–26) in the chapter entitled "Inside a Mission Statement." Make a note of the words that would be applicable to your company's statement.
   - Reread the chapter entitled "How to Write a Mission Statement" (page 33) with its step-by-step instructions so you can stay focused, especially if you're working with a committee. Many of the steps can be delegated.

2. If you're trying to update or rewrite your organization's statement:
   ♦ Do all of the above with your current mission by your side. You may be surprised how many parts of the old mission are worth retaining. Plus, integrating some of the old mission with the new will provide continuity. This can go a long way to comforting employees/members/stockholders who may have questions about changes in the way they are being asked to perceive your organization.

Finally, this resource can help you initiate dialogue, conversation, and debate among your colleagues to determine exactly what kind of statement is appropriate for your group—or if more than one statement should be drafted. That's when you can truly put together the words and phrases that make a statement as distinctive as your organization.

A FEW WORDS ABOUT MISSION STATEMENTS AND NONPROFIT ORGANIZATIONS

Every organization, whether it is a company in business to make a profit or a charitable organization with nonprofit status, needs a mission statement.

In fact, many nonprofit groups, social agencies, and service organizations *do* have mission statements. These statements herald the purpose of the group to the public and provide direction for its employees, members, and volunteers.

Creating a mission statement will also aid a nonprofit group in its applications for grants and other forms of financial aid. In some cases, a grant proposal isn't complete unless it includes a mission statement.

Although this book is devoted primarily to the nation's largest corporations, members of nonprofit organizations setting out to write a mission statement will also find the information, how-to instructions, and examples from other companies quite valuable.

IN THE BEGINNING...THERE WAS THE MISSION STATEMENT

MISSION STATEMENTS HAVE been a part of working life and human history since the beginning of time. Perhaps the very first mission statement is recorded in Genesis, with the command "Be fruitful, and multiply..."

More recently, Shakespeare wrote a mission statement for Marc Anthony, which he proclaims when he begins to eulogize Julius Caesar:

> Friends, Romans, countrymen, lend me your ears;
> I come to bury Caesar, not to praise him.

The Preamble to the Constitution of the United States is a kind of mission statement, establishing the reason for the creation of the historical document:

> We the People of the United States, in Order to form a more perfect Union, establish Justice, insure domestic Tranquillity, provide for the common defense, promote the general Welfare, and secure the Blessings of Liberty to ourselves and our Posterity, do ordain and establish this Constitution for the United States of America.

One of contemporary culture's best-known mission statements is far ahead of its time:

> Space, the Final Frontier ... These are the voyages of the Starship *Enterprise*. Its five-year mission: To explore strange new worlds, to seek out new life and new civilizations, to boldly go where no man has gone before.

When Gene Roddenberry wrote *Star Trek*, he also authored a mission statement that would become familiar to millions.

Ultimately, whenever and wherever men and women have endeavored to achieve something purposefully, a statement of mission or purpose is pronounced. It precedes the first step in a long march. And it is etched in stone over the entrances of great buildings.

People, by their very nature, seem to ennoble a task by endowing it with a stated mission.

COMPANIES ARE LIKE PEOPLE. THEY NEED A MISSION.

Corporations as entities and people as individuals share certain characteristics. Over time, they develop personalities that shape their philosophies and motivate their actions. And without a purpose or a mission, both a person and a company will flounder.

Shaping the identity of a corporation really begins with defining its mission. Its reason for being. Its purpose. Focus. Goal.

Every company, no matter how big or small, needs a mission statement as a source of direction, a kind of compass that lets its employees, its customers, and even its stockholders know what it stands for and where it's headed.

A mission engenders a company with a sense of purposefulness, that there is a reason for working—aside from compensation.

A mission also serves to unify people in a company, especially when it is comprised of many different kinds of people, in different parts of the country and the world, with varying job titles as well as different levels of training and education.

As a unifying touchstone, a mission likewise provides the company and its employees with a sense of identity.

And finally, a mission, simply by its very existence, *provides a foundation* on which the company can build its future.

BRIDGING BORDERS

The unifying aspect of a mission statement cannot be overemphasized, especially for companies that are international in scope.

Johnson Wax (the most familiar brand name from the S.C. Johnson Company) publishes an eye-opening brochure, "This We Believe." In its introduction, the company states the important role a mission statement can play in unifying a worldwide company and bridging borders:

> ...our statement of corporate philosophy has been translated and communicated around the world—not only within the worldwide company, but also to key external audiences. It has served us well by providing all employees with a common statement of the basic principles which guide the company in all the different cultures where we operate. It has also provided people outside the company with an understanding of our fundamental beliefs. It communicates the kind of company we are.

A BLUEPRINT FOR SUCCESS

There's another way of perceiving what a mission is all about. Consider a mission as part of the *set of fundamental principles* by which a business operates. The rest of the set could include a vision, goal, slate of objectives, ethics statement, an environmental policy, operating policies, and a basic business philosophy—among many other statements.

Thinking of a mission statement as part of a company's overall blueprint for success—and communicating that to employees, customers, and the public—gives a company a head start on *achieving* that success.

Pfizer produces a large booklet entitled "Our Vision" that details the company's mission, purpose, and values. In the introduction, company Chairman and CEO William C. Steere Jr. explains what the company's vision means, "Our Vision is not a new focus for Pfizer, but rather a restatement of the principles that have brought us tremendous success and will serve as our guideposts in coming years."

A mission can be strengthened with other statements that support how the mission is to be achieved. Ford Motor Company follows its mission statement with its statement of values, introduced by the conviction, "How we accomplish our mission is as important as the mission itself."

GUIDING PRINCIPLES

National Semiconductor Corporation designs, manufactures, and markets semiconductors for the computer and electronics industry. Kevin Wheeler, the Director of National Semiconductor University (described in its own publication as "an international network of employee development professionals chartered to enhance human capability"), explains the importance of a set of guiding principles to his company:

> We have spent a great deal of time over the past three years developing a corporate vision, a set of guiding principles and beliefs, and a mission statement that will help us achieve that vision.

> We believe that a set of guiding principles must be firmly in place if a company is to prosper. Indeed, all companies have guiding principles whether or not they are explicit. However, implicit principles can be counterproductive if they are in conflict with the vision.

> Many companies go through transition without examining these foundation principles by which all work gets done. To do so is dangerous—much like sailing a ship through a narrow channel without benefit of charts or pilot. Better to make them explicit—challenge them or reaffirm or change them openly for all to see and understand.

And, of course, all of these beliefs have to be translated into behavior—into clear understandings of what each employee must do and not do. The process to achieve this must be interactive and must involve the very bottom of the organization as well as the very top. A set of descriptive terms will not suffice.

We are in the midst of that process today. I believe that it takes five to ten years to achieve a complete shift from one set of beliefs to another, and I also believe that it is one of the most difficult things for a company to do successfully.

Winnebago Industries also has a set of guiding principles that includes the line, "We must not only satisfy customers, we must also surprise and delight them."

THE CORE VALUES

Deluxe Corporation provides every employee with a booklet, "Commitment the Deluxe Way," which includes the company's vision, mission, and other company positioning statements. In the introduction, Deluxe Chairman and CEO Gus Blanchard explains what the booklet and statements mean:

> Right now we are creating the future of Deluxe. As we work through this massive retooling and mobilization of our work force, however, we need to keep in mind a common understanding of why we exist as a corporation and what we wish to accomplish.

> That's the purpose of this booklet. In the following pages, you'll find simple definitions of our vision, envisioned future, mission, core values, and strategic business principles. You'll also find the tenets that mold our business conduct and our personal accountabilities. Whether you work in production, sales, data processing, product development, or some other

vital niche within our organization, you should find here the core of what it means to be a Deluxer.

THIS VISION IS ALSO SHAPING THE FUTURE...

The impact of a company's own vision can be dramatic. Microsoft Corporation's vision statement is a single sentence: "A computer on every desk and in every home."

Microsoft includes an explanation of their vision:

We are single-minded in our commitment to this vision. And we have maintained that singular focus ever since our company was founded in 1975.

This vision has created a revolution that's changed how people around the world do business . . .

This vision is also shaping the future . . .

SO WHAT EXACTLY *IS*
A MISSION STATEMENT?

AND HOW DOES it vary from a Vision Statement, Business Philosophy, Objectives, Values, Strategies, Pledge, Tactics, Purpose, Promise, Beliefs, Standards, Code of Ethics, Idea, Call to Action, Guidelines, Direction, Focus, Commitment, Policy, Discipline, Covenant, Standards of Performance, or Credo? Or are all these titles just variations on the same theme?

Anyone who has ever been asked to write a company's mission statement sooner or later comes to these questions.

Fortunately, others have already tread this uphill path. Collectively, they've produced an astonishingly rich, varied, and colorful palette of definitions.

The following companies have embraced the challenge of defining a mission statement (and other related statements) prior to composing one. Although they vary individually in premise and tone, dovetailed together, they comprise a solid frame for housing this mission statement compendium.

Please note: I have used the term "mission statement" to include a broad range of approaches and titles by a wide variety of companies. Some companies put their vision and values before their mission, if they have one. Simply by shaping a "statement," these companies are stating or implying their corporate mission.

EXAMPLE #1: | Aeroquip-Vickers, Inc. (formerly TRINOVA Corporation)

TRINOVA Corporation became Aeroquip-Vickers, Inc. in the mid-1990s. This company remains a manufacturer of engineered components, headquartered in Maumee, Ohio. Under the new name, the company still produces a booklet that states its Corporate Mission Statement, Statement of Purpose and Goals, and Core Values, which are essentially unchanged from the TRINOVA version. As TRINOVA the company booklet also included a section that asked and answered the following questions for the benefit of employees:

♦ What is a mission statement?
♦ What is "our mission"?
♦ Does this replace other TRINOVA mission statements?
♦ What do we do with the mission?
♦ Who developed our mission?
♦ Do other corporations have mission statements?
♦ How is our mission different?

Here is a sample of the text of the questions and answers.

What is a mission statement?

A mission statement is an enduring statement of purpose for an organization that identifies the scope of its operations in product and market terms, and reflects its values and priorities.

A mission statement will help a company to make consistent decisions, to motivate, to build an organizational unity, to integrate short-term objectives with longer-term goals, and to enhance communication.

What is "our mission"?

(See Aeroquip-Vickers, Inc.'s mission statement in Part II.) Our mission is stated quite simply. It defines our key goals and defines our values. It is also forward-looking. Our mission is uniquely the property and the heritage of TRINOVA employees. And, it is the foundation upon which we can all build a strong and successful future for TRINOVA and for ourselves.

What do we do with the mission?

It is the responsibility of each of us to make the mission a guide to our decision making and action. To accomplish this, we must each become proponents of the mission and exemplify it in our words and actions. Make its goals our goals, and make the six core values the very essence of how we act and how we expect others in TRINOVA to act.

Who developed our mission?

The Corporate Management Committee wrote our mission with considerable input from other managers throughout TRINOVA.

Do other corporations have mission statements?

Yes. Many corporations have adopted mission statements. Some have been successful while others have not. We take our mission seriously and we intend to live by it now and in the future.

How is our mission different?

Our mission captures our values; it does not invent new ones! It is not intended to radically alter TRINOVA. Rather, it is intended to make sure that we capitalize on our strengths and that we all move in the same direction. Our mission will be enduring and will become a natural part of our work.

If we can—over time—internalize our values and meet our goals, we will have the distinction of being a truly excellent company.

Pennsylvania Power & Light Company (PP&L) is an electric utility serving 29 counties in Southeastern Pennsylvania. The entry for PP&L in Part II of this book includes both the current Vision, Values, and Principles plus the earlier versions of the company's Vision, Values, Mission, and Philosophy developed in the 1980s (with the expressed written permission of the company).

One of the reasons for doing this is to present portions of PP&L's extraordinary nine-page brochure produced in the 1980s that not only articulated the company's vision, values, mission, and business philosophy, but defines the terms as well.

These definitions of vision, values, mission, and business philosophy read as follows:

Vision

The vision of an organization is a concise word picture of the organization at some future time, which sets the overall direction of the organization. It is what the organization strives to be. A vision is something to be pursued, while a mission (defined later) is something to be accomplished.

Values

Values are the collective principles and ideals which guide the thoughts and actions of an individual, or a group of individuals. Values define the character of an organization—they describe what the organization stands for.

Mission

A mission is a statement that specifies an organization's purpose or "reason for being." It is the primary objective toward which the organization's plans and programs should be aimed. A mission is something to be accomplished, while a vision (defined earlier) is something to be pursued.

Business Philosophy

The business philosophy establishes the "rule of conduct" for operating the organization. It translates the values of the organization into more concrete descriptions of how the values will be applied to run the business.

In the chapter "How to Write a Mission Statement" (page 33), you'll find an interview with PP&L's former Director of Corporate Communications, James Marsh, in which he explains how the company revised its vision, values, mission, and philosophy statements.

EXAMPLE #3: American United Life Insurance Company

American United Life Insurance Company (AUL) has prepared an excellent brochure for their employees entitled "Aspire," which explains the company's vision, mission, shared values, and overall objectives. The introduction uses a warm, empathetic, and conversational tone to explain what the company vision is and why it is important. Of special note are two lines that should ring true for any company, "Words on paper that become dusty while sitting on a shelf do no good. To create value, each of us needs to understand the company's vision, adopt it as our own, and use its principles to help us be increasingly effective."

Here is the entire text:

As a team member at AUL, you probably have a general idea of what the company does and how your job and department fit into the overall plan. However, you may be less certain about some other equally important things, such as: what the company stands for, what values it holds most highly, and whether its objectives are ones you are pursuing.

The answers to these questions are important to your success, as well as the success of AUL. A company of this size, which touches the lives of so many people—employees, producers and customers—has succeeded for some very definite reasons. To promote success, and to ensure that those of us here are working toward the same goals as the company, these reasons have been documented. Together, these items form the AUL vision.

This vision—which includes our mission, shared values and overall objectives—is intended to serve as the guidepost for action and decision making at all levels within the company. Each of us is encouraged to find ways to make the vision live in our daily work. Words on paper that become dusty while sitting on a shelf do no good. To create value, each of us needs to understand the company's vision, adopt it as our own, and use its principles to help us be increasingly effective.

Working together as a team is important. This is a document we can and should use to bring focus to the results we are trying to achieve. Weave this vision into your daily work life. If it is helpful as a reminder, display this information in your work area. All of us are vital to the company's success. When we raise our aspirations and live the vision, we'll be helping to ensure that AUL's future—and our own—are as strong as we can make them.

See Part II for the full text of AUL's vision statement.

A Special Logo to Symbolize the Vision

AUL has actually created a vision logo. It is extraordinary and merits special attention. I can recall no other company that has done this. The logo demonstrates the company's serious commitment to its vision. A black and white version of the full-color logo is presented below.

The AUL "Aspire" brochure includes an explanation of the logo:

The AUL vision logo was created to help symbolize our company principles. The three sides of the triangular logo represent the three major elements of our vision statement.

These three components—mission, values and objectives—are also designed into this version of the logo. The graphic display of the rising sun helps exemplify illumination—illumination of the challenges before us and our chosen approaches for meeting them. The company colors help identify the logo as truly belonging to AUL.

OTHER EXAMPLES

Weyerhaeuser defines what a vision statement means in the introduction to the company's statements, "Our Vision" and "Our Values":

A vision describes the desired future state of an organization. To be valid, a vision statement must endure and not change with every business cycle.

Meridian Bancorp explains, "Our Vision is Meridian's statement of core values that defines the company's culture and the Meridian way of working."

Bausch & Lomb devotes a lengthy portion of text explaining the definition, importance, and role of "Values" in the introduction of its company publication "The Values We Share at Bausch & Lomb." See Part II and the Bausch & Lomb entry for the entire text.

Wisconsin Public Service Corporation is an electric and gas utility company. In their statement, "Our Vision," the company says, "A vision is a mental image of the company we want to be. It's intended to give all employees, as well as everyone else the company works with and serves, a consistent picture of the company we are creating." The company also defines the words behind their mission statement: "A mission describes the aim of our current business practices. It offers us direction."

CMS Energy of Jackson, Michigan, is the nation's fourth largest combination electric and gas utility. Their comprehensive publication

"Our Strategic Plan" includes the company's vision, goals, strategies, and creed. They explain each term, as follows:

- Our Vision declares how we as a company will operate in philosophical terms—in decision making, serving customers and measuring success.
- Our Goals describe what we will do to cement positive relationships with our stakeholders.
- Our Strategies explain how we will reach our goals.
- Finally, the company Creed is our pledge of performance. Good service and value to our customers is a must.

Clearly, defining terms and explaining the purpose of a mission, vision, principle, or strategy helps to communicate the statement more effectively and with greater impact.

INSIDE A MISSION STATEMENT

IDEALLY, A company's mission statement should be as unique as the company itself, so it stands to reason that no two mission statements are exactly alike.

As Part II of this book will illustrate, there is great variety in the ways that companies compose, present, and distribute their missions.

The differences become apparent when you examine the four basic elements that comprise and distinguish a mission statement: *target audience, length, tone,* and *format.*

TARGET AUDIENCE: THIS MISSION'S FOR YOU

Who is the mission statement intended for? The employees of a company? The general public? Stockholders? Some companies compose a mission that's intended for all audiences. Others purposefully create a mission for employees' eyes only. Still others post their missions in annual reports, where they'll be seen only by stockholders or prospective investors.

AMP, in its brochure that describes the company's mission, values, and vision, starts with a letter from the Chairman and CEO that begins, "To Our Customers . . ."

Other CEOs precede their company's mission with the salutation, "Dear (Company) Employee . . ."

The Knight-Ridder Promise, which accompanies the Knight-Ridder statement of values, is directed

To Our Customers

To Our Employees

To Our Shareholders

To Our Communities

To Our Society

In the same vein, Warner-Lambert states "Our Creed" and addresses each of the target audiences to which the company commits itself:

To Our Customers

To Our Colleagues

To Our Shareholders

To Our Business Partners

To Society

The target audience has a significant impact on the length, tone, and visibility of the mission statement.

Sometimes the target audience is specifically mentioned in the mission statement itself. This is true for Kmart, which states, "Kmart will become the discount store of choice for middle-income families with children by satisfying their routine and seasonal shopping needs as well as or better than the competition."

LENGTH: HOW LONG IS LONG ENOUGH?

According to a popular folk legend, when Abraham Lincoln was president, he was asked by a reporter, "How long should a man's legs be?" Lincoln is said to have responded, "Long enough to reach the ground."

The same is true for a mission statement.

For some companies, a single sentence is sufficient. Others have produced great, lengthy documents that begin with a mission and include vision statements, values, philosophies, objectives, plans, and strategies in supporting roles. And still others are somewhere in between, longer than one line but contained within one page.

All that's necessary is that the mission be long enough to reach the target audience.

Companies with More Than One Mission

A company *can* have more than one mission statement. That is, it may be appropriate for *each division* of a corporation to have its own mission, vision, values, and objectives—especially if that corporation is heavily diversified.

Consolidated Freightways provides a mission for each of its three divisions, for example. And Ben & Jerry's has a product mission, a social mission, and an economic mission.

TONE: AVOIDING FLAT NOTES

The tone of a mission statement is a crucial part of its makeup. It takes a certain tone to resonate with the target audience.

Should a statement be conversational? Formal? Originate from the office of the Chief Executive Officer? The President? The head of Human Resources? The Corporate Communications Manager? It all depends on the company and, again, the target audience.

If the language is too lofty, haughty, or ponderous, it won't be taken very seriously. And, more significantly, it will defeat its very purpose.

So what kind of language should one employ? That is best answered by examining the individual parts that comprise a mission statement. These include the title, key words, and phrases.

Title

Establishing the right tone requires the deliberate choice of specific words that give a statement its own character. The *title* itself can set the tone. It's certainly sufficient to entitle a mission statement with the prominent headline "Mission Statement." (And hundreds of companies presented in these pages do exactly that.) But a significant number of companies apply their own stamp to the genre.

Northwestern Mutual Life's mission is entitled "The Northwestern Mutual Way."

Johnson Wax provides a booklet with its mission, entitled "This We Believe."

Bausch & Lomb orients employees with a publication, "The Values We Share at Bausch & Lomb."

Kellogg's has a company booklet entitled "The Kellogg Company Philosophy." It begins with a quote from founder W.K. Kellogg: "We are a company of dedicated people making quality products for a healthier world."

Ingersoll-Rand's "Our Way to Excellence" brochure includes the company's vision and mission as well as statements entitled "Our Passion" and "Our Guiding Principles."

American Express lists its values under the title "Blue Box Values." The blue box is a reference to the graphic branding emblem for the American Express logo.

The brochure published by AMP, previously mentioned, is entitled "The Journey." The trek referred to here is the company's "Journey to Excellence," which is supported by its mission, values, and vision.

Gannett Company Inc. presents its "Strategic Vision" and "Operating Principles" as part of "Gannett's Basic Game Plan."

Nalco Chemical Company has a "Nalco Philosophy of Operations."

Hibernia Bank supports its mission and purpose statements with "Ten Commandments" for behavior, each starting with an active verb.

Key Words

Key words and phrases also set the tone for a statement. A list of key words is included below along with the number of times that word appears in the 301 mission statements in Part II.

- Ability—25
- Accomplished—6
- Asset—36
- Best—94
- Change—41
- Commitment—91
- Communicate—15
- Communities—97
- Conscience—1
- Corporate citizen—32
- Customers—211
- Dedicated—32
- Dedication—18
- Dignity—32
- Direct—34
- Diversity—33

- Employees—158
- Empower—27
- Enthusiasm—7
- Ethics—22
- Excellence—77
- Exciting—3
- Fair—68
- Fun—44
- Future—33
- Goal—81
- Goodwill—3
- Growth—116
- Harmony—3
- Individual—78
- Initiative—27
- Innovation—64
- Joy—2
- Leader—106
- Leadership—63
- Life—49
- Long-term—66
- Mission—207
- Mutual—36
- Passion—13
- Performance—82
- Potential—27
- Pride—29

- Principles—37
- Productivity—21
- Profit—111
- Quality—169
- Relationships—48
- Reliable—16
- Respect—109
- Return on equity—18
- Risk—35
- Security—17
- Serve—83
- Service—206
- Shareholders—111
- Solution—26
- Strategy—21
- Strength—60
- Success—106
- Support—69
- Team—100
- Teamwork—66
- Tomorrow—7
- Trust—59
- Unique—17
- Value—185
- Values—85
- Vision—110

Phrases

As you read through the various mission statements in Part II, you'll encounter certain phrases that stand out in tone and spirit.

For instance, National Semiconductor urges its employees to "Be curious, imaginative, and courageous in challenging our current thinking."

Both Nike, the shoe company, and Comerica, a banking corporation, have mission statements that refer to "enriching people's lives." Imagine, two companies devoted to completely different businesses, but with nearly identical phrasing in their mission statements.

Vons Supermarkets urges employees in their vision statement to have a "give a darn" attitude.

Robert Mondavi Winery has an excellent set of mission, vision, values, and management philosophy statements. Among its values, the company states, "We believe it essential to listen to our customers for opportunities to add value" and to "consider all employees ambassadors of the company . . ." Every business would do well to communicate the importance of employees having a high awareness of their role as ambassadors of the company brand.

IMC Global has five Strategic Goals in its "Pursuing the Vision" company publication. Among them are "Creating a High Performance Culture" that makes IMC "A company where you want to come to work . . . every day."

The Pillsbury Company has a vision statement that reflects their friendly, likable branding, "We Make Lips Smile Everywhere By Making Everyday Food Special."

Sundstrand Corporation states that one of its "Beliefs" is "Developing and maintaining relationships rather than just executing transactions."

In addition to a mission statement, Lucent Technologies cites four company values. The first one is "an obsession with serving our customers."

General Electric has a series of "GE Values" statements that explain that GE leaders "Have a passion for excellence and hate bureaucracy."

U.S. Bancorp of Minneapolis declares that one of its official values is "Diversity." And although dozens of companies endorse the merits of diversity, this company states, "We value individual differences and work to leverage their inherent creative potential."

Corning Incorporated stands behind its list of company values, including integrity, by saying, "Integrity is the foundation of Corning's reputation."

Coachmen Industries' "Principles" statement includes, "Our deep-seated philosophy is that 'Business goes where it is invited and stays where it is well cared for.'"

Merrill Lynch's Principles include "Respect for the Individual" and is summed up by "It means following the Golden Rule."

There are hundreds of other fascinating phrases, lines, and statements in the samples of mission statements that follow in Part II.

FORMAT: WHAT SHOULD A MISSION STATEMENT LOOK LIKE?

How a company regards its mission statement is often reflected in the manner it's presented to customers, employees, stockholders, and the public at large. In other words, looks do mean everything.

Some statements are printed principally in the company's annual report (many of these are featured on the cover). Others appear in the annual report and in other formats and venues so they can be distributed, promoted, and championed as representative of the company's profile.

Suitable for Framing

Some companies print their mission statement on high-quality, 8½ by 11-inch paper so it is suitable for framing.

The oldest mission for an American company cited in this book is from Northwestern Mutual Life, which composed its statement in 1888. To dignify this legacy, the company publishes its mission statement on card stock, in the 8½ by 11-inch format, with a calligraphic, hand-lettered style.

And where should a framed mission or other statements be displayed? In the lobby? In each employee's office? In the lunchroom or cafeteria? It all depends on the company's particular culture.

How many companies go to the trouble and minor expense of presenting their mission statement in a formal, "dressed up" format?

Here is a list of just some companies profiled in Part II that feature their mission statements in "presentation mode":

AlliedSignal
Airborne Express
American Express
American Protective Services
Anheuser-Busch Companies
Aristech Chemical Corporation
Avis
Bethlehem Steel
Chevron
Commercial Federal Corporation
CUNA Mutual Insurance Group
Deere & Company (John Deere)
Edwards (A.G. Edwards & Sons, Inc.)
Ethyl Corporation
Hormel
Litton Industries
Minnesota Mining and Manufacturing (3M)
Nalco
Rhône-Poulenc Rorer
Safety-Kleen
Sanwa Bank
Southern Company
Southwest Airlines
Sundstrand
TRW

Levi Strauss uses a paperstock with a blue denim tone.

Westin Hotels presents their vision statement with a beautifully scripted text in a 8½ by 6-inch horizontal format.

Honeywell's vision, mission, values, and goals are printed on an 11 by 17-inch poster.

Have Mission Will Travel

Many companies produce their mission, vision, values, goals, and objectives in both the large card-stock format and again in a small format that's appropriate for each employee to carry in a wallet or purse.

Total Systems Services, Inc. is a company devoted to credit card processing. So its mission statement appears on—guess what?—a plastic credit card. This medium has been adopted by other companies as well.

And although not all companies produce their statements on a card the size and weight of a credit card, many do imprint their statements in miniature form. Some of these companies include Ace Hardware, AMETEK, Atlanta Gas Light Company, Diamond Shamrock, Federal-Mogul, General Public Utilities Corporation, Goodyear, Lucent Technologies, Southern California Edison, Sprint, Staples, Tultex, Vons, and Warner-Lambert Company.

Butler Manufacturing Company and Rollins Inc. both have their mission statements printed on the back of employees' business cards.

Inland Paperboard & Packaging's mission, values, vision, and objectives are printed on a 3 by 5-inch laminated card, so it is especially durable as well as portable. Pillsbury also distributes its mission statement on a laminated card.

American Family Insurance Group produces its mission statement on a 3 by 4-inch magnet, suitable for attaching to any metallic surface.

Brochures, Booklets, and Handbooks

To give greater visibility and credibility to their statements, many companies publish brochures, booklets, and handbooks in various sizes and formats that are separate from the annual report.

Like the suitable-for-framing sheets on heavy stock, these formats have great impact and are custom-made for easy distribution to a variety of target audiences.

So it's not surprising that they appear in a wide variety of sizes too:

- 8½ by 11 inches
- 8½ by 8½ inches
- 7½ by 11 inches
- 7 by 4⅜ inches
- 5½ by 8½ inches
- 4½ by 9½ inches
- 3⅞ by 9 inches
- 3⅝ by 8½ inches
- 3½ by 5½ inches

Companies with separate booklets for their statements include Borg-Warner, Centerbank, Centura Banks, CMS Energy, Comerica, Corning, Delta Air Lines, First Interstate Bancorp, Fleming Companies, Gillette, Kansas City Power & Light, Lafarge Corporation, Rubbermaid, Sprint, and Weyerhaeuser.

Multiple Formats

Many companies publish their mission, vision, and values statements in more than one format. They may produce the text in a brochure, an 8½ by 11-inch poster, and a wallet-sized card, and, of course, in their annual report. This permits the statements to be distributed in a number of ways.

Most notable today is the appearance of the mission statement (or vision, values, credo, etc.) on a company's website.

For international companies, communicating the mission statement can be a challenge. Haworth, Inc., the worldwide manufacturer of office products, produces its "Our Principles" brochure in seven different languages.

COPYRIGHTS

Remember that all the statements a company publishes, whether in the form of a mission, values, vision, principles, creed, etc., are the property of that company. All of the statements reprinted here are done so with the expressed written permission of each company.

Hormel (Geo. A. Hormel & Co.), Borg-Warner, Chemical Banking Corporation, and Gibson Greetings Inc. are just some of the companies that have a copyright mark (©) accompanying their mission statements. But you should consider a copyright implicit with all company statements.

Please respect the copyrights of the mission statements included in Part II. And be sure to copyright your own mission statement. For more information about copyright law and registration, consult your local library's reference section.

HOW TO WRITE A MISSION STATEMENT (OR MISSION *NOT* IMPOSSIBLE)

IN THE COURSE of conducting research for this book and talking with people from all walks of business, I encountered a lot of enthusiasm. I also heard a lot of stories about companies that started the process of creating a mission statement but never quite finished.

People kept asking me, "Is this going to be a 'How to Write a Mission Statement' book? And when will it be available?"

Many people seem to get stopped in their tracks by a kind of mission-statement-writing-process quagmire. This dilemma was confirmed by firsthand accounts. But, happily, the following examples demonstrate how companies can set out to complete the task.

EXAMPLE #1: | Keyport Life Insurance Company

Keyport is a specialty life insurance company that provides retirement savings products, including fixed and variable annuities. In 1998, the company revised its mission statement, creating a simpler, more concise statement. Here are the company's old and new mission statements. John Rosensteel, President and CEO, explains how and why the process took place.

OLD MISSION STATEMENT

Keyport is a customer-focused, premier provider of innovative annuity and life insurance products that enable customers, in selected market segments, to reach their long-term financial goals. We provide outstanding product value and quality service to our customers and a rewarding environment for all employees, while optimizing shareholder value.

NEW MISSION STATEMENT

Helping People Create Their Own Future ... A Certain Future.

Q: How would you describe what a mission statement is and its purpose?
JR: In my opinion, it's intended to speak to why our organization exists, our purpose and what are we here for. It clarifies what and who this company is and what it does.

Q: Why is it important for your company to have one?
JR: I think it's important for every company to have a mission statement. It helps to shape the direction and strategy of the company. It helps to align both management and employees and rally them around what you're trying to accomplish. And it unifies everyone around a common set of values that define the company's culture.

Q: What led to the decision to update and change your mission statement?
JR: Mission statements, like anything else, are subject to a certain degree of evolution as a company grows. You need to constantly be attentive to changing markets and changing trends to make sure both where you are and where you're headed are still in sync. The *process* we went through in writing the original statement was probably as important as the statement itself. However, the original was not a statement that lent itself to a quick recollection. It was a bit wordy and technical. The new one has evolved to capture everything we want to say in spirit and tone but does so with greater economy. And that makes it easier to remember.

Q: Who determined the process?
JR: It started from our senior management group. It didn't just happen one day. It was an evolutionary process. Since arriving at Keyport, I've had an annual meeting of the senior management team. We've taken the opportunity to go away and really talk about where we are as a company as a part of business planning. We've taken a close look at who we are, what we're trying to accomplish, and what we can become. A day spent

like this gets your team aligned. And out of this kind of process we consider how to communicate our conclusions and vision back through the organization and get everyone on track together. It has a major impact on our ability to achieve our short-term and long-term business objectives.

Q: What was the process like?

JR: At the end of the day it was a fairly satisfying one. There are moments when it can be like being at the dentist because it is truly like pulling teeth when you're spending time on semantics, weighing different viewpoints, trying to get consensus on what we mean and where we want to go. Let's face it. Articulating these points in a way that everyone can agree on is a challenge. Fortunately, there is a lot to be gained from just going through the process.

While we started the process at the senior management level, we made sure that we got a lot of opinions from employees at all levels of our company. We created a "Voice Committee" and assembled a group of seven people to figure out a way to create a single, distinctive, and consistent voice for communicating our mission and goals. Making sure we heard all the voices from within our company was the best way to speak with one voice to the rest of the company and to our customers.

And I've been especially impressed with the way the next level of management picked up our newly defined theme and found ways to communicate it within the organization. For instance, our "Certainty" theme and new logo were unveiled together at an all-employee meeting that became a very positive event for everyone at our company.

Q: How long did it take to rewrite the statement?

JR: It truly evolved over time, happening in two parts: the creation and the roll-out. As I mentioned, the evolution of the mission statement was the result of the two-to-three-day, off-site meeting with my senior executive team. This really started five years ago. Each time we had our annual meeting, we revisited the basic issues of where we were as a company and where we wanted to go.

When we first created our original mission statement, it certainly took longer than two to three days because we had a great deal of varying views of who we were and where we were headed. That took about six months to sort out. After we decided we had something to share with the rest of the organization, we spent two months rolling it out, getting employee groups together and getting feedback. This resulted in some polishing and some editing of the original statement. Clearly that was instructive and valuable to get people talking and thinking about these issues in a collective way. Over the years, the rewriting process has been smoother. Once the statement was in place it was easier to rewrite because we didn't have to start with a blank sheet of paper.

Q: What other company mission statements did your group take a look at?
JR: We looked at a wide variety of mission statements from other companies, and at background articles.

Q: What was the best part of going through this process?
JR: The increased level of communication among the senior management team. The first time I did this I had seventeen of our senior managers in a room. And then it dawned on me that this meeting was the first time they'd all been together. In that sense, we've all come a long way together in building consensus, expressing varying opinions, and creating a position that generates enthusiasm.

Q: How was the new statement introduced to employees?
JR: We've historically had an annual meeting of all employees where we have done a little bit of celebrating of the results achieved in the previous year while we set the stage for the challenges of the coming year. This year, instead of focusing on that, we utilized this opportunity to roll out the new mission statement and unveil the new positioning statement with the theme "Certainty." This theme has a lot of application to the business we're in: financial certainty in a potentially uncertain future, recognizing that retirement is a significantly longer period than it used to be, the transfer of the risk of longevity.

Q: How is the mission statement featured at the company or in company publications?

JR: We unveiled the new statement and new logo at our company meeting. We also displayed our new company literature. When employees showed up for work on the following Monday, each one found a mouse pad imprinted with the new logo and the tagline "A Certain Future," which is part of the new statement. Each also got a gym bag with our new logo.

In our lobby we display banners with the new logo and "A Certain Future" featured prominently. And we have a new trade advertising campaign that embodies the new mission.

Q: What has been the response of employees, customers, and stockholders?

JR: The feedback has been very positive. People really like the new logo. The "Certainty" theme is viewed as a very provocative positioning statement, and it has stimulated discussion about our mission statement.

EXAMPLE #2: | **The Case of Pennsylvania Power & Light Company (PP&L)**

Pennsylvania Power & Light Company went through the process of updating their vision and values statements. Jim Marsh, former Director of Corporate Communications, explains why and how the company went about drafting and finalizing the new statements. (Both the older and updated vision and values statements are included in the entry for PP&L in Part II.)

Q: What led up to the decision to update and change your vision and values statements?

JM: The Energy Act of 1992 provided for the eventual deregulation of the electric utility industry and it drove us toward a more competitive environment. We moved from regulated rates to rates for electricity driven by the marketplace. Our statements needed to change to reflect the changes in our industry and how we changed to deal with the new, competitive environment.

Q: Who determined the process?

JM: Our corporate management committee, which is five senior officers, got together at the beginning of the year and worked with a facilitator, an outside consultant. We looked at what a vision statement should be and do, and we kept pounding away at it at meetings over several months. We came up with a new draft, sent it out for comments among the staff, and then out for focus group testing among employees, which gave us even more input. The responsibility for developing this material rests with senior management, but it was developed with the input of a wide section of employees. PP&L has 7,600 employees.

Q: In 1992, PP&L had vision, values, mission, and philosophy statements. Now the company has created new vision and values statements. Will there be a mission and philosophy statement eventually, too?

JM: We haven't by design dropped them, we just started with the vision and values. They superseded the philosophy statement. It doesn't mean we won't work on it. The principles are about the same as those developed for our Continuous Performance Improvement Process, PP&L's "quality" program. We put together a union/labor partnership that developed CPIP. Our Corporate Principles are close to this.

As I mentioned, since publication of our vision, values, mission, and philosophy in the '80s, the Energy Act of 1992 changed our industry. We had to go through a revision of the vision statement to reflect this changing industry.

So, we have an updated vision and values statement. Now, we're working on a financial strategy. We may be going back and looking at a philosophy. This is a living thing and as it becomes appropriate we may make changes and improvements. As for the other statements, our business philosophy is kind of rolled into the values statement.

Q: How did you end up finding a facilitator to help your company create the new statements?

JM: We went out and sent a proposal to a number of outside business consultants and facilitators. They came in with a "process." They did just what is implied. They facilitated the thought process and rationale, rather than doing the actual writing. The back-and-forth revisions and drafts were with our top management people.

Q: What was the best part of going through this process?

JM: As Director of Corporate Communications it was my responsibility to be actively involved. It's really exciting just looking at what a vision statement is supposed to do. It is supposed to be a few words that are energizing to an organization. I was very excited with what we came up with.

Q: What else did your company do differently than last time to get new statements drafted?

JM: This time management went out a number of times and sought input and feedback directly from employees. That feedback *did* change the content to some extent.

Q: Have there been positive employee comments?

JM: Very definitely positive. They saw the process in the context of a lot of things we're trying to do to change the culture around here to emphasize teamwork and partnership. As you may know, the electric utility industry is a conservative culture. In order to be successful, we're going to have to be able to get more of a buy-in from employees and make them feel that they're truly part of the process.

The statements are different, but the commitment is not different. As times change, we feel the need to change with them and have a more up-to-date vision that's reflective of this company and what's in it for everyone.

EXAMPLE #3: | The Case of Deluxe Corporation

Deluxe Corporation is a provider of integrated risk management, electronic transaction, and paper payment services to the financial services and retail industries. The story behind Deluxe Corporation's mission statement, included in the company publication "Commitment the Deluxe Way," is provided by Stuart Alexander, Vice President of Corporate Communications.

> In 1997, our company formed a group of people from across the company. This team, dubbed the Guiding Coalition, was responsible for redefining Deluxe's culture and values. As our chief executive officer, Gus Blanchards, said, "It's time to discuss terms such as 'mission' and 'vision' and to reach a common understanding of why we exist as a corporation and what we want to accomplish."
>
> The Guiding Coalition, working by consensus, then put down in writing what Deluxe stands for and where it is heading. Members of the Guiding Coalition were recommended by the corporate management team. The coalition, which is ongoing, includes people from all levels, business units, and geographical areas of the company. In searching for members of the coalition, managers looked for "change agents" who were looked upon as credible leaders by their coworkers.
>
> In composing a mission, vision, core values, and business principles, the coalition took care to make sure the principles touched every person at Deluxe. Members weren't satisfied until the wording reflected the work done by every person in every part of the company. The coalition's overriding goal was to make sure that all employees understood Deluxe's direction and future.
>
> Of course, writing a new and more comprehensive statement didn't mean getting rid of the company's core values. Many of our "new" values are the same ones Deluxe and its subsidiaries have always had, but other things were added so that employees

would be better prepared to serve our customers. Following the introduction of the Deluxe Way, the Guiding Coalition began working on ways to promote positive change and to maximize formal and informal communications channels at Deluxe.

EXAMPLE #4: | The Case of *Architectural Record*

Architectural Record, headquartered in New York, is a professional magazine for architects. In the September 1993 edition, in his column "Notes from Behind the Scenes," publisher Roscoe C. Smith III gave an account of the process by which that magazine attempted to produce a mission statement:

> Starting in early May and proceeding through August, a series of meetings was held for the purpose of writing a definitive plan for the future of this magazine involving every aspect of what we produce. We're looking at how the magazine can be improved, expanded in its usefulness, even transformed into other useful products—print or electronic, all based on the needs expressed by our "customers"—you, our readers, and you, our advertisers. Above all, it was agreed that it must be a plan that management and staff can unanimously endorse and execute.
>
> Attending our meetings were people from editorial, marketing, circulation, advertising sales, production, and accounting. Twelve in all . . . but our titles were left outside the meeting-room door. One person, one vote. Total agreement was our goal. The first order of business was to draft a precise and clear mission statement. To start the process, each attendee was asked to submit his or her thoughts on the matter in writing. We all assumed it would then be an easy task to combine our ideas and reconcile the differences. And, with that out of the way, go on to the planning stages.
>
> We were mistaken. It wasn't that easy.

However, weeks later—with the Fourth of July looming on the horizon and having more than once recalled a group that also met through a long, hot summer (in Philadelphia)—it was agreed by all concerned to adopt the following statement. Every word having been weighed, every thought examined, and very resource considered . . . over and over again. I want to share it with you:

> The mission of *Architectural Record* is to provide original, reliable, and useful information to the architectural marketplace worldwide, in timely and easy-to-use formats which:
>
> ♦ Create an industry-wide forum.
> ♦ Set the standards for excellence in architectural design.
> ♦ Present insights and practical solutions for current challenges in design, building construction, and business practice.
> ♦ Build success for our readers, our advertisers, our associates and investors, and ourselves.
> ♦ Establish the authoritative record of architecture.

With this commitment in hand, we are in the process of rethinking every part of what we do.

These examples point out how much work goes into the creation of a mission statement. But the rewards provide a great return on the investment in time and effort.

A STEP-BY-STEP GUIDE TO WRITING A MISSION STATEMENT

Writing any document can be a daunting and arduous task. Just because someone is a good engineer, chemist, shop foreman, salesperson, or loan officer doesn't mean he or she is very comfortable with putting words down on paper.

Even the Founding Fathers became exasperated with trying to write the Declaration of Independence by committee and finally left things in the hands of Thomas Jefferson. Their problem was they had no recipe, formula, or blueprint for creating a new form of government.

But history is on your side. Others have blazed a trail before you and left an easy step-by-step method for writing a mission statement.

Step 1:
Decide who is going to write the mission statement

Is this a solo task or a group effort? Take a lesson from the real-life examples of other companies and consider the advantages of creating a committee with representatives from every department in your company. That way, everyone will have a chance to feel like they had a voice in the statement's creation and will be more likely to embrace its content and spirit.

Step 2:
Agree on when the statement is going to be written

During business hours or in evening sessions? In a single weekend? At the office or off-site where there will be fewer distractions? And how much time will you allow?

A single afternoon or evening? A weekend? A month? Six months? A year? Impose a deadline and stick to it.

Step 3:
Determine the target audience(s)

Employees of your company? Customers? Suppliers? Stockholders? The general public? You have to figure out *who* you're talking to before you can figure out *what* to say.

Step 4:
Decide what kind of language is appropriate

Start with a list of key words and phrases that apply to your business. Bring a group of people together, roll out an easel, invite a free flow of ideas, and write down words and phrases that come to mind. Refer to the list of key words provided earlier.

This may lead to a discussion about what kind of statement you're writing in the first place and what its title should be. You may wish to create a mission statement that describes your company's purpose or goal. But you may also want to include a Vision Statement that addresses the issues of people, service, and the future of the company, that is, how your company is going to achieve its goal. That's only the beginning. Remember, there are value statements, statements of principles, philosophies, ethics, environmental policies, and more.

It's ultimately up to you to decide the nature, length, and tone of the document.

Step 5:
Adopt a format

Will the mission statement be presented to the target audience in the annual report? Beautifully printed on quality paper, designed for framing and distribution? In a brochure or pamphlet? As a wallet-size card? Embedded in a Lucite paperweight? Printed on a company calendar or coffee mugs? Silk-screened on T-shirts? Emblazoned on a banner? Engraved in granite? Displayed at the front door?

If you're proud of your official mission statement, you'll want to communicate its message in a variety of ways that reflect your company's distinctive culture.

Like most any task, breaking down the process into smaller steps makes it easier to accomplish. Ultimately, by focusing on your company's goals, you'll achieve this one as well: "Be fruitful and multiply."

This ancient mission statement, mentioned near the beginning of this book, is still very much to the point. In fact, it's an excellent place from which to begin writing your own mission. Consider the ways and means your company can be fruitful in the sense of growing your business. Determine the strategies to multiply your profitability.

And you're on your way toward the creation of a successful mission statement.

LET ME HEAR FROM YOU

I welcome the opportunity to consider the mission statements of other companies, nonprofit organizations, colleges and universities, municipalities, and government agencies for future editions of *The Mission Statement Book.* Submissions should include a description of the organization, revenue and employee data, a specific contact, and written permission for me to use the submitted material. Submissions should be mailed to me at

> Jeffrey Abrahams
> c/o Ten Speed Press
> P.O. Box 7123
> Berkeley, California 94707

PART II

THE COMPANIES
AND THEIR STATEMENTS

THE MORE THAN 300 companies presented here represent a wide variety of industries. But in order to present each one in a consistent manner, I have included the company's statement(s) and a profile of the company.

I put this data to use in Part III. There you'll find indexes that arrange the companies by industry and state.

The corporate descriptions are most often presented in the companies' own words found in their annual report. For additional details, I recommend you contact the companies directly or look up their websites.

In categorizing each company, I had the dilemma of placing companies that contributed to more than one type of industry. In some cases, the company has been placed in an industry category that was listed first by the company itself in its own corporate description. In other cases, I categorized the company by the industry it was most closely associated with (for instance, General Motors makes locomotives as well as cars, but it seemed most logical to place it in the Motor Vehicles and Related category). You may wish to refer to several related headings in Part III to find companies that straddle industry categories.

Please note: No attempt has been made to analyze whether or not these companies actually "practice what they preach" and conduct business by the terms of their mission statements, vision, values, objectives, goals, etc. That is an entirely different kind of book. My intention here is to focus on the nature and content of the mission statement genre and provide a reference resource for people attempting to write a statement for their own company or organization.

Ace Hardware Corporation

The Ace corporate mission is to be a retail support company ... providing independent Ace dealers with quality products, programs and services that focus on retail success. The philosophies of low up-front pricing and highly efficient, productive manIBMagement will always guide our basic operating decisions.

We are committed to offering the best overall program to Ace retailers. To do so, we must maintain our market share and expand it where possible by supporting our existing dealers, as well as broadening our dealer base, where appropriate.

We are also committed to understanding the dynamics of retailing, the effects of intense competition, and the importance of improving communication with Ace dealers. We are here to serve the Ace dealer, we know our success is based on our independent retailer's success, and we are committed to that success.

CORPORATE DESCRIPTION

Ace Hardware Corporation operates as a wholesaler of hardware and related products, and manufactures paint products. As a dealer-owned cooperative, Ace sells its products retail to the public through 4,100 individual retailers who own 5,000 Ace stores.

ADDRESS   2200 Kensington Ct.
Oak Brook, IL 60521

INDUSTRY CATEGORY   Retail

◆   ◆   ◆   ◆   ◆   ◆   ◆

Adia Personnel Services

| Vision

Passion for quality.
Dedication to innovation.
Commitment to employees.

| Goal

To translate Adia's vision into increased market share, long-term profitability, and employee loyalty.

| **Mission Statement**

Adia will be recognized as the industry leader by consistently providing service excellence to our customers. We will be our clients' first choice for personnel services.

Adia will be known as the easiest personnel services company to do business with. We are committed to removing barriers between us and our customers.

Adia will be identified as a company which improves client productivity by providing highly skilled temporary and full-time workers.

Adia will be perceived as the preferred company to work for in the industry. Our commitment to management and staff autonomy, extensive training, internal promotions and generous benefits will translate into unparalleled ownership and pride by our employees. These programs will result in high staff retention, positive morale and exceptional company loyalty.

Adia will provide franchises with a high level of support resulting in an appreciation of their Adia affiliation and recognition of the value of services provided by Adia. Adia will actively solicit franchisees' advice and suggestions.

Adia will be regarded as the industry leader for innovation throughout its operations. We will integrate successful industry traditions with progressive programs and management.

Adia will attract and retain the highest level of temporary employees by providing benefits and programs customized for the unique requirements of this segment of our work force. Worker satisfaction will result in outstanding Adia representation.

Adia will achieve significant market share while consistently producing operating results and profits that exceed industry norms.

CORPORATE DESCRIPTION

Adia is in the personnel services business, providing temporary and full-time workers.

ADDRESS   100 Redwood Shores Parkway
Redwood City, CA 94065

INDUSTRY CATEGORY   Business Services

◆ ◆ ◆ ◆ ◆ ◆ ◆

Advest, Inc.

STATEMENT | **Advest's Mission**

We are committed to be the best at helping people build wealth, primarily toward retirement, through the highest quality, most effective professionals in the industry.

CORPORATE DESCRIPTION

Advest, Inc. is one of the country's leading regional brokerage and investment banking firms and a wholly owned subsidiary of The Advest Group, Inc. The Company provides investment banking, securities brokerage, trading and other financial advisory services to individual, corporate and institutional clients.

ADDRESS   90 State House Square
Hartford, CT 06103

INDUSTRY CATEGORY   Financial Investment Services

◆ ◆ ◆ ◆ ◆ ◆ ◆

Aeroquip-Vickers, Inc.

STATEMENT | **Our Mission**

The mission of Aeroquip-Vickers, Inc. is to create economic value for our shareholders through superior growth and profitability.

To accomplish our mission, we will develop strategies that create sustainable competitive advantage; and we will build an organization fully capable of implementing these strategies.

Our success will not be a matter of chance, but of commitment to the core values that distinguish us:

CUSTOMER ORIENTATION. We listen to our customers and respond to their needs.

QUALITY. We provide quality in everything we do.

TECHNOLOGY. We invest in technology to enhance our productivity and effectiveness.

INNOVATION. We take personal initiative for constructive change.

INTEGRITY. We conduct ourselves ethically, respect the dignity of the individual and are responsible community citizens.

TEAMWORK. We work as a team across functions, businesses and cultures.

By personalizing these core values and by working hard, we will win and we will all share in our success.

CORPORATE DESCRIPTION

Aeroquip-Vickers, Inc. is two companies, Aeroquip Corporation and Vickers, Incorporated, worldwide manufacturers and distributors of engineered components and systems to industrial, automotive and aerospace markets.

ADDRESS   3000 Strayer
P.O. Box 50
Maumee, OH 43537-0050

INDUSTRY CATEGORY   Manufacturing

◆　◆　◆　◆　◆　◆　◆

Airborne Express

| **Airborne Express Statement of Values**

Airborne Express is its people, teamed to satisfy the worldwide shipment and delivery needs of their customers. Every employee is an important and valued member of the Airborne team. Each strives to perform with excellence and to ensure reliable, economical, quality service. All take pride in being the industry's premier provider of customer satisfaction, in fact and by reputation.

Airborne Values are the foundation for the corporate drive to excel.

Customer Satisfaction is the top priority of every employee and the purpose of every job. Cost effective ongoing achievement of customer satisfaction is the foundation of our business.

♦ ♦ ♦

Strategies, goals and objectives, established to ensure consistent customer satisfaction, corporate financial health, and employee development and support, are clearly defined, communicated and understood.

♦ ♦ ♦

Management believes in, promotes and pursues excellence throughout the organization. Excellence is expected in the quality and quantity of work done by every employee in every function, both for our customers and our fellow employees. "Doing it right the first time" is the dominant pattern in every activity.

♦ ♦ ♦

Initiative and ingenuity applied to the conduct of business and the resolution of problems are encouraged and supported throughout the organization.

♦ ♦ ♦

The roles and responsibilities of every employee are clearly defined. Aggressive cooperative fulfillment on behalf of our customers and in support of Airborne strategies and goals is valued and commendable.

♦ ♦ ♦

Reward structures recognize contribution to and achievement of results that enhance customer satisfaction, improve cost effectiveness and strengthen profitability.

♦ ♦ ♦

The outcomes of living the Airborne Values are:

Quality service for our customers.
A rewarding work environment for our people.
Adequate return to our shareholders.

CORPORATE DESCRIPTION

Airborne Express provides door-to-door express delivery of small packages and documents throughout the United States and to most foreign countries. The company also acts as an international and domestic freight forwarder for shipments of any size. Most of the company's domestic shipments are transported on its own airline and fleet of ground transportation vehicles through its company-owned airport and central sorting facility in Wilmington, Ohio. Airborne Express's responsibility begins with pickup at point of origin and extends through delivery to the consignee. Throughout all transactions, the customer has access to progress reports every step of the way.

ADDRESS　　3101 Western Ave.
P.O. Box 662
Seattle, WA 98111

INDUSTRY CATEGORY　　Package Delivery Service

♦ ♦ ♦ ♦ ♦ ♦ ♦

Alliant Techsystems, Inc.

The mission of Alliant Techsystems is to be the leading supplier of defense products and services to the U.S. government and its allies. We will:

- Be an outstanding employer
- Lead in the markets we serve
- Continuously improve the quality of everything we do
- Be a positive force in the communities where we live and work

And by so doing, we will achieve consumer satisfaction, superior financial performance, and enhanced shareholder value.

CORPORATE DESCRIPTION

Alliant Techsystems' businesses have supplied high-quality defense products and systems to the U.S. government and its allies for more than 50 years. Today, the company ranks as the largest munitions supplier to the U.S. Department of Defense and the world's leading developer and manufacturer of lightweight torpedoes.

ADDRESS   600 Second St. NE
Hopkins, MN 55343-8384

INDUSTRY CATEGORY   Industrial, Specialized

◆　◆　◆　◆　◆　◆　◆

AlliedSignal Inc.

STATEMENT | **Our Vision**

We will be one of the world's premier companies, distinctive and successful in everything we do.

| **Our Commitment**

We will become a Total Quality Company by continuously improving all our work processes to satisfy our internal and external customers.

| **Our Values**

CUSTOMERS Our first priority is to satisfy customers.

INTEGRITY We are committed to the highest level of ethical conduct wherever we operate. We obey all laws, produce safe products, protect the environment, practice equal employment, and are socially responsible.

PEOPLE We will help our fellow employees improve their skills, encourage them to take risks, treat them fairly, and recognize their accomplishments, stimulating them to approach their jobs with passion and commitment.

TEAMWORK We build trust and worldwide teamwork with open, candid communications up and down and across our organization. We share technologies and best practices, and team with our suppliers and customers.

SPEED We focus on speed for competitive advantage. We simplify processes and compress cycle times.

INNOVATION We accept change as the rule, not the exception, and drive it by encouraging creativity and striving for technical leadership.

PERFORMANCE We encourage high expectations, set ambitious goals, and meet our financial and other commitments. We strive to be the best in the world.

CORPORATE DESCRIPTION

AlliedSignal Inc. manufactures a variety of specialized materials for the Aerospace, Automotive, and Engineered Materials markets serving the needs of consumer, military, and commercial customers. Allied has more than 400 facilities in the United States and 40 other countries and territories.

ADDRESS   101 Columbia Rd.
Morristown, NJ 07962-1057

INDUSTRY CATEGORY   Industrial, Specialized

◆ ◆ ◆ ◆ ◆ ◆ ◆

American Express

STATEMENT | **American Express Company Vision**
"To Become the World's Most Respected Service Brand"

| **American Express Blue Box Values**
All our activities and decisions must be based on, and guided by, these values.

- Placing the interests of Clients and Customers first.
- A continuous Quest for Quality in everything we do.
- Treating our People with respect and dignity.
- Conduct that reflects the highest standards of Integrity.
- Teamwork—from the smallest unit to the enterprise as a whole.
- Being Good Citizens in the communities in which we live and work.

To the extent we act according to these values, we believe we will provide outstanding service to our clients and customers, earn a leadership position in our businesses and provide a superior return to our shareholders.

CORPORATE DESCRIPTION

American Express is a global travel, financial and network services provider. Founded in 1850, the company provides individuals with charge and credit cards, travelers cheques and other stored value products. It also offers financial planning, brokerage services, mutual funds, insurance and other investment products.

ADDRESS   American Express Tower
World Financial Center
200 Vesey St.
New York, NY 10285

INDUSTRY CATEGORY   Financial Investment Services

◆ ◆ ◆ ◆ ◆ ◆ ◆

American Family Insurance Group

STATEMENT | **Vision Statement**

Strong, growing and friendly

| **Mission**

The mission of the American Family Insurance Group is to provide financial protection for qualified individuals, families and business enterprises. We will do so on a profitable basis in an expanding geographic territory. Our primary business focus will be to deliver personal lines insurance products through an exclusive agency force. To fulfill our Mission, we are committed to improvement of our business so that we represent a best value to consumers and a strong, growing and friendly organization to our customers, agents and employees.

CORPORATE DESCRIPTION

American Family Insurance Group is a multi-line insurance provider with a wide variety of products for individuals, families, and businesses. It offers financial services and property, auto, commercial, health and life insurance in fourteen states.

ADDRESS   6000 American Parkway
Madison, WI 53783

INDUSTRY CATEGORY   Insurance

◆ ◆ ◆ ◆ ◆ ◆ ◆

American Protective Services, Inc.

STATEMENT | **American Protective Services, Inc.**
Company Philosophy

QUALITY SERVICE
To provide the finest service that money can buy, yet still be affordable to our market.

STANDARDS OF ETHICS
To conduct ourselves with unfailing commitment to the highest ethical and professional standards. To always treat others as we would like to be treated.

OUR MOST IMPORTANT RESOURCE
To place maximum emphasis on our uniformed personnel . . . our most important resource. To keep the profit motive of our free enterprise system in harmony with the needs of our people, and when necessary, to err in favor of human considerations rather than monetary ones.

PROFESSIONAL DEVELOPMENT
To provide good jobs for our people; jobs that are challenging, but safe, and that provide a realistic expectation of career development.

REASONABLE PROFIT

To realize a reasonable profit for all our hard work and for the risks that we assume in providing our service.

JOB SATISFACTION

To be proud that we have given our work our best effort and had fun along the way.

CORPORATE DESCRIPTION

American Protective Services is a privately held contract security company. It provides security officers for a wide variety of businesses, including ships, warehouses, shopping center, high-rise office buildings, hospitals, airports, construction projects, radio, television, and motion picture studios, hotels, country clubs, residential communities, hi-tech and research facilities, government and public utilities, factories, and retail stores.

Their business is to assist their clients in theft prevention, access control, safety and a host of other essential services.

ADDRESS　　7770 Pardee Ln.
Oakland, CA 94621-1454

INDUSTRY CATEGORY　　Security

◆　◆　◆　◆　◆　◆　◆

American United Life Insurance Company

STATEMENT | **Mission**

We the people of AUL provide security and peace of mind to our customers by offering insurance and other financial products and services. We will be the company of choice by providing value and building the highest level of trust with our customers.

| Values

ACHIEVEMENT

We will be one of the top companies in the financial services industry.

STEWARDSHIP

We will always be strong in order to keep our long-term promise to pay.

PARTNERSHIP

We will work together as a team with our producers to serve our customers.

INTEGRITY

We will act with the highest ethical standards.

RESPONSIVENESS

We will listen to our customers and respond to their needs.

EXCELLENCE

We will be distinguished as a quality company and good corporate citizen.

| Objectives

CUSTOMER

Maximize the value to our customers by providing superior quality in products and services.

GROWTH

Grow revenue and assets on a profitable basis. Increase our number of customers.

PARTNERS

Grow and strengthen our partnerships.

PEOPLE

Cultivate an environment which values, develops and retains high-quality people.

CORPORATE DESCRIPTION

American United Life Insurance Company is a mutual company with headquarters in Indianapolis. It was founded in 1877 and currently is licensed to sell in 45 states and the District of Columbia.

ADDRESS   P.O. Box 368
Indianapolis, IN 46206-0368

INDUSTRY CATEGORY   Insurance

◆ ◆ ◆ ◆ ◆ ◆ ◆

Ameritas Life Insurance Corp.

STATEMENT | **Ameritas Vision**

Through the combined efforts of all associates, Ameritas will Be the Best in our targeted markets by exceeding the expectations of our customers. We will be a leader in the design and delivery of select insurance and financial products and services.

CORPORATE DESCRIPTION

Ameritas and its subsidiaries offer a full line of life insurance, group dental and vision products, annuities, pension products including 401(k) retirement plans, and a wide variety of investment products and services.

ADDRESS   5900 O St.
P.O. Box 81889
Lincoln, NE 68510

INDUSTRY CATEGORY   Insurance

◆ ◆ ◆ ◆ ◆ ◆ ◆

Ameritech

STATEMENT | **Our Vision**

Ameritech will be the world's premier provider of full-service communications for people at work, at home or on the move. Our goal is to improve the quality of life for individuals and to increase the competitive effectiveness of the businesses we serve. As we move and manage information for our customers, we set standards for value and quality. Ameritech's competence reaches worldwide, building on our strength in America's vibrant Upper Midwest. Customers can be assured that we will assume only those tasks we can do exceedingly well.

CORPORATE DESCRIPTION

Ameritech is one of the world's leading information companies, providing full-service communication and advanced information services to about 12 million customers in the Midwest. Ameritech also has operations in international markets.

ADDRESS   30 South Wacker Dr.
                Chicago, IL 60606

INDUSTRY CATEGORY   Communications and Telecommunications

◆   ◆   ◆   ◆   ◆   ◆   ◆

AMETEK Inc.

To achieve enhanced, long-term shareholder value by building a strong operating company serving diversified markets to earn a superior return on assets and to generate growth in cash flow.

Strategies & Objectives

♦ Succeed with the shareholder value enhancement plan, including reducing the cost of capital with debt levels consistent with AMETEK's strong case flow.

♦ Realize over the long term a 30% Return on Assets (Operating Profit divided by Assets) for all operating businesses.

♦ Optimize cash flow for investment in growth and debt reduction.

♦ Build competitive advantages by investing in the growth of current businesses to evolve and extend core products and manufacturing technologies into new products, niche markets and new applications.

♦ Continue to apply Total Quality Management throughout the Company to nurture new product development, manage change and continual improvement, and make cost reductions an integral part of planning and control.

♦ Capitalize on the competitive advantages of floor care, specialty metals and water filtration products. Build on unique advantages in other product lines and other niche markets.

♦ Multiply the benefit of operational resources with a global market expansion, especially in Europe and the Pacific Rim. Employ strategic alliances and joint ventures to manage risk, especially for international growth.

♦ Maintain a flat, decentralized organization focused on the customer. Seek business synergies that create strength and reduce costs.

♦ Link incentive compensation with qualitative and quantitative business performance.

CORPORATE DESCRIPTION

AMETEK designs, builds and sells:

- ♦ Motors for vacuum cleaners, furnaces, electric lawn tools, computers and business machines;
- ♦ Water filtration systems for home, commercial and industrial use;
- ♦ High-purity metal in strip and powder form for the electronics and telecommunications industry;
- ♦ Instruments for aerospace, automotive, manufacturing, utility and petrochemical industries.

ADDRESS   Corporate Office
Station Square
Paoli, PA 19301

INDUSTRY CATEGORY   Manufacturing

♦   ♦   ♦   ♦   ♦   ♦   ♦

Amgen

STATEMENT | **Mission**

To be the world leader in developing and delivering important, cost-effective therapeutics based on advances in cellular and molecular biology.

(The company explains its mission in its annual report, as follows:) Our mission statement serves as the foundation for our business strategy, drives our operational objectives and guides our daily decisions. We constantly strive "to be the world leader in developing and delivering important, cost-effective therapeutics based on advances in cellular and molecular biology." We have pursued this mission for more than a decade. It has served us well and provides direction as we face the future.

CORPORATE DESCRIPTION

Amgen Inc. is a global biotechnology company that discovers, develops, manufactures, and markets human therapeutics based on advances in cellular and molecular biology.

ADDRESS   One Amgen Center Dr.
Thousand Oaks, CA 91320-1789

INDUSTRY CATEGORY   Pharmaceutical/Biotechnology

◆　◆　◆　◆　◆　◆　◆

AMP Incorporated

STATEMENT | **Our Mission**

AMP Incorporated is in the business of designing, manufacturing, marketing and selling interconnection components, subassemblies and services for electrical, electronic and optical applications. These are supplied both direct to customers and through distributors and subcontractors.

AMP's customer base includes original equipment manufacturers and businesses which install and maintain electrical and electronic equipment throughout the world.

AMP's business is customer-driven, technology-influenced and engineering-oriented, coupled with world-class manufacturing.

In order to achieve the core company goals, various business units have been created. These business units consist of sectors, groups, divisions, departments, companies and strategic alliances, which have the responsibility for developing cohesive missions, quantifiable objectives and comprehensive strategies through adopting the guiding principles within the following key result areas:

Total Customer Satisfaction
Continuous Quality Improvement
Human Resource Excellence
Growth
Profitability
Cost Reduction
Innovation/Technological Leadership
Public Responsibility/Corporate Citizenship

Our Vision

We share a vision of AMP Incorporated as a Worldwide Team of People who are:

Motivated to pursue the path to excellence through continuous improvement in all that we do.

Empowered to think globally and act locally as we address the true needs of our markets.

Inspired to provide our customers with products and services so outstanding that we will be the supplier of choice.

Our Voice

At AMP we believe in ...

Earning our leadership position in the interconnection industry by continuing to develop innovative products and services and by meeting and surpassing our customers' expectations.

Maintaining steadfast commitment to excellence in every product and every service we provide as a means of earning the confidence and loyalty of our customers.

Serving our customers' global needs by offering them our foundation of worldwide support.

Encouraging personal and team ownership of problem identification, prevention, and solution.

Creating a climate of trust and respect that empower our people to develop to the fullest, while sharing the responsibilities of success and the rewards of achievement.

Keeping each individual and function informed about AMP, its customers, suppliers, and competitors.

Forming lasting, mutually beneficial relationships with our customers and suppliers, based on fairness and integrity.

Achieving the growth and profit that guarantee our financial stability and competitive strength to maximize the long-term return to shareholders.

Fulfilling our responsibilities as a good corporate citizen by being a positive, powerful force in our communities worldwide and helping conserve our natural environment.

CORPORATE DESCRIPTION

The world leader in electrical/electronic connection devices, AMP supplies well over 100,000 types of and sizes of devices to 200,000 electrical/electronic equipment makers—and tens of thousands of customers who install and maintain equipment. AMP has 160 facilities in 32 countries.

ADDRESS   P.O. Box 3608
Harrisburg, PA 17105-3608

INDUSTRY CATEGORY   Electronics

◆   ◆   ◆   ◆   ◆   ◆   ◆

AMR Corporation (American Airlines)

STATEMENT | **AMR Corporate Vision**

We will be the global market leader in air transportation and related information services.

That leadership will be attained by:

- Setting the industry standard for safety and security.
- Providing world class customer service.
- Creating an open and participative work environment which seeks positive change, rewards innovation, and provides growth, security and opportunity to all employees.
- Producing consistently superior financial returns for shareholders.

CORPORATE DESCRIPTION

AMR Corporation is the parent company of American Airlines. One of the largest scheduled passenger airlines in the world, American provides jet service to approximately 180 destinations worldwide.

ADDRESS   P.O. Box 619616
Dallas/Fort Worth Airport
Dallas, TX 75261-9616

INDUSTRY CATEGORY   Transportation

◆ ◆ ◆ ◆ ◆ ◆ ◆

Anheuser-Busch Companies, Inc.

STATEMENT | **Vision**

Through all our products, services and relationships, we will add to life's enjoyment.

| **Mission**

The mission of Anheuser-Busch is to:
+ Be the world's beer company
+ Enrich and entertain a global audience
+ Deliver superior returns to our shareholders

| **Values**

We believe in ...
+ Quality in everything we do.
+ Exceeding customer expectations.
+ Trust, respect and integrity in all of our relationships.
+ Continuous improvement, innovation and embracing change.
+ Teamwork and open, honest communication.
+ Each employee's responsibility for contributing to the company's success.
+ Creating a safe, productive and rewarding work environment.
+ Promoting the responsible consumption of our products.
+ Preserving and protecting the environment and supporting communities where we do business.

CORPORATE DESCRIPTION

Anheuser-Busch, Inc. is a St. Louis-based diversified corporation whose subsidiaries include the world's largest brewing organization, the country's second-largest producer of fresh-baked foods and the country's second-largest theme park operator.

ADDRESS   One Busch Pl.
St. Louis, MO 63118-1852

INDUSTRY CATEGORY   Food/Beverage

◆ ◆ ◆ ◆ ◆ ◆ ◆

Apple Computer

STATEMENT | **Corporate Mission**

Apple is committed to bring the best personal computing products and support to students, educators, designers, scientists, engineers, businesspersons and consumers in over 140 countries around the world.

(Information provided courtesy of Apple Computer, Inc.)

CORPORATE DESCRIPTION

Apple Computer, Inc., ignited the personal computer revolution in the 1970s with the Apple II, and reinvented the personal computer in the 1980s with the Macintosh. Apple is now recommitted to its original mission—to bring the best personal computing products and support to students, educators, designers, scientists, engineers, businesspersons and consumers in over 140 countries around the world.

ADDRESS   1 Infinite Loop
Cupertino, CA 95014

INDUSTRY CATEGORY   High Technology

◆ ◆ ◆ ◆ ◆ ◆ ◆

Aristech Chemical Corporation

STATEMENT | **Mission**

Aristech Chemical Corporation's mission is to provide products of the highest value and consistent quality to our customers and to continually improve every work process in our system which develops, produces, markets and services these products.

The people of Aristech, utilizing their skill, experience, creativity and knowledge, are the key to Aristech's success. Participative leadership demonstrating integrity provides an environment where employees can develop their talents, find pride and fulfillment in work and contribute through teamwork. Our stakeholders—including Customers, Employees, Owners, and Suppliers—are valued in an environment of cooperation, communication and partnership.

Excellence is achieved by aligning the organization on these goals:

- Be a leader in customer satisfaction.
- Focus resources and efforts in our core businesses.
- Form long-term strategic alliances.
- Constantly improve technology, skills, and safety, health and environmental performance.

In pursuit of this mission, Aristech will achieve for its stakeholders the long-term goals of continuous development and maximized values.

CORPORATE DESCRIPTION

Aristech Chemical Corporation is a diversified producer of chemicals and plastics serving a large number of industrial and consumer firms.

ADDRESS   600 Grant St.
Pittsburg, PA 15219-2704

INDUSTRY CATEGORY   Chemicals

◆ ◆ ◆ ◆ ◆ ◆ ◆

Armstrong World Industries, Inc.

| **Our Operating Principles**

To respect the dignity and inherent rights of the individual human being in all dealings with people.

To maintain high moral and ethical standards and to reflect honesty, integrity, reliability and forthrightness in all relationships.

To reflect the tenets of good taste and common courtesy in all attitudes, words and deeds.

To serve fairly and in proper balance the interests of all groups associated with the business—customers, stockholders, employees, suppliers, community neighbors, government and the general public.

Our Corporate Mission

We will be a fast and flexible learning organization committed to ever-improving the value of Armstrong for our employees, customers and shareholders.

We will be a world leader in all our businesses by excelling in customer satisfaction, innovation, marketing and manufacturing.

These capabilities, our people, and our commitment to quality will be our global platform for growth.

Our Strategies for Success

Build a human resource and leadership development program that will assure continuous learning, agile thinking and positive change.

Develop marketing expertise that will give us a competitive advantage year after year.

Forge strong and superior relationships with all our customers.

Improve our process to understand consumers and other end users and to create compelling offers for them.

Invest in the tools of technology and the methods of world-class manufacturing.

Invest in capital, innovation and marketing where returns are in line with our shareholders' expectations.

Seek alliances, products and brands which will gain strength from our capabilities in customer relationships, innovation, marketing and manufacturing.

CORPORATE DESCRIPTION

Armstrong is primarily a manufacturer and marketer of interior furnishings. Its products include floor coverings, building products and furniture.

ADDRESS   P.O. Box 3001
Lancaster, PA 17604-3001

INDUSTRY CATEGORY   Manufacturing

♦ ♦ ♦ ♦ ♦ ♦ ♦

AT&T Corp.

STATEMENT | **AT&T MISSION STATEMENT**

We aspire to be the most admired and valuable company in the world. Our goal is to enrich our customers' personal lives and to make their businesses more successful by bringing to market exciting and useful communications services, building shareowner value in the process.

| **Our Vision**

Build shareholder value by providing "universal communications services" that put our customers in touch with the people or the information they need, whenever they want, wherever they are, in the form most useful to them, and at a competitive price.

CORPORATE DESCRIPTION

AT&T Corp. is the world's premier voice and data communications company, serving more than 80 million customers, including consumers, businesses and government. With annual revenues of nearly $52 billion and 110,000 employees, AT&T provides services to virtually every country and territory around the world.

AT&T runs the world's largest, most sophisticated communications network and the largest digital wireless network in North America. The company is a leading supplier of data and Internet services for businesses and the nation's largest direct Internet service provider to consumers.

AT&T provides outsourcing, consulting and networking-integration services to large businesses. The company offers outbound local calling to businesses in 49 states and, as a result of its July 1998 merger with Teleport Communications Group, plans to integrate complete local service into its business offers throughout 66 U.S. markets by early 1999.

AT&T's businesses are backed by the research and development capabilities of AT&T Labs, which is working to create the information services and communications network of tomorrow.

ADDRESS   32 Avenue of the Americas
New York, NY 10013-2412

INDUSTRY CATEGORY   Communications and Telecommunications

◆ ◆ ◆ ◆ ◆ ◆ ◆

Atlanta Gas Light Company

STATEMENT | **Our Company's Vision**

Atlanta Gas Light Company will become America's **leading** natural gas and energy services company by being the **provider of choice** for customers, employees, and investors.

To be the provider of choice ... Atlanta Gas Light Company must change ...

- For Customers
  —From ... Emphasis on regulation ... to emphasis on competition
  —From ... Offering what we think customers want ... to providing what customers value
- For Employees
  —From ... Being "good enough" ... to being the best
  —From ... Rewarding for longevity ... to rewarding for performance
- For Investors
  —From ... "We have always done it this way" ... to "How can it be done better?"
  —From ... Business as usual ... to increasing shareholder value

CORPORATE DESCRIPTION

Atlanta Gas Light Company is the largest natural gas distribution company in the southeastern United States, serving more than 12 million customers in 228 cities and communities in Georgia. Through its subsidiary, Chattanooga Gas Company, the Company serves more than 40,000 customers in Chattanooga and Cleveland, Tennessee.

ADDRESS   P.O. Box 4569
             Atlanta, GA 30302

INDUSTRY CATEGORY   Utility

◆ ◆ ◆ ◆ ◆ ◆ ◆

Autodesk, Inc.

| **Vision**

To create software tools that transform ideas into reality.

| **Mission**

To create quality software solutions and support services that foster innovation, creativity and productivity for customers and partners around the world.

| **Philosophy/Values**

At Autodesk we work to excite and inspire our CUSTOMERS worldwide with INNOVATIVE software that defines the market. We strive to produce the best QUALITY products and processes. We're committed to our employees, customers, partners and vendors, as we consider them an integral part of our business. We are flexible in our approaches, practice responsible risk-taking and learn from our mistakes. We're alert to PROFITABLE ideas, and are able to forego short-term gain in favor of long-term vitality for our shareholders.

We are direct, clear and ETHICAL in our communication and actions. We will not deceive anyone—not even our competitors. We speak with honesty, courage and care. We're accountable for our words, our work and our processes—building a challenging and rewarding work environment.

We RESPECT individuality both inside and outside the corporation, honoring diverse lifestyles and workstyles. We believe our vitality depends on capitalizing on everyone's unique talents. Through collaboration and TEAMWORK we continually create ourselves, our company and our success.

CORPORATE DESCRIPTION

Autodesk, Inc. develops, markets and supports a family of design automation and multimedia software products for use on personal computers and workstations. The Company distributes its products primarily through a network of dealers and distribution and has operations in the Americas, Europe and Asia/Pacific.

ADDRESS   2320 Marinship Way
Sausalito, CA 94965

INDUSTRY CATEGORY   High Technology

◆　◆　◆　◆　◆　◆　◆

Avis Rent A Car

STATEMENT | **AVIS® Vision**

To Become the World's Pre-eminent Rent A Car Brand

| **AVIS® Mission**

To Ensure A Stress-Free Rental Experience By Providing Safe, Dependable Vehicles And Special Services Designed To Win The Customers' Loyalty.

| **AVIS® Values**

INTEGRITY

We will honor all commitments to our customers, employees and shareholders.

We will conduct our business with unwavering high standards of honesty, trust, professionalism, and ethical behavior.

We will communicate openly and frequently with all constituents with a principle of communicating what we know, when we know it.

QUALITY

We will place the interests of our customers first.

We will be dedicated to building a rewarding and lasting relationship with each and every customer.

We will maintain a continuous quest for world class quality to assure customer satisfaction to earn the unwavering loyalty of our customers.

SHAREHOLDER VALUE

We will deliver value in all we do to assure consistently high returns to our shareholders.

We will be dedicated to continuous innovation to assure we explore new ideas and opportunities to accelerate profitable growth.

We will recognize and reward excellent performance, which drives superior results.

TEAMWORK

We will work as one cohesive Team from the smallest unit to the enterprise as a whole.

We will develop and retain leaders who continually raise the bar, provide direction, remove barriers, and empower people to successfully accomplish goals.

We will assure a sharing of ideas, skills, and resources throughout the company.

We will respect the structure and reporting relationship in the company, yet assure that organization boundaries never become a barrier to success.

RESPECT FOR THE INDIVIDUAL

We will treat each person with whom we work with respect and dignity.

We will communicate expectations to employees and provide honest and timely feedback on performance.

We will embrace a diversity of ideas, cultures, ethnicity, and background to enhance our promise and value to customers.

We will provide career development opportunities for employees who show initiative and performance results to help them individually manage their own career to maximize their potential.

COMMUNITY RESPONSIBILITY

We will be active participants in the communities in which we live and work.

We will encourage employee involvement in civic and charitable activities.

We will be role model business leaders in the countries and communities in which we operate the business.

We will develop and implement business practices consistent with safeguarding the environment.

CORPORATE DESCRIPTION

Avis Rent A Car, Inc. operates the second largest general use car rental business in the world, based on total revenue and volume of rental transactions. The Company, based in Garden City, New York, rents vehicles to business and leisure travelers in the United States, Canada, Puerto Rico, the U.S. Virgin Islands, Argentina, Australia, and New Zealand.

ADDRESS   900 Old Country Rd.
Garden City, NY 11530

INDUSTRY CATEGORY   Transportation

◆ ◆ ◆ ◆ ◆ ◆ ◆

Avon Products, Inc.

STATEMENT | **Our Vision**

To be the Company that best understands and satisfies the product, service and self-fulfillment of women—globally.

CORPORATE DESCRIPTION

Avon is the world's leading direct seller of beauty and related products with $4.0 billion in annual revenues. Avon markets to women in more than 100 countries through 1.7 million independent representatives.

ADDRESS   9 W. 57th St.
New York, NY 10019

INDUSTRY CATEGORY   Consumer Goods and Services

◆ ◆ ◆ ◆ ◆ ◆ ◆

Baldor Electric Company

STATEMENT | **To be the best, as determined by our customers ...**

Our mission is: To be the best (as determined by our customers) marketers, designers and manufacturers of electric motors and drives. To achieve this, we must:

♦ Provide better value to our customers than any of our competitors.

♦ Attract and retain competent employees dedicated to reaching our goals and objectives.

♦ Produce good, long-term results for our shareholders.

CORPORATE DESCRIPTION

Baldor Electric Company designs, manufactures and markets a broad line of energy-efficient electric motors and electronic drives. From the home office in Fort Smith, Arkansas, the Company supports the sales offices and warehouses that stock Baldor products worldwide to supply distributors and original equipment manufacturers. Baldor does business in more than 55 countries.

ADDRESS   P.O. Box 2400
Fort Smith, AR 72902

INDUSTRY CATEGORY   Manufacturing

♦   ♦   ♦   ♦   ♦   ♦   ♦

Ball Corporation

STATEMENT | **Mission**

To create shareholder value by being the first-choice provider to our stakeholders of the products, services and expertise that we offer.

| **Strategy**

- Invest in businesses which we believe will earn a return in excess of our cost of capital.
- Operate our North American beverage and food can businesses for earnings growth and positive cash flow by manufacturing low-cost, high-quality products while maintaining technical excellence.
- Manage our PET container operations and extensive international packaging operations for significant sales and earnings growth.
- Capitalize on the world-class capabilities of our aerospace and technologies subsidiary.

CORPORATE DESCRIPTION

Ball Corporation is a manufacturer of metal and plastic packaging, primarily for beverages and foods, and a supplier of aerospace and other technologies and services to commercial and governmental customers. The company was founded in 1880.

ADDRESS 10 Longs Peak Dr.
Broomfield, CO 80021

INDUSTRY CATEGORY Manufacturing

♦ ♦ ♦ ♦ ♦ ♦ ♦

Banta Corporation

STATEMENT | **Banta Corporate Mission**

Banta Corporation, a leader in the graphic communications industry, provides quality printing and other image services to publishers, merchandisers, and consumer products companies. The vitality of this business depends upon providing targeted products and services on a timely basis, in a quality manner, at a competitive value.

Banta's very existence depends on providing superior products and services to customers. Banta businesses serve a broad spectrum of graphic communication needs for educational, general book and magazine publishers, and for advertising, catalog, other direct marketing and consumer products companies. The Corporation delivers professionalism, accuracy, timeliness, quality products, appropriate technology and value. It has built credibility, relationships and reputation that distinguish it from the competition. Banta will not knowingly compromise its value by promulgating inappropriate graphics or content.

As a publicly-owned corporation, Banta's ultimate responsibility is to its shareholders. Banta's goal, in this regard, is to earn a superior return on investment through profit improvement and growth. Corporate focus and strategic positioning consistent with prudent yet aggressive asset management create the value placed on Banta common stock in the securities market.

Banta's success depends on honest, thoughtful, hard-working people who work as a team and are dedicated to the importance of setting and achieving higher goals. Banta feels a deep, personal responsibility to all its associates and will reward employees commensurate with their contributions to the success of the business. As an equal opportunity employer, it seeks to create and maintain an environment where every person has the opportunity to reach his or her potential.

Banta is committed to honesty and integrity in its relationship with suppliers of raw materials, goods and services. The Corporation evaluates suppliers on the basis of quality, price, service and innovation.

Banta encourages associates to become involved in activities that make their communities a better place to live and do business. Support of worthwhile projects in areas where the Corporation operates enhances the general health, education and well-being of the communities. Banta's Corporate Foundation selectively supports national, regional and community civic and cultural activities and educational institutions.

Banta Corporation's stated objective is to perform at superior levels. Profit increases the value of shareholder's investment and is essential to business reinvestment and employee security. Growth is necessary to provide opportunities on an ever-increasing scale for all associates. Banta Corporation, therefore, is committed to achieving profitable growth.

CORPORATE DESCRIPTION

Banta Corporation is one of North America's leading providers of printing and graphic services. It serves publishers of educational and general books, special-interest magazines, consumer and business catalogs, and direct marketing materials. Its other businesses offer pre-press services, computer software packages, multimedia kits, point-of-purchase displays, product labels, postage stamps and single-use products.

ADDRESS   225 Main St., River Place
P.O. Box 8003
Menasha, WI 54952-8003

INDUSTRY CATEGORY   Media

◆　◆　◆　◆　◆　◆　◆

Bard (C.R. Bard, Inc.)

STATEMENT | **Mission**

Bard's Mission is to advance the delivery of health care by profitably developing, manufacturing and marketing value-driven products which meet the quality, integrity and service expectations of our customers while providing opportunities for employees. As a result, we will optimize shareholder value and be a respected worldwide health care company.

CORPORATE DESCRIPTION

C.R. Bard, Inc. is a leading multinational developer, manufacturer and marketer of health care products. Bard holds strong positions in cardiovascular, urological and surgical products.

ADDRESS   730 Central Ave.
Murray Hill, NJ 07974

INDUSTRY CATEGORY   Health Care

◆   ◆   ◆   ◆   ◆   ◆   ◆

Barnett Banks, Inc.

STATEMENT | **Mission Statement**

The mission of Barnett is to create value for its owners, customers and employees as a major financial service provider in the United States.

We will strengthen our position in existing markets by providing a full range of financial services, by acquiring other financial institutions, and by capitalizing on our market knowledge and our commitment to entrepreneurial market ownership.

Our focus will be on satisfying our customers' total financial needs by offering differentiated benefits driven by a sales and service process that solidifies and expands the total customer relationship.

Barnett will aggressively pursue diversified income opportunities which include internal initiatives, acquisitions, and alliances in attractive markets throughout the country which complement, leverage, and expand our core capabilities.

By the year 2000, Barnett will be a fully diversified financial services organization with the acknowledged leadership position in the evolving banking business in its markets and with a diversified group of other financial businesses throughout the nation.

CORPORATE DESCRIPTION

Barnett Banks, Inc. operates 616 banking offices in Florida and Georgia. With $38 billion in assets, it is the leading financial institution in Florida and the 22nd largest in the United States.

ADDRESS   50 North Laura St.
P.O. Box 40789
Jacksonville, FL 32203-0789

INDUSTRY CATEGORY   Banking

◆ ◆ ◆ ◆ ◆ ◆ ◆

Bausch & Lomb Incorporated

STATEMENT

(From the company booklet entitled "The Values We Share at Bausch & Lomb")

| Value Defined

val'ue (val'yoo) n.—belief, principle or conviction that has fundamental worth to people. For instance, loyalty to one's family is a value many share. Honesty or sincerity is another common value.

The Importance of Values

The concept of values is vital in most areas of society. Our standards of behavior, even our laws, spring from our values. If we accept certain values as important, then we will strive to protect and defend them, even when they are rejected or ignored by others.

Shared values bind the members of a group together. Individual and group activities are thus directed along a common path. Values jointly shared also provide a framework for making decisions, encourage constructive patterns of behavior and define avenues for personal and business success.

The Role of Values at Bausch & Lomb

At Bausch & Lomb, we've inherited a strong company whose values have shaped a tradition of excellence and quality that spans more than 135 years. A clear understanding of those values will help us meet the obligation we have to preserve and enhance what we have inherited, especially the Bausch & Lomb name and all that it represents. It also enables us to pass on a company that continues to reach its highest potential for future generations of employees and shareholders.

Although our company operates in an ever-changing environment, our values remain constant. They don't shift with time or circumstance. They don't yield to whim or convenience. They apply to all areas of our business. Bausch & Lomb's values are clearest when viewed in relation to these elements: customers and quality; employees; profits; innovation; and community.

We'll discuss these areas in the pages to follow.

The Importance of Customers & Quality

The trust, respect and loyalty of customers worldwide is vital to Bausch & Lomb's long-term success. We earn and maintain these attributes by making conformance to customer's expectations our number one priority, as expressed in two ways.

- ♦ First, we totally commit ourselves to our customers, including those within the company, by identifying their expectations; remaining attuned and responding to changing demands; developing relationships based on trust and mutual respect; and by assuming a leadership role in advancing their knowledge and skills and championing the success of their activities or business.

♦ Second, we pursue quality as a way of life at Bausch & Lomb. Quality is more than a word used to describe our products and services. It's an attitude that affects everything we do. Since 1853, Bausch & Lomb products have been known throughout the world for their quality. To continue this tradition we will:

   ♦ Require strict attention to quality in every department and every functional area, at all levels.
   ♦ Provide the highest quality products and services.
   ♦ Select suppliers according to their quality and total cost, not just price.

Our commitment to our customers and to quality is constant and consistent. We define Quality as consistently conforming to the expectations of our Customers.

A Partnership with Employees

Bausch & Lomb's employees are the company's most important corporate resource. Their efforts produce more than products and service—they produce the company's success and lead it towards the future. Bausch & Lomb and its employees have a partnership, built upon mutual trust and respect. To maintain this relationship, the company and the employees must be committed to upholding certain principles . . . on every level, worldwide.

The first and most important principle is that every employee's contribution is valuable. Each individual is necessary to the success of the company as a whole.

In recognition of that principle, we are committed to helping each employee reach his or her full potential by providing job opportunities and salary advancement on the basis of merit, without bias or discrimination of any kind. We are further committed to diversity throughout the company, and to implementing specific programs to increase the representation of women and minorities, especially in senior management.

As individuals, we must be committed to upholding high standards of personal conduct at work and to carrying out our responsibilities in the best possible manner. In addition, we must treat our fellow employees with trust, respect and dignity.

We are committed to encouraging creativity and initiative by providing an environment for all employees to develop skills and abilities. As individuals, we are asked to contribute ideas and suggestions continually to seek a better way to improve the company, its products and its work methods.

As partners, the company and employees must be sensitive to each other's needs and concerns. We believe in recognizing the achievements of individual employees and in compensating employees fairly. We will recognize employees' concerns for employment continuity by making layoffs and position eliminations measures of last resort.

Together, we will support a positive image of Bausch & Lomb in its worldwide community. We will also show sensitivity to the needs of the company's customers at all times.

Finally, the company and employees, as partners, will join together to make Bausch & Lomb a safe, healthy place to work.

The Role of Profits

Bausch & Lomb is in business to make a profit. That is the only way the company can pay its employees a fair wage, provide an attractive return to shareholders, and invest in future growth. It is also the only way the company can sustain itself to carry out its business mission and citizenship responsibilities.

The company has become known in recent years for high standards of growth and profitability. The company will be managed with the intent of maintaining such high standards, and management and employees will be challenged to contribute toward these goals.

Although we remain focused on the need to maximize performance, Bausch & Lomb will balance its needs for current earnings with its desire for consistent long-term growth. The company will not mortgage its future for the sake of short-term gain.

Innovation and Finding a Better Way

Innovation and creativity are essential catalysts for Bausch & Lomb's future success. Our search for new products and services, and for business methods which better meet the needs of our customers must reach into every sector of our company.

Bausch & Lomb is committed to encouraging the teamwork, initiative and entrepreneurial spirit which fosters innovation, and to nurturing emerging businesses which creates significant growth for the company. This requires the company to provide an atmosphere which allows individuals to challenge the status quo and to assume reasonable risk, and which permits new ideas to surface in an unrestricted manner. It further obligates Bausch & Lomb to adequately fund the prices of discovery, and to provide the tools of research and to find progress in ideas which have failed as well as in those which succeed.

Our Company and Our Community

Bausch & Lomb believes that the company and its employees have a shared responsibility to work for the betterment of their communities. When the company and the community work together, there can be significant benefits for both parties.

To reinforce this commitment, the company will operate in an ethical manner, carefully observing all laws and regulations; will be sensitive to community needs; and will act in partnership with other businesses, agencies of government, and civic organizations to improve the quality of life for everyone.

Accordingly, the company encourages individual employee involvement in community activities at all levels. Utilizing corporate resources, Bausch & Lomb will engage in a selected range of philanthropic activities in its home communities, seek appropriate leadership roles, and remain in close contact with other private sector and governmental leaders.

CORPORATE DESCRIPTION

Bausch & Lomb manufactures and distributes products for the Healthcare and Optics business.

The Healthcare segment consists of three sectors:

♦ The Personal Health Sector: Consists of branded products purchased directly by consumers. Products include contact lens solutions, oral care products, eye care products, and non-prescription medications.

♦ The Medical Sector: Consists of contact lenses, ophthalmic pharmaceuticals, hearing aids, dental implants, and other products sold to healthcare professionals, or which are obtainable by consumers only through a prescription.

♦ The Biomedical Sector: Includes products and services supplied to customers engaged in the research and development of pharmaceuticals and the production of genetically engineered materials.

The Optics Segment consists primarily of products used by consumers for the protection or enhancement of vision, such as sunglasses, binoculars and telescopes.

ADDRESS One Chase Square
P.O. Box 54
Rochester, NY 14601-0054

INDUSTRY CATEGORY   Scientific, Photo, and Control Equipment

♦   ♦   ♦   ♦   ♦   ♦   ♦

Baxter Healthcare Corporation

STATEMENT | **Vision Statement**

Our businesses hold leading positions in high-growth global markets. Driving this leadership are talented, dedicated people, all pursuing the same vision—to be recognized worldwide as a leader in providing select, innovative health-care technologies, products and services to improve lives.

CORPORATE DESCRIPTION

Baxter International Inc. (NYSE: BAX) is a global medical products and services company that focuses on critical therapies for life-threatening conditions. Baxter's products and services in blood therapies (biopharmaceuticals and blood collection, separation and storage devices), cardiovascular medicine, medication delivery and renal therapy are used by health-care providers and their critically ill patients in 112 countries.

ADDRESS   One Baxter Pkwy.
Deerfield, IL 60015-4633

INDUSTRY CATEGORY   Medical Products and Services

◆ ◆ ◆ ◆ ◆ ◆ ◆

Bay View Capital Corporation
(Bay View Federal Bank)

STATEMENT | **Mission Statement**

The mission of Bay View Federal Bank is to operate a successful, safe and sound regional bank serving the financial needs of the California communities in which it is located.

| **Directional Statements**

To accomplish this mission, management and the staff will, with respect to the following constituencies:

1. <u>Shareholders</u> – Generate through earnings sufficient capital to sustain the growth objectives of the Bank and achieve equitable returns to shareholders. Increase the value of the retail franchise through expansion of products, services and markets served. Prudently manage the risk components of the balance sheet in order to ensure the long term viability of the Bank.

2. <u>Customers</u> – Meet customer needs by investing prudently in research, development and sales programs that increase market penetration. Emphasize quality of service in all dealings with customers.

3. <u>Regulators</u> – Maintain favorable regulatory ratings that will allow the bank to pursue its business plan.

4. <u>Employees</u> – Invest in the human resources of the Bank to accomplish corporate objectives and enhanced career opportunities for employees.

CORPORATE DESCRIPTION

Bay View Capital Corporation is the holding company for Bay View Federal Bank, a federally chartered savings bank with $2.6 billion in assets. Bay View operates 25 branches and 4 loan production offices principally in the San Francisco Bay Area.

ADDRESS   2121 S. El Camino Real
San Mateo, CA 94403

INDUSTRY CATEGORY   Banking

◆ ◆ ◆ ◆ ◆ ◆ ◆

Becton Dickinson and Company

STATEMENT | **At Becton Dickinson, Superior Quality Is the Only Way**

Our mission as a Company is to provide the many markets we serve with products of consistently superior quality at price levels that are fair and competitive. Achieving this mission is a responsibility we all share and is necessary to meet the expectations of our customers, ourselves, and our shareholders. With this uncompromising dedication to superior quality, we have a focus for our actions that unifies us, adds value to our work, and enriches our lives.

CORPORATE DESCRIPTION

Becton Dickinson and Company manufactures and sells a broad range of medical supplies and devices and diagnostic systems for use by health-care professionals, medical research institutions and the general public.

ADDRESS 1 Becton Dr.
Franklin Lakes, NJ 07417-1880

INDUSTRY CATEGORY Scientific, Photo, and Control Equipment

◆ ◆ ◆ ◆ ◆ ◆ ◆

Ben & Jerry's Homemade, Inc.

STATEMENT | **Ben & Jerry's Statement of Mission**

Ben and Jerry's is dedicated to the creation and demonstration of a new corporate concept of linked prosperity. Our mission consists of three interrelated parts:

PRODUCT MISSION

To make, distribute and sell the finest quality all-natural ice cream and related products in a wide variety of innovative flavors made from Vermont dairy products.

SOCIAL MISSION

To operate the company in a way that actively recognizes the central role that business plays in the structure of society by initiating innovative ways to improve the quality of life of a broad community: local, national, and international.

ECONOMIC MISSION

To operate the company on a sound financial basis of profitable growth, increasing value for our shareholders and creating career opportunities and financial rewards for our employees.

Underlying the mission of Ben & Jerry's is the determination to seek new and creative ways of addressing all three parts, while holding a deep respect for individuals, inside and outside the company, and for the communities of which they are a part.

CORPORATE DESCRIPTION

Ben & Jerry's Homemade, Inc., a Vermont corporation, makes Ben & Jerry's super-premium ice cream, Ben & Jerry's lowfat frozen yogurt, and ice cream novelties. The company's products are available in unique as well as traditional flavors, and are marketed through supermarkets, grocery stores, convenience stores, and restaurants. The company also franchises Ben & Jerry's ice cream scoop shops.

ADDRESS   P.O. Box 240
                 Waterbury, VT 05676

INDUSTRY CATEGORY   Food/Beverage

◆ ◆ ◆ ◆ ◆ ◆ ◆

Bethlehem Steel

STATEMENT | **Vision**

To Be the Premier Steel Company

| **Objectives**

◆ Increase stockholder value
◆ Serve our customers
◆ Partnerships among employees
◆ Be a good citizen

| **Strategy**

◆ Concentrate on steel
◆ Rebuild our financial strength
◆ Improve continuously safety and total quality

CORPORATE DESCRIPTION

Bethlehem produces high-quality steel for a variety of industries, including automotive, construction, office furniture, home appliance, farm equipment, container, heating/air-conditioning, machinery, shipbuilding, oil and gas pipeline, tubing, and railroad cars and rail transportation.

ADDRESS   1170 Eighth Ave
Bethlehem, PA 18016

INDUSTRY CATEGORY   Manufacturing

◆ ◆ ◆ ◆ ◆ ◆ ◆

Betz Laboratories, Inc.

STATEMENT | Betz Corporate Strategies

The primary mission of Betz Laboratories, Inc. is to utilize value-added services and concepts to promote growth of its basic businesses profitably while maintaining existing net margins:

Betz will continue to provide its customers a return on their Betz investment through value added programs and concepts.

Betz will continue to build on its strengths and focus most of its resources into the basic businesses and product lines.

Betz will continue to specialize through decentralization wherever it makes sense from a marketing or technology standpoint as a method to improve its market penetration and profit growth.

Betz will continue to strive to be the highest quality company in all aspects of its people, products, services, and technology.

Betz will continue to help preserve the environment and maintain our dedication to the safe and prudent use of our chemicals in our technical and commercial programs.

CORPORATE DESCRIPTION

Betz is a multinational company that is a technological leader in the worldwide specialty chemical market. The Company's business is the engineered chemical treatment of water, wastewater, and process systems operating in a wide variety of industrial and commercial applications, with particular emphasis on the chemical, petroleum refining, paper, automotive, electrical utility and steel industries.

ADDRESS   4636 Somerton Rd.
Trevose, PA 19053-6783

INDUSTRY CATEGORY   Chemicals

◆　◆　◆　◆　◆　◆　◆

Blockbuster Inc.

STATEMENT | **Mission**

To be a global leader in rentable home entertainment by providing outstanding service, selection, convenience and value.

CORPORATE DESCRIPTION

Blockbuster Inc. and various affiliates of Blockbuster Inc. own and operate BLOCKBUSTER VIDEO® stores worldwide. Blockbuster is a unit of Viacom Inc., one of the world's largest entertainment and publishing companies and a leading force in nearly every segment of the international media marketplace.

ADDRESS   1201 Elm St.
Renaissance Tower
Dallas, TX 75270

INDUSTRY CATEGORY   Consumer Goods and Services

◆   ◆   ◆   ◆   ◆   ◆   ◆

Borg-Warner Security Corporation

STATEMENT |

Any business is a member of a social system, entitled to the rights and bound by the responsibilities of that membership.

Its freedom to pursue economic goals is constrained by law and channeled by the forces of a free market. But these demands are minimal, requiring only that a business provide wanted goods and services, compete fairly, and cause no obvious harm.

For some companies, that is enough. It is not enough for Borg-Warner.

We impose upon ourselves an obligation to reach beyond the minimal. We do so convinced that by making a larger contribution to the society that sustains us, we best assure not only its future vitality, but our own.

This is what we believe ...

We believe in the dignity of the individual.

However large and complex a business may be, its work is still done by people dealing with people. Each person involved is a unique human being, with pride, needs, values, and innate personal worth. For Borg-Warner to succeed we must operate in a climate of openness and trust, in which each of us freely grants others the same respect, cooperation, and decency we seek for ourselves.

We believe in our responsibility to the common good.

Because Borg-Warner is both an economic and social force, our responsibilities to the public are large. The spur of competition and the sanctions of the law give strong guidelines to our behavior, but alone do not inspire our best. For that we must heed the voice of our natural concern for others. Our challenge is to supply goods and services that are of superior value to those who use them; to create jobs that provide meaning for those who do them; to honor and enhance human life; and to offer our talents and our wealth to help improve the world we share.

We believe in the endless quest for excellence.

Though we may be better today than we were yesterday, we are not as good as we must become. Borg-Warner chooses to be a leader—in serving our customers, advancing our technologies, and rewarding all who invest in us their time, money and trust. None of us can settle for doing less than our best, and we can never stop trying to surpass what already has been achieved.

We believe in continuous renewal.

A corporation endures and prospers only by moving forward. The past has given us the present to build on. But to follow our visions to the future, we must see the difference between traditions that give us continuity and strength, and conventions that no long serve us—and have the courage to act on that knowledge. Most can adapt after change has occurred; we must be among the few who anticipate change, shape it to our purpose, and act as its agents.

We believe in the commonwealth of Borg-Warner and its people. Borg-Warner is both a federation of businesses and a community of people. Our goal is to preserve the freedom each of us needs to find personal satisfaction while building the strength that comes from unity. True unity is more than a melding of self-interests; it results when values and ideals are also shared. Some of ours are spelled out in these statements of belief. Others include faith in our political, economic, and spiritual heritage, pride in our work and our company; the knowledge that loyalty must flow in many directions; and a conviction that power is strongest when shared. We look to the unifying force of these beliefs as a source of energy to brighten the future of our company and all who depend on it.

About these statements

In September 1981, Borg-Warner chairman James E. Beré asked about 100 senior managers to help him define the company's basic business principles. He asked each of them to reflect on what values and beliefs should underlie Borg-Warner's business decisions, to send him these ideas in writing, and to take part in interviews on the subject.

This testimony was compiled by the corporate staff throughout the winter of 1981–82, and interwoven with Beré's own ideals for the company. Beré and staff then grouped the ideas into major themes and developed these into the five statements listed inside [above]. The preamble was added to sum up both the philosophy that launched this process and the goal the five tenets are meant to serve.

The statements are intended to help guide all who act on Borg-Warner's behalf. As Beré said in announcing them at a management meeting in May 1982, the beliefs are "our promise to the future."

(Copyright © 1982 Borg-Warner Corporation)

CORPORATE DESCRIPTION

Borg-Warner Security Corporation is the nation's largest security company, with 87,000 employees serving more than 150,000 customers from nearly 600 offices located throughout the United States and in Canada, the United Kingdom and Colombia. Guard, alarm, armored and courier services are provided under the Wells Fargo®, Burns®, Pony Express® and Bel-Air names, which represent the best in technology, service and performance.

ADDRESS   200 S. Michigan Ave.
                Chicago, IL 60604

INDUSTRY CATEGORY   Security

◆   ◆   ◆   ◆   ◆   ◆   ◆

Bruno's, Inc.

STATEMENT | **Mission**

Bruno's Inc. is a leading southeastern supermarket chain that utilizes multiple store formats to cater to all consumers. We will always offer our customers the best possible values. Our perishable departments will be superior, offering the freshest and highest quality products unmatched by any competitor. We will treat our family of employees fairly, and we will be customer and community minded. We will use selected technology to enhance our efficiencies and to support our future growth. Through these means we will continue to provide added value to our customers, our shareholders, our employees, and our communities.

CORPORATE DESCRIPTION

Bruno's, Inc. is a leading regional food retailer, operating a total of 258 supermarkets in Alabama, Georgia, Mississippi, Florida, South Carolina, and Tennessee.

ADDRESS   800 Lakeshore Pkwy.
                Birmingham, AL 35211

INDUSTRY CATEGORY   Food/Beverage

◆   ◆   ◆   ◆   ◆   ◆   ◆

Burlington Northern Santa Fe Corporation

STATEMENT | **Vision**

Our vision is to realize the tremendous potential of the Burlington Northern and Santa Fe Railway by providing transportation services that consistently meet our customers' expectations.

We will know we have succeeded when:

- Our customers find it easy to do business with us, receive 100-percent on-time, damage-free service, accurate and timely information regarding their shipment, and the best value for their transportation dollar.
- Our employees work in a safe environment free of accidents and injuries, are focused on continuous improvement, share the opportunity for personal and professional growth that is available to all members of our diverse work force, and take pride in their association with BNSF.
- Our owners earn financial returns that exceed other railroads and the general market as a result of BNSF's superior revenue growth, an operating ratio in the low 70s, and a return on invested capital which is greater than our cost of capital.
- The communities we serve benefit from our sensitivity to their interests and to the environment in general, our adherence to the highest legal and ethical standards, and the participation of our company and our employees in community activities.

CORPORATE DESCRIPTION

The Burlington Northern and Santa Fe Railway Company was formed in December 1996 following the merger of Santa Fe Pacific Corporation and Burlington Northern Inc. in September 1995. Headquartered in Fort Worth, Texas, the company is one of the world's leading providers of high-quality rail and transportation services.

ADDRESS   PO Box 961057
Fort Worth, TX 76161-0057

INDUSTRY CATEGORY   Transportation

◆ ◆ ◆ ◆ ◆ ◆ ◆

Butler Manufacturing Company

STATEMENT | **Corporate Mission Statement**

Butler Manufacturing Company's mission is to be the value and service leader for building systems, specialty components, and construction services for nonresidential construction customers.

CORPORATE DESCRIPTION

Butler Manufacturing Company is a leader in the marketing, design, and production of systems and components for nonresidential structures. Products and services are provided within the commercial, community, industrial, and agricultural markets.

Butler was founded in 1901, and currently operates manufacturing, engineering, and service centers throughout the United States and twelve foreign countries. The Company's products are primarily sold, installed, and serviced through approximately 4,000 independent dealers in the United States and throughout the world. Butler also provides complete design/build construction services directly to large customers with multiple sites or with projects of unusual size or complexity.

ADDRESS   BMA Tower, Penn Valley Park
P.O. Box 419917
Kansas City, MO 64141-0917

INDUSTRY CATEGORY   Construction

◆　◆　◆　◆　◆　◆　◆

Cabot Corporation

Vision/Mission Statement

To build successful businesses by developing and using our market knowledge, and our operating, financial, and technical competencies.

To lead in quality, safety, innovation, employee involvement, operating standards, and financial performance.

To be recognized as the preferred supplier, customer, and employer; as a valued member of the community; and as a quality company by stockholders and the financial community.

Operating Cultures

- Principles, which require adherence to ethical, legal, and environmental standards and the maintenance of decent, safe, and healthy working conditions in all facilities.
- Employees, who are accountable, creative, entrepreneurial, profit-conscious, highly skilled, and quick.
- Management, which is customer-focused, urgent, empowering, simple, and governed by mutual respect and Total Quality methods.

Strategies for Base Business Development

- Total cost improvement, declining real unit costs
- Market segmentation, creative margin improvement, Market Driven Management (MDM)
- Customer/supplier partnerships where possible/appropriate
- Basic technology improvement and protection
- Employee development
- Sharing of knowledge and competence within the company
- Task alignment, Added Value Analysis (AVA)
- Exploitation of global position
- Creation of interdivisional opportunities
- Development of sales/distribution skills
- Development of business unit extensions
- Expansion of existing commercial relationships

CORPORATE DESCRIPTION

Cabot Corporation has operations in specialty chemicals and materials, and energy.

ADDRESS   75 State St.
Boston, MA 02109-1806

INDUSTRY CATEGORY   Chemicals

◆ ◆ ◆ ◆ ◆ ◆ ◆

Carpenter Technology Corporation

STATEMENT | **Vision**

Our vision is to be a major, profitable and growing international producer and distributor of specialty alloys, materials and components by providing specialty material and service solutions for our customers, integrating our growing knowledge of materials science, customer needs, user industries and engineering applications.

CORPORATE DESCRIPTION

Carpenter Technology Corporation is a leading international manufacturer of specialty alloys and engineered products for use in aerospace, automotive, industrial and consumer products industries.

ADDRESS   P.O. Box 14662
Reading, PA 19612-4662

INDUSTRY CATEGORY   Industrial, Specialized

◆ ◆ ◆ ◆ ◆ ◆ ◆

Caterpillar Inc.

STATEMENT | **Business Mission**

Provide customers worldwide with differentiated products and services of recognized superior value.

Pursue businesses in which we can be a leader based on one or more of our strengths.

Create and maintain a productive work environment in which employee satisfaction is attained with high levels of personal growth and achievement while conforming to our "Code of Worldwide Business Conduct and Operating Principles."

Achieve growth and provide above-average returns for stockholders resulting from both management of ongoing businesses and a studied awareness and development of new opportunities.

Note: The Caterpillar Inc. Business Mission Statement was reprinted with the expressed written permission of Caterpillar Inc.

CORPORATE DESCRIPTION

Caterpillar Inc. together with its consolidated subsidiaries operates in three principal business segments:

1. Machinery—Design, manufacture, and marketing of earthmoving, construction, and materials handling machinery.
2. Engines—Design, manufacture, and marketing engines for earthmoving and construction machines.
3. Financial Products—Provides financing alternatives for Caterpillar and noncompetitive related equipment sold through Caterpillar dealers, and extends loans to Caterpillar customers and dealers.

ADDRESS   100 N.E. Adams St.
Peoria, IL 61629

INDUSTRY CATEGORY   Construction

◆　◆　◆　◆　◆　◆　◆

CBI Industries, Inc.

STATEMENT | **Purpose**

CBI Industries is a world-wide business enterprise whose purpose is to enhance shareholder value by safely and profitably providing products and services of the highest value through its contracting, industrial gases and terminaling businesses principally to customers who process, store and/or use liquids and gases. To achieve this purpose, CBI's decisions focus on sustaining customer satisfaction, maximizing employee contribution and maintaining the highest degree of integrity in its conduct.

Guiding Principles

1 To prudently manage our assets to provide a fair return to our shareholders.
2 To be continually responsive to the changing needs of our customers.
3 To emphasize the importance of our employees by:
    Providing an environment where people realize their full potential, where they feel good about their work, are challenged and well trained, and are able to grow both professionally and personally, thereby maximizing their contributions.
    Promoting employee ownership to enhance a mutuality of interest with other shareholders.
    Developing and maintaining appropriate compensation, benefit and retirement programs to promote long-term employment.
4 To encourage innovation which improves our business processes, practices, and products and services, in order to achieve a clear competitive advantage.
5 To foster a work environment which emphasizes integrity, quality, safety, training and productivity as important and ongoing practices throughout CBI.

6 To develop close relationships with our suppliers, treating them with fairness and respect, enabling them to support our commitments to our customers.

7 To carry out work consistent with responsible behavior toward the environment.

8 To encourage and support the activities of our employees in civic, social and professional organizations where they live and work.

CORPORATE DESCRIPTION

CBI Industries has subsidiaries operating in the construction of metal plate structures and other contracting services, industrial gases, oil blending and storage, and other investments.

ADDRESS   800 Jorie Blvd.
Oak Brook, IL 60521-2268

INDUSTRY CATEGORY   Industrial, Specialized

◆ ◆ ◆ ◆ ◆ ◆ ◆

Cenex, Inc.

STATEMENT | **Cenex Purpose**

To strengthen the economic well-being of our member-owners.

| **Our Mission**

To anticipate and meet the agronomy, petroleum and related product and service needs of farmers, ranchers and rural communities through local cooperatives.

To be the preferred supplier of those products and services through local cooperatives.

To build and maintain a financially strong cooperative system.

CORPORATE DESCRIPTION

Cenex serves 320,000 farmers and ranchers through more than 1,800 local cooperatives in 15 states from the Great Lakes to the Pacific Northwest. Through the Cenex/Land O'Lakes marketing venture, essential supplies are provided to rural America including refined fuels, lubricants, propane, tires and vehicle accessories, plant food, crop protection products, and information/technology services.

ADDRESS   P.O. Box 64089
St. Paul, MN 55164-0089

INDUSTRY CATEGORY   Agriculture

◆　◆　◆　◆　◆　◆　◆

Centerbank

STATEMENT | **Our Company Vision**

Our company will continue to endeavor to be a provider of financial services and products that customers need and want. The company will maintain strategic and organizational flexibility to meet the challenges associated with the dynamics of the changing industry landscape.

In pursuing its vision, the company will endeavor to maintain an environment which encourages employee integrity, creativity, a spirit of excitement, and personal growth; rewards high performance; and ensures a high level of customer satisfaction.

CORPORATE DESCRIPTION

Centerbank is a diversified financial services company committed to enhancing long-term profitability and increasing shareholder value. Incorporated in 1850, it comprises banking and commercial finance operations in Connecticut as well as nationwide mortgage banking and equipment leasing businesses. With assets of $2.8 billion, deposits of $2.2 billion, a $6.0 billion mortgage service portfolio, and shareholders' equity of $173.6 million, Centerbank is one of the larger independent financial institutions based in Connecticut.

ADDRESS   60 N. Main St.
Waterbury, CT 06702

INDUSTRY CATEGORY   Banking

◆ ◆ ◆ ◆ ◆ ◆ ◆

Centura Banks, Inc.

STATEMENT | **The Centura Commitment**

WE ARE COMMITTED to helping our customers achieve all of their financial goals. Customers are the reason we exist, and we must go above and beyond their expectations to create positive, memorable experiences for them. We must listen to their needs, provide them with creative, appropriate financial solutions and serve them in a friendly, caring way.

WE ARE COMMITTED to doing what's right, without exception. Every decision we make, and every action we take, must follow the highest ethical and moral standards. We must tell the truth, keep all commitments and use our time and resources to make our world a better place to live.

WE ARE COMMITTED to creating an exceptional place to work. The power of each individual must be allowed to grow and develop to its potential. We must respect human dignity, reward outstanding performance and empower our people to make the most beneficial decisions for their customers, the company and themselves.

WE ARE COMMITTED to excellence in everything we do. There is always a better way. We must think creatively, continuously improve and pursue new ideas to achieve uncommon breakthroughs. We must thrive on change, shun bureaucracy and strive to surpass our competitors. We must grow our knowledge, learn from our mistakes and emphasize quality in all aspects of our work.

WE ARE COMMITTED to following these principles to make a profit. We must profit to remain in business, grow and meet our responsibilities to all who have a stake in our success—namely our employees, our customers, our communities and our shareholders.

CORPORATE DESCRIPTION

Centura is a bank holding company headquartered in Rocky Mount, North Carolina, which provides a full range of financial services for businesses and individuals.

ADDRESS   134 N. Church St.
P.O. Box 1220
Rocky Mount, NC 27802

INDUSTRY CATEGORY   Banking

◆　◆　◆　◆　◆　◆　◆

Chase Manhattan Corporation

STATEMENT | **The Chase Vision**

| **Purpose**

We provide financial services that contribute to the success of individuals, businesses, communities and countries around the world. By creating solutions for our customers, opportunities for our employees, and superior returns for our shareholders, we help each to achieve their goals.

| **Mission**

Our mission is to be the premier global financial services company in the markets we serve.

Values

Our behavior is guided by fundamental values that flow from a total commitment to integrity:

- Customer Focus
- Respect for Each Other
- Teamwork
- Initiative
- Professionalism
- Quality

CORPORATE DESCRIPTION

Founded in 1799, The Chase Manhattan Corporation, with more than $366 billion in assets, has operations in over 50 countries, clients in 180, and relationships with more than 30 million households across the U.S.

ADDRESS   270 Park Ave.
New York, NY 10017-2070

INDUSTRY CATEGORY   Banking

◆　◆　◆　◆　◆　◆　◆

Chemfab Corporation

STATEMENT | **Mission Statement**

Our mission is to deliver superior value to our customers through preeminence in polymer-based flexible advanced materials and related manufacturing process technologies.

CORPORATE DESCRIPTION

Chemfab Corporation and its consolidated subsidiaries is an international advanced performance materials company. It designs, manufactures, and markets a wide range of products for use in extreme service environments. These products are based on the Company's flexible composite materials and specialty films which exhibit exceptional thermal, chemical, electrical, mechanical and release characteristics. The Company's flexible composite materials typically consist of woven fiberglass or other high-strength reinforcements coated or laminated with thermoplastics and elastomers. Worldwide end-use applications are in aerospace, architectural, chemical processing, communications, electronics, food processing, military, protective clothing, and other industrial markets.

ADDRESS   701 Daniel Webster Hwy.
P.O. Box 1137
Merrimack, NH 03054-1137

INDUSTRY CATEGORY   Manufacturing

◆   ◆   ◆   ◆   ◆   ◆   ◆

Chemical Banking Corporation

STATEMENT | **Chemical Banking Corporation**
1992 Mission Statement

"Our mission is to be the best brand-based financial institution, a leader in our chosen markets.

We value the highest ethical standards and leadership, excellence and quality in everything we do while creating and maintaining mutually valuable customer relationships.

We are committed to an environment marked by teamwork, accountability, innovation, openness and empowerment that provides an opportunity for personal challenge and growth."

CORPORATE DESCRIPTION

Chemical Banking Corporation is a broad-based financial institution with three core business franchises—the Global Bank, the Regional Bank and Texas Commerce Bancshares. Chemical's Global Bank is a leading bank for large U.S. corporations and foreign-based multinationals, with significant product franchises.

ADDRESS   270 Park Ave.
New York, NY 10017

INDUSTRY CATEGORY   Banking

◆ ◆ ◆ ◆ ◆ ◆ ◆

Chevron Corporation

STATEMENT   Chevron Corporation
Our Mission, Vision, Values, Strategies

Mission

Chevron is an international petroleum company. Our mission is to achieve superior financial results for our stockholders, the owners of our business.

Vision

Our vision is to be Better than the Best, which means:
- *All employees are proud of their work.*
- *Competitors respect us.*
- *Customers and Suppliers prefer us.*
- *Investors are eager to invest in us.*
- *Communities welcome us.*
- *Continuous Quality Improvement is the process we will use to achieve our vision.*

Values

How we pursue our mission, building on our basic values, is as important as the mission itself.

- *Employees*—the key to success—providing the fundamental strength, vitality and reputation of our Company.
- *Customers*—our basic focus—achieving a lasting partnership means a commitment to excellence in everything we do.
- *Community*—the respect of the community is critical— requiring the highest ethical standards of business, social and environmental responsibility.

Strategies

Our primary objective is to achieve superior operating and financial results so that our stockholders' return exceeds the performance of our strongest competitors. Our goal for the period 1994–1998 is to be number one relative to our competitors in Total Stockholder Return. We believe a 15% per year average return will be required to achieve this goal. In pursuing this objective we will balance long-term growth and short-term profits.

Guided by Chevron's Corporate Strategic Plan we will reach this objective by:

- *Building a committed team to accomplish the Corporate mission.* Built on mutual trust and respect for our differences, we will foster a work environment where communication is open and effective, our maximum contributions are valued and rewarded and teamwork is practiced in support of the common good. We will accept our individual responsibility for personal growth, alignment of our goals with the Company's strategies and the success of the business.
- *Focusing attention on customers.* We will anticipate and respond quickly to the changing needs of our customers— providing quality products and services to customers inside and outside the Company.

- *Ensuring that all operations meet the challenge of the strongest competitors.* We will gain a competitive edge through superior asset management, effective cost control and effective use of technology.
- *Identifying and improving our key work processes.* We will continuously benchmark best practices, improve productivity, measure progress, and communicate results and experiences.
- *Decentralizing decision making and accountability.* We will effectively communicate Corporate objectives and policies, move operational goals and decision making to strategic business units and stress the importance of meeting specific goals.
- *Giving high priority to environmental, public and government concerns.* Compliance is not enough—we will look ahead, anticipate change and develop innovative responses to safety, environmental, public and governmental concerns.

CORPORATE DESCRIPTION
Chevron is an international petroleum company.

ADDRESS   225 Bush St.
San Francisco, CA 94104

INDUSTRY CATEGORY   Oil and Gas

♦ ♦ ♦ ♦ ♦ ♦ ♦

Citicorp

STATEMENT | **Citicorp's Vision**

To be a global bank, unique in worldwide presence ... dedicated to our customers ... financially strong ... consistent ... committed to our staff and its development ... delivering sustained superior performance to investors.

Unique, Global

Unique is being global, operating both locally and collectively around the world in delivering financial services for the benefit of both individual and corporate consumers; unique also in spirit.

Customer Dedication

Dedicated to serving the financial needs of our customers. Our success depends upon our importance to them. Customer needs define position, product and service offerings. We seek to build sustained relationships and recognize the importance of continuity of people. We are committed to competitive excellence, delivering customer satisfaction, and investing in the business, people and technology required to meet our customer needs.

Financially Strong

Our balance sheet and earnings will be a source of strength; recognized internally, by customers, investors, competitors, rating agencies, and regulators. Control, executional excellence and productivity improvements are acknowledged objectives.

Consistent

Consistent and dependable: in our commitment to our people, with our customers, in the development and execution of our strategy, and in our risk profile.

Staff and Its Development

We seek to recruit, develop and retain the most talented people from around the world. We will reward people based on merit, teamwork, results, and shared values. We are accountable: We will take responsibility for our actions and the exercise of judgment. We treat people with trust, openness and respect, and maintain the highest ethical standards in dealing with customers, the community and each other.

Delivering Sustained Superior Performance to Our Investors

Our objective is to achieve superior returns on shareholders' equity. We seek the reality and reputation of being well-managed, being consistently sound in our risk-taking judgments, and being seen as one of the most respected financial institutions in the world; a unique global bank.

CORPORATE DESCRIPTION

Citicorp, with its subsidiaries and affiliates, is a global financial services organization. Its staff of 81,500 serves individuals, businesses, governments, and financial institutions in over 3,300 locations including branch banks, representative offices, and subsidiary and affiliate offices in 93 countries throughout the world.

Citicorp, a U.S. bank holding company, is the sole shareholder of Citibank, N.A. (Citibank), its major subsidiary.

ADDRESS   399 Park Ave.
New York, NY 10043

INDUSTRY CATEGORY   Banking

◆ ◆ ◆ ◆ ◆ ◆ ◆

The Clorox Company

STATEMENT | **Organization**

We recognize that our continued success as a company depends upon the abilities and best efforts of the people at our U.S. and International operations.

We strive, therefore, to maintain the kind of organization in which our people can perform to the best of their ability to help the Company achieve its objectives. A number of principles guide us in structuring the organization for managing our business and for encouraging the performance necessary for the Company's success.

| **Principles**

We will maintain within the organization the flexibility to take full advantage of our opportunities and make the best use of our strengths and resources.

To most effectively develop, manufacture and market our products, we have established profit centers and the centralized staff functions to support them. When justified by promising business opportunities, we will establish new profit centers and sales organizations, and new central staff services groups.

We will delegate responsibility with accountability to the lowest practical level with the proper balance of management control to assure optimum coordination and use of our resources worldwide.

We will encourage an innovative spirit throughout the organization.

We will encourage our people to take the initiative in their work, understanding that some risk is involved, but also recognizing that the potential benefits to the business often outweigh such risks.

We continually will focus on productivity improvement, cost reduction, and quality in our operations.

We will strive for and encourage throughout the entire Company a working alliance among all levels of the organization to achieve our common goals. We will use the "team approach" in all our work.

Every job in our organization should permit us to earn respect and recognition, to maintain individuality and dignity, and to experience the deep satisfaction of working with others for a common purpose.

CORPORATE DESCRIPTION

The Clorox Company is a dynamic international organization whose principal business is developing, manufacturing and marketing products that provide excellent value for consumers. These products are sold primarily in grocery stores and other retail outlets in many parts of the world.

The Company's line of domestic retail products includes many of the country's best known brands of laundry additives, home cleaning products, cat litters, insecticides, charcoal briquets, salad dressings, sauces and water filter systems. The great majority of the Company brands either lead or are a strong second in their categories.

The Company's Professional Products unit is focused on expanding many of its successful retail franchises in cleaning and food products into new channels of distribution such as the institutional and professional markets and the food service industry.

ADDRESS   1221 Broadway
Oakland, CA 94612

INDUSTRY CATEGORY   Consumer Goods and Services

◆ ◆ ◆ ◆ ◆ ◆ ◆

CMS Energy

STATEMENT | **Our Strategic Plan**

**Our Vision, Goals, Strategies and Creed Join
Together to Form our Strategic Plan**

- Our Vision declares how we as a company will operate in philosophical terms—in decision making, serving customers and measuring success.
- Our Goals describe what we will do to cement positive relationships with our stakeholders.
- Our Strategies explain how we will reach our goals.
- Finally, the company Creed is our pledge of performance. Good service and value to our customers is a must.

| **Our Vision**

CONSUMERS POWER COMPANY improves the quality of life and prosperity of its customers by providing energy and related services that are reliable, attractively priced and tailored to the needs of the customer.

The FOUNDATION of our growth is the TERRITORY THAT WE SERVE. We improve the vitality of our customer base by providing rates and services that meet our customers' needs. We bring energy-related technology and services to our customers that improve their ability to compete and thrive in the global marketplace. We accomplish this by being highly efficient, by fostering innovation, and by maximizing our ability to work and learn together.

As **EMPLOYEES,** we are *skilled* in carrying out the actions necessary to serve our customers, and we are *expected to participate* in the creation and execution of processes, policies, and procedures with the flexibility to meet changing customer needs.

Our **INVESTMENT** decisions are made with a priority on *reducing product price, improving the quality of service* we provide our customers, and expanding our services portfolio to meet changing customer needs.

The measure of our **SUCCESS** is *shareholder return.* As our service territory prospers and as our customers benefit from competitive rates, reliable energy and innovative service, our shareholders are rewarded by earning an outstanding return on their investment, by receiving a dividend that is predictable, sustainable and substantial, and by continued growth in the value of their investment.

GOAL 1 | Maintain a Positive MPSC Working Relationship

Strategies

- Resolve issues with MPSC on a timely basis.
- Share plans regularly with MPSC and staff.
- Openly acknowledge acceptance of MPSC authority.
- Utilize careful, limited judicial appeal strategy.
- Review work plan accomplishments with MPSC staff.
- Work closely and openly with Commission and staff on issues and trends of general industry interest, with emphasis on regulatory impacts of competitive issues.

GOAL 2 | Earn Employee Trust and Confidence

Strategies

- Create an environment where decisions are expected to meet the criteria implicit in the Strategic Plan (Corporate Vision, Creed, Goals and Strategies).
- Establish general behavior consistent with the Corporate Creed (as determined by subordinates, peers, supervisors and customers) as important to continued career success.

- Establish and maintain a constructive union relations environment by working with union leadership to develop mutually beneficial goals, strategies and timetables for improved employment practices which enable employees to better meet the changing needs of our customers.
- Maintain a focus on wellness and family to promote healthy lifestyles.
- Promote a learning environment where employees understand the changing nature of the utility business, contribute to defining the company's responses to these changes, and receive fair access to career development opportunities.
- Establish equitable compensation programs which recognize and reward individual and team performance and appropriately reflect increased responsibility.

GOAL 3 | **Achieve Customer Satisfaction Through Superior Service at Competitive Rates**

Strategies

- Focus corporate resources on understanding and meeting the needs of customers from the customers' perspective.
- Aggressively work to retain and add customers within profitability criteria.
- Engage all employees in the identification of customer service, margin growth and cost-saving opportunities.
- Reengineer business processes to improve our ability to add, serve and retain customers.
- Develop rates and pricing structures which enhance Consumer Power Co.'s flexibility and competitive position.
- Aggressively manage production costs to attain competitive advantage over alternative power suppliers.
- Expand customer service beyond the meter.

GOAL 4 | Continually Achieve Authorized Shareholder Return

Strategies

♦ Successfully market uncommitted MCV capacity.

♦ Establish performance-based incentive regulation with balanced incentives for customer and shareholder.

♦ Obtain MPSC acceptance of financial goals and strategies that are attractive to investors.

♦ Reduce debt and achieve a balanced capital structure.

♦ Make financially prudent capital investments that reduce product price, improve service quality and expand our services portfolio to meet changing customer needs.

♦ Maximize the value of our utility-related core competencies in current and new markets.

GOAL 5 | Maintain Safety Leadership

Strategies

♦ Build individual and collective employee commitments to achieve an injury- and incident-free work place.

♦ Increase public safety and customer safety education programs.

♦ Work with regulators and other stakeholders to develop clear definitions of safety requirements, and meet those requirements.

♦ Involve employees who use the tools/equipment in purchase decisions and in operating procedure development.

♦ Increase the understanding by management and all employees of the technical, procedural and cost aspects of safety issues.

♦ Implement electric shock task for recommendations.

GOAL 6 | **Enhance the Economic, Social and Environmental Progress of the Communities We Serve**

Strategies

- Encourage and recognize the community leadership positions and volunteer efforts of employees and retirees.
- Support and implement programs and activities which enhance the quality of education with emphasis on math and science studies.
- Assist the communities we serve in achieving improved economic attractiveness and prosperity.
- Develop and pursue a corporate-wide strategy for environmental stewardship.
- Develop a communication and education strategy to address emerging energy issues of public concern (EMF, stray voltage, rad-waste, etc.).
- Improve Michigan business climate to enhance economic development.

Our Creed

We, The People of CMS Energy and Consumers Power, believe that providing superior service and excellent value to our customers, in a safe way, are our most important priorities.

In doing so, we maximize the likelihood of a prosperous company that can provide substantial benefits to our shareholders, employees, and the communities we serve.

In conducting our business, we pledge the following to our customers, employees, shareholders, regulators and other government officials, suppliers, and neighbors:

- TO COMMUNICATE honestly and conduct our business with the highest standards of ethics, trust, and integrity.
- TO RESPECT the dignity of the individual, nurture diversity, facilitate training and career development, and promote employee fulfillment.

- TO PROMOTE a sense of ownership, accountability, and responsibility for the company's success by recognizing and encouraging achievement and excellence.
- TO STRIVE constantly to improve our performance by encouraging innovation, responsible risk-taking, and teamwork among all who contribute to our success.
- TO STRIVE to achieve a superior return to our shareholders to encourage their continued support and investment.
- TO PROVIDE a safe, clean, and productive work environment.
- TO PROTECT the environment, and the locations where we operate to preserve them for the benefit of the communities we serve.
- TO BE GOOD corporate citizens through charitable giving and voluntary service to our communities, our state and our nation.

CORPORATE DESCRIPTION

CMS Energy is a $7 billion (asset) group of growing energy companies with operations in electric generation and distribution, natural gas distribution and storage, oil and gas exploration, independent power and utility services. Its principal subsidiary, Consumers Power, is the nation's fourth-largest combination electric and gas utility.

ADDRESS   212 W. Michigan Ave.
Jackson, MI 49201-2277

INDUSTRY CATEGORY   Utility

♦ ♦ ♦ ♦ ♦ ♦ ♦

CNA Insurance Companies

Introduction

The insurance contract, at its heart, is a specific commitment on CNA's part that allows our customers to better fulfill their own diverse commitments. Recognition of this fact has led us to adopt the phrase For All The Commitments You Make as a reflection of our view of that basic value we provide our customers. In the process of serving our customers, we also make commitments to many others, such as producers, employees, stockholders, and our communities. By their very nature, commitments must be kept. We believe that the following values and strategies allows us to make our commitments with confidence that we will indeed keep them, now and in the future.

Values

1. Integrity

We believe in maintaining the utmost integrity in dealing with our policyholders, producers, employees, stockholders and communities where we do business.

2. Focus on Underlying Economic Value

We manage our business to maximize its underlying economic value. We do not let short-term profit considerations override long-term profit opportunities.

3. Long-term Relationships

We value long-term relationships with our customers, producers, reinsurers and employees. We pursue strategies designed to foster long term relationships with customers and with producers. We recognize loyalty among employees in our personnel management practices.

4. Excellence in Execution

We are committed to being the best in what we do. In planning or in execution, we want our people to be the best they can be. Our decision-making process requires solid information and rigorous analysis. We provide an environment that allows every one of our employees an opportunity to realize his or her potential to the fullest extent.

5. Organizational Responsibility

We believe that great plans are most surely achieved in the long run by an organizational system of checks and balances (thereby minimizing the probability of big mistakes), by taking controlled risks and by reducing our risk through not depending too much on any one business.

6. Pre-eminence of the Customer

We recognize that any business can succeed only if it can create and keep customers. While the insurance product alone provides a valuable service that is in the public interest, we must provide more than just another insurance product. Cost-effective methods of doing business; cost containment; value-added, caring service all are needed to fully serve and satisfy our customers.

Strategies

1. Insurance Rather than Financial Services

In the absence of market need, we do not want to be a broad-based financial services company. We want to focus on risk management needs. For example, we do not want to provide stock brokerage or real estate brokerage services.

2. Multi-line Operation

We want to pursue segments of both the commercial and individual markets. We also want to meet selected needs in property, liability, life, health and pension areas.

Our strategy of being a multi-line company follows from our desire to maximize the value of our businesses in place and our desire to control the risk from changes in the environment.

3. Capitalizing on Strengths

We want to focus our efforts and resources on businesses where we have strong competitive position and management expertise. This requires that we focus on businesses where we have or can build a large enough volume to be competitive. Wherever CNA's expertise and competitive position allow, we want to provide products to meet all the risk management needs for our customers.

4. Partnership with Distributors

We want to cultivate long term, genuine partnership relationships with our distributors. HPA (High Performance Agency) and LSA (Life Select Agency) programs are examples of this strategy.

5. Cost-effective Methods of Doing Business

We seek cost-effective methods of doing business by maintaining a lean functional organization and by improving productivity through work flow streamlining and automation. Expense reduction can provide significant competitive advantages as long as other goals, such as excellence in execution, are not compromised.

6. Cost Containment

We feel a responsibility to our customers to bring about changes in the costs of goods and services that make up the underlying price of the insurance producer. We recognize that the insurance consumer today seeks more than just spread of risk in an insurance product. In order to make products more affordable, we are willing to take an assertive, public position.

7. Value-added, Quality Service

We want to provide our customers value-added, quality, caring service; individual attention; and positive, meaningful communications. More than most, insurance is a people business. Our product is intangible. We seek to differentiate CNA by the quality of individual contracts with our customers.

CORPORATE DESCRIPTION

CNA Financial Corporation is the parent company of the multi-line CNA Insurance Companies, which rank among the 15 largest insurance organizations in the United States, with 1993 property-casualty and life-health premiums of $8.9 billion.

ADDRESS   CNA Plaza
Chicago, IL 60685

INDUSTRY CATEGORY   Insurance

◆   ◆   ◆   ◆   ◆   ◆   ◆

Coachmen Industries, Inc.

STATEMENT | **Corporate Mission & Guiding Principles**

Mission:

Coachmen Industries, Inc. is a leading manufacturer of recreational vehicles, modular homes, and related products. Our mission is to design, market and continually advance our products to be the value leader in the industries we serve. This, in turn, allows us to prosper as a business and to offer opportunities to our employees as well as provide a reasonable return to our shareholders.

Principles:

How we accomplish our mission is as important as the mission itself. Fundamental to success for the Company are those basic values which have guided our progress since our founding.

♦ **Our Corporate motto is "Dedicated to the Enrichment of Your Life."**
This means we will do our best to provide quality products and services which will improve the lifestyle of our users.

♦ **Our word is our bond.**
Our dealers and suppliers are our partners. We endeavor to practice the Golden Rule in all of our relations with others.

♦ **Quality is our first priority.**
We must achieve customer satisfaction by building quality products. This will allow us to compete effectively in the marketplace. We will always remember: No sale is a good sale for Coachmen unless it fulfills our customers' expectations.

♦ **Customers are the focus of everything we do.**
As a Company we must never lose sight of the commitment we make to those who buy our products. Our deep-seated philosophy is that "Business goes where it is invited and stays where it is well cared for."

- **Integrity is our commitment.**
  The conduct of our Company's affairs must be pursued in a manner that commands respect for its honesty and integrity.
- **Profits are required for the company to grow and flourish.**
  Profits are our report card of how well we provide customers with the best products for their needs.

CORPORATE DESCRIPTION

Coachmen Industries, Inc. manufactures a full line of recreational vehicles and van conversions through seven divisions with manufacturing facilities located in Indiana, Georgia, Michigan, and Oregon. These products are marketed through a nationwide dealer network. The Company's housing divisions, with locations in Indiana, Ohio, North Carolina, Tennessee, and Iowa, supply modular housing to builder/dealers in nineteen adjoining states. The Company's parts and supply divisions concentrate primarily on providing parts and supplies to the recreational vehicle and van conversion industries, and also have an important interest in the office furniture market.

ADDRESS   P.O. Box 3300
Elkhart, IN 46515

INDUSTRY CATEGORY   Motor Vehicles and Related

◆ ◆ ◆ ◆ ◆ ◆ ◆

Coca-Cola

We exist to create value for our share owners on a long-term basis.

We refresh the world. We do this by developing superior beverage products that create value for our Company, our bottling partners and our customers.

In creating value, we succeed or fail based on our ability to perform as worthy stewards of several key assets:

1. Coca-Cola and our other highly valuable trademarks
2. The world's most effective and persuasive distribution system
3. Satisfied customers, who make a good profit selling our products
4. Our people, who are ultimately responsible for building this enterprise
5. Our abundant resources, which must be intelligently allocated
6. Our strong global leadership in the beverage industry in particular and in the business world in general.

CORPORATE DESCRIPTION

Coca-Cola is the global soft-drink industry leader, with world headquarters in Atlanta, Georgia. The Company's businesses also include The Minute Maid Company, the world's leading marketer of juices and juice drinks.

ADDRESS   One Coca-Cola Plaza
Atlanta, GA 30313

INDUSTRY CATEGORY   Food/Beverage

◆ ◆ ◆ ◆ ◆ ◆ ◆

Columbia/HCA Healthcare Corp.

STATEMENT | **Mission**

♦ To attain international leadership in the health care field.
♦ To provide excellence in health care.
♦ To improve the standards of health care in communities in which we operate.
♦ To provide superior facilities and needed services to enable physicians to best serve the needs of their patients.
♦ To generate measurable benefits for:
> The Community
> The Employee
> The Medical Staff
> and, most importantly, The Patient.

CORPORATE DESCRIPTION

Columbia/HCA is a leading hospital management company committed to the delivery of quality patient care at a reasonable rate.

ADDRESS   One Park Plaza
P.O. Box 550
Nashville, TN 37202-0550

INDUSTRY CATEGORY   Health Care

♦ ♦ ♦ ♦ ♦ ♦ ♦

Comerica Incorporated

STATEMENT | **Mission**

To forge a cohesive team dedicated to being the standard for exceptional customer service.

Vision

We define ourselves as a relationship-driven financial services organization. Our customers are our first priority. Our employees will be known for their teamwork and will be faithful to our core values and beliefs. We are leaders in the communities we serve. Our board of directors are the shareholders' representatives; we are accountable to them. We will consistently produce returns on equity in the top quintile of the top U.S. bank holding companies.

Purpose

We are in business to enrich people's lives.

Core Values and Beliefs

Comerica is a company where . . . integrity, trust and open communication prevail; customer needs drive our business—we strive to exceed their expectations; we value lasting relationships with our customers, employees, communities and shareholders; we are colleagues, respecting each other and working as a team; we are innovative, flexible and constantly striving to improve; we are entrusted with our responsibilities, held accountable and rewarded fairly; and, we are proud to be members of the team and enjoy coming to work.

CORPORATE DESCRIPTION

Comerica Incorporated is a bank holding company headquartered in Detroit. It operates financial institutions under the Comerica name in Michigan, California, Florida, Illinois and Texas.

ADDRESS   P.O. Box 75000
Detroit, MI 48275-3352

INDUSTRY CATEGORY   Banking

◆   ◆   ◆   ◆   ◆   ◆   ◆

Commercial Federal Corporation

STATEMENT | **VISION**

Commercial Federal Bank is a full-service community bank that is dedicated to providing customers with 100% of their financial needs.

| **MISSION**

We will ensure that the customer comes first, and that we provide service in the easiest possible way—when and where the customer wants.

| **PRINCIPLES**

To enhance long-term shareholder value, we are a bank that is responsive to the needs of the communities wherein decisions are made by local market managers who are aware of those unique needs by being closely connected to the communities and customers they serve.

We are a Company that focuses on delivering an extraordinary degree of customer service.

In addition, we want to continue to attract, motivate and retain outstanding people. We want to create an environment that inspires great things from great people who enjoy what they do!

CORPORATE DESCRIPTION

Commercial Federal Corporation is the parent company of Commercial Federal Bank, a federal savings bank headquartered in Omaha, Nebraska. Founded in 1987, it is one of the largest financial institutions in the Midwest. Commercial Federal is a full-service community bank that emphasizes single-family residential and construction real estate lending, business banking, consumer lending, commercial real estate lending, retail deposit activities, including demand deposit accounts and mortgage banking.

ADDRESS   2120 S. 72nd St.
Omaha, NE 68124

INDUSTRY CATEGORY   Banking

♦ ♦ ♦ ♦ ♦ ♦ ♦

Comptek Research, Inc.

STATEMENT | **Our Mission**

Our mission is to provide innovative electronic and telecommunications products and services which distinguish Comptek on the basis of quality and commitment.

CORPORATE DESCRIPTION

Comptek Research, Inc. includes three wholly owned subsidiaries which provide advanced technology products and services to customers throughout the world.

Comptek Federal Systems, Inc. provides electronic warfare and battle management systems to the U.S. Department of Defense and allied military services.

Comptek Telecommunications, Inc. provides data communications products and services to the financial industry and other commercial customers.

Industrial Systems Service, Inc. manufactures electronic assemblies and systems for a broad range of military and commercial applications.

ADDRESS   2732 Transit Rd.
Buffalo, NY 14224-2523

INDUSTRY CATEGORY   Communications and Telecommunications

◆ ◆ ◆ ◆ ◆ ◆ ◆

Computer Sciences Corporation

+ Leadership in the solution of client problems in information systems technology
— Offer a full spectrum of services from business reengineering and I.T. strategy to systems integration, operations management outsourcing and professional services
— Respond to each client with the combination of services that is best for him

Management Principles

The corporate purpose of Computer Sciences Corporation is to be preeminent in the solution of client problems in information systems technology. This demands that we make an absolute commitment to excellence in our contract performance and products. We will achieve our purpose by observing these principles:

We commit to client satisfaction as our most important business objective.

We recognize that CSC's accomplishments are the work of the people who comprise CSC. We will encourage initiative, recognize individual contribution, treat each person with respect and fairness, and afford ample opportunity for growth in CSC.

We in turn will require of our people the highest standards of professionalism and technical competence.

We will maintain the highest standards of ethics of business conduct, and operate all times within the laws of the United States and all other countries in which we do business.

We will identify and respond aggressively to new opportunities, and commit to success in each undertaking.

Finally, our success as a company requires that we achieve profits and growth commensurate with a leadership position in our industry.

(Signed)

William R. Hoover
Chairman and CEO

CORPORATE DESCRIPTION

Computer Sciences Corporation (CSC) solves client problems in information systems technology. Its broad-based services include management consulting in the strategic use of information technology; the development and implementation of complete information systems; and outsourcing, covering the full range of a client's information technology activities.

ADDRESS   2100 E. Grand Ave.
El Segundo, CA 90245

INDUSTRY CATEGORY   High Technology

◆ ◆ ◆ ◆ ◆ ◆ ◆

Computervision Corporation

STATEMENT

Computervision's Customer Commitment is to help customers gain a time-to-market advantage by continuously improving the productivity of their people, processes and technologies.

CORPORATE DESCRIPTION

Computervision Corporation is a leading international supplier of desktop and enterprise-wide product development software and services. For more than 25 years, the company's product and process data management (PDM) and design automation (CAE/CAD/CAM) software solutions have helped manufacturers improve product quality and reduce time to market. Computervision Services provides best practices consulting programs to support product development process reengineering and technology implementation. Computervision Services also supports applications systems and networks in heterogeneous computing environments.

ADDRESS   100 Crosby Dr.
Bedford, MA 01730

INDUSTRY CATEGORY   High Technology

◆ ◆ ◆ ◆ ◆ ◆ ◆

ConAgra

STATEMENT | **Mission**

Our mission is to increase stockholders' wealth. Our job is to feed people better.

CORPORATE DESCRIPTION

ConAgra is a diversified international food company. Among its divisions are food brands that are household names, such as Banquet, Butterball, Hebrew National, Healthy Choice, Orville Redenbacher's, Hunt's, Wesson, Peter Pan, Knott's Berry Farm, Armour, and La Choy among others.

ADDRESS　　One ConAgra Dr.
　　　　　　　Omaha, NE 68102

INDUSTRY CATEGORY　　Food/Beverage

◆　◆　◆　◆　◆　◆　◆

Conner Peripherals, Inc.

STATEMENT | **Mission**

Conner's mission is to be the leading supplier of computer storage solutions by providing a comprehensive line of disk drives, tape drives, disk arrays and data protection and storage management software for the entry, value, performance and portable market segments.

CORPORATE DESCRIPTION

Conner is a leading supplier of storage solutions for the computer industry.

ADDRESS　　3081 Zanker Rd.
　　　　　　　San Jose, CA 95134

INDUSTRY CATEGORY　　High Technology

◆　◆　◆　◆　◆　◆　◆

Consolidated Freightways, Inc.

| **[For MotorFreight] Mission Statement**

CF MotorFreight will continue to distinguish itself as the premier long-haul LTL motor carrier in North America. The Company will maintain this position by embracing a no-compromise philosophy of customer satisfaction. Evidence of our success is the marketplace perception that CF MotorFreight is a preferred service company with which to do business.

[For Con-Way Transportation Services] Mission Statement

The Con-Way Transportation Services Mission is to expand and diversify its transportation and support services, including LTL regional trucking, full truckload transportation and international shipping.

Con-Way Transportation Services will balance short and long range objectives, optimize profitability, and develop dominant market position through product leadership and effective integration of human, capital and material resources.

Key Elements

+ People
+ Service
+ Capacity
+ Technology
+ CFI Support

[For Emery Worldwide] Mission Statement

Our mission is to exceed our customers' expectations. We believe they deserve nothing less. Whether we meet in the customer's office, on the dock or over the telephone, we're honest and professional. Individually, we are proud of our work and our history of innovations. Together, we are a team of dedicated people working to satisfy our customers.

Emery Worldwide is an international and domestic transporter of packages, parcels and freight. We also will handle envelopes for customers who require transportation of packages, parcels and freight. No shipment is too large to be handled by Emery Worldwide. The company serves business customers.

Emery Worldwide strives to provide total freight transportation to customers. Inbound packages, parcels and freight are as important as our outbound.

We clearly understand each location's expense of performing service on behalf of each of our customers and govern our sales efforts and operational activities accordingly.

CORPORATE DESCRIPTION

Consolidated Freightways, Inc. is a $4.1 billion diversified transportation company specializing in the movement of less-than-truckload freight through 11 independent companies that provide transportation services for commercial and industrial shipments by land, sea and air throughout North America and the world. The principal operating companies are: CF Motor Freight, Con-Way Transportation Services, and Emery Worldwide.

ADDRESS   3240 Hillview Ave.
Palo Alto, CA 94304

INDUSTRY CATEGORY   Transportation

◆　◆　◆　◆　◆　◆　◆

Continental Airlines

STATEMENT | **Corporate Vision**

To Be Recognized as the Best Airline in the Industry by our Customers, Employees and Shareholders.

CORPORATE DESCRIPTION

Continental Airlines was the nation's fifth largest air carrier in 1992, as measured by revenue passenger miles.

ADDRESS   2929 Allen Pkwy., Ste. 2010
Houston, TX 77019

INDUSTRY CATEGORY   Transportation

◆　◆　◆　◆　◆　◆　◆

Continental Medical Systems, Inc.

STATEMENT | **Mission Statement**

Acting as a diversified provider of medical rehabilitation and physician activities, the Mission of Continental Medical Systems is to ensure high quality and cost effective outcomes to those we serve while providing a favorable return to our stockholders.

CORPORATE DESCRIPTION

The Company is a diversified provider of comprehensive medical rehabilitation and physician services. The Company has a significant presence in each of the rehabilitation industry's three principal sectors—inpatient rehabilitation care, contract services and outpatient rehabilitation care. Additionally, the Company is the largest provider of physician locum tenens services in the United States.

ADDRESS   P.O. Box 715
Mechanicsburg, PA 17055

INDUSTRY CATEGORY   Health Care

◆　◆　◆　◆　◆　◆　◆

Cooper Tire & Rubber Company

STATEMENT | **Business Creed**

Over the years, Cooper Tire & Rubber Company has maintained a consistent style of doing business. This reliability and steadiness is rooted in the Company's rich history as one of America's pioneer tire and rubber products manufacturers.

In a 1926 interview, I. J. Cooper, former president for whom the Company is named, outlined three planks in Cooper's business platform:

- Good Merchandise—because it doesn't pay to make, sell or use an inferior article.
- Fair Play—prices that satisfy the user, leave the dealer with a profit and the maker with a margin to cover his labor, thought and investment.
- Square Deal—to everyone, every time because you can't beat a natural law and still progress and prosper.

CORPORATE DESCRIPTION

Cooper Tire & Rubber Company, founded in 1914, specializes in the manufacturing and marketing of rubber products for consumers and industrial users. Products include automobile and truck tires, inner tubes, vibration control products, hoses and hose assemblies, automotive sealing systems and specialty seating components.

ADDRESS   Findlay, OH 45840-2315

INDUSTRY CATEGORY   Motor Vehicles and Related

♦ ♦ ♦ ♦ ♦ ♦ ♦

Copperweld Corporation

Copperweld Corporation is recognized worldwide as a leading manufacturer of mechanical and structural tubing and bimetallic wire products. Our mission is to provide superior products and services in response to our customers' needs. By continuous improvement of all aspects of our performance, we anticipate our customers' critical requirements and maintain competitive advantage in the markets we serve. Our goal is to be an ever-vital and prosperous business providing an innovative, productive, and rewarding environment for our people; real value for our customers and suppliers; and a reasonable ongoing return for our shareholders.

In accomplishing our business mission, we are guided by the following basic principles:

Customers are the ultimate focus of all of our business activities.

Quality in products, services, and all of our business transactions is first priority.

Integrity is never compromised.

People provide the strength, energy, and essential resource to ensure a successful business.

Employee involvement, trust, recognition and teamwork, drive, personal growth, contribution, accomplishment, and sustained superior performance.

Continuous Improvement is our way of life; change is valued for the competitive opportunities it presents.

Value created for our customers and suppliers is a prerequisite to the continuing generation of value for our enterprise.

Critical Appraisal of the Competitive Environment is essential for ongoing success to provide clear focus on necessary change and to define the associated resource deployment.

CORPORATE DESCRIPTION

Copperweld Corporation is a manufacturer of structural, mechanical and welded-mechanical steel tubing, and bimetallic rod, wire, and strand.

ADDRESS   Four Gateway Center, Ste. 2200
Pittsburgh, PA 15222-1211

INDUSTRY CATEGORY   Manufacturing

◆ ◆ ◆ ◆ ◆ ◆ ◆

Corning Incorporated

STATEMENT | **[From the Corning Publication "Our Values"]**
Who we are

Our Purpose

Our purpose is to deliver superior, long-range economic benefits to our customers, our employees, our shareholders, and to the communities in which we operate. We accomplish this by living our corporate values.

Our Strategy

Corning is an evolving network of wholly and jointly owned businesses which owes its continued existence to shared values, a core competence in science and technology, and an unending spirit of innovation in all aspects of our corporate life.

Corning will focus on four strategies that will enable the corporation to reach its long-term financial goals:

Growth Markets. Invest aggressively in growing markets in which we are or expect to be #1 or #2 and in which we are the high-quality, low-cost supplier. These markets are: Communications, Environment, Life Sciences.

Traditional Businesses. Mange our traditional businesses for cash to support these growth investments.

Core Science and Technology. Nurture our science and technology so that it drives our growth markets and also creates as-yet unidentified future opportunities.

Corporate Investments. Hold our investments in Dow Corning and Pittsburgh Corning for optimal growth and cash generation over time.

Our corporate network adds value to its component parts through our company's name and reputation, a common dedication to our core values, a coherent overall strategy, and shared financial and human resources.

What we value

Our Values

We have a set of enduring beliefs that are ingrained in the way we think and act. These values guide our choices, defining for us the right courses of action, the clearest directions, the preferred responses. Consistent with these values we set our objectives, formulate our strategies, and judge our results. By living these values we will achieve our purpose.

Quality

Total Quality is the guiding principle of Corning's business life. It requires each of us, individually and in teams, to understand, anticipate, and surpass the expectations of our customers. Total Quality demands continuous improvement in all our processes, products, and services. Our success depends on our ability to learn from experience, to embrace change, and to achieve the full involvement of all our employees.

Integrity

Integrity is the foundation of Corning's reputation. We have earned the respect and trust of people around the world through more than a century of behavior that is honest, decent, and fair. Such behavior must continue to characterize all our relationships, both inside and outside the Corning network.

Performance

Providing Corning shareholders a superior long-term return on their investment is a business imperative. This requires that we allocate our resources to ensure profitable growth, maintain an effective balance between today and tomorrow, deliver what we promise, and tie our own rewards directly to our performance.

Leadership

Corning is a leader, not a follower. Our history and our culture impel us to seek a leadership role in our markets, our multiple technologies, our manufacturing processes, our management practices, and our financial performance. The goods and services we produce are never merely ordinary and must always be truly useful.

Innovation

Corning leads primarily by technical innovation and shares a deep belief in the power of technology. The company has a history of great contributions in science and technology, and it is this same spirit of innovation that has enabled us to create new products and new markets, to introduce new forms of corporate organization, and to seek new levels of employer participation. We embrace the opportunities inherent in change, and we are confident of our ability to help shape the future.

Independence

Corning cherishes—and will defend—its corporate freedom. That independence is our historic foundation. It fosters the innovation and initiative that has made our company great, and will continue to provide inspiration and energy to all parts of our network in the future.

The Individual

We know that in the end the commitment and contribution of all our employees will determine our success. Corning believes in the fundamental dignity of the individual. Our network consists of a rich mixture of people of diverse nationality, race, gender, and opinion, and this diversity will continue to be a source of our strength. We value the unique ability of each individual to contribute, and we intend that every employee shall have the opportunity to participate fully, to grow professionally, and to develop to his or her highest potential.

Where we want to go

Our Financial Goals

Performance

We will be consistently in the top 25 percent of the Fortune 500 in financial performance as measured by return on equity and long-term growth in earnings per share.

Capital Structure

We will maintain a debt-to-capital ratio of approximately 30 percent and a long-term dividend payout of 33 percent.

We will issue new shares of stock on a limited basis in connection with employee ownership programs and acquisitions with a clear strategic fit, and we will repurchase shares on the open market as appropriate.

CORPORATE DESCRIPTION

Corning Incorporated is a diversified products and services company with a strong tradition of technological innovation. Although historically a glass and specialty materials manufacturer, Corning today concentrates on the three key global markets that account for 60 percent of its revenues: optical communications, life sciences and the environment.

ADDRESS   One Riverfront Plaza
Corning, NY 14831

INDUSTRY CATEGORY   Manufacturing

◆　◆　◆　◆　◆　◆　◆

Cray Research, Inc.

STATEMENT | **Cray's Mission Statement**

Cray Research provides the leading supercomputing tools and services to help solve our customers' most challenging problems.

CORPORATE DESCRIPTION

Cray Research produces supercomputers with very powerful computational capacities.

ADDRESS   655 Lone Oak Dr.
Eagan, MN 55121

INDUSTRY CATEGORY   High Technology

◆ ◆ ◆ ◆ ◆ ◆ ◆

CSX Corporation

STATEMENT | **CSX Mission Statement**

CSX is a transportation company committed to being a leader in railroad, inland water and containerized distribution markets.

To attract the human and financial resources necessary to achieve this leadership position, CSX will support our three major constituencies:

- ◆ For our customers, we will work as a partner to provide excellent service by meeting all agreed-upon commitments.
- ◆ For our employees, we will create a work environment that motivates and allows them to grow and develop and perform their jobs to the maximum of their capacity.
- ◆ For our shareholders, we will meet our goals to provide them with sustainable, superior returns.

The primary responsibility of every CSX employee is to serve customers in the spirit of partnership in order to understand and satisfy their needs.

We must provide quality execution on a consistent basis over the long term through:

- An organization that values its employees and respects their dignity.
- A commitment to teamwork, openness and candor.
- A commitment to increased quality and continuous improvement.
- Increased empowerment and personal accountability.
- A commitment to ethical conduct.
- A willingness to innovate and change in well-planned ways that yield a competitive advantage.
- A sense of urgency and bias for action.

Only by carrying out these values will CSX be able to fulfill our ultimate responsibility to provide sustainable, superior returns to our shareholders.

CORPORATE DESCRIPTION

CSX Corporation is an international transportation services company offering a wide variety of rail, container-shipping, intermodal, barging, trucking, contract logistics and related services worldwide. Business units include CSX Transportation Inc., Sea-Land Service Inc., CSX Intermodal Inc., American Commercial Lines Inc., and Customized Transportation Inc.

ADDRESS   One James Center
901 E. Cary St.
Richmond, VA 23219-4031

INDUSTRY CATEGORY   Transportation

◆　◆　◆　◆　◆　◆　◆

CUNA Mutual Insurance Group

STATEMENT | **Mission**

Creating financial security

| **Vision**

To be the best at serving credit unions and members.

| **Corporate Objectives**

1. Provide excellent, innovative products and services
2. Build productive partnerships with credit unions and credit union organizations
3. Increase dramatically the financial security provided to credit unions, members and policyholders through strategies of growth and distribution
4. Enable employees to achieve their potential through training, empowerment and teamwork
5. Achieve superior efficiency and productivity
6. Ensure our financial integrity and strength

| **Team Shared Commitments**

We are:

Committed to making our organization the best in the financial services industry—recognizably differentiating it from others—and to serving credit unions, members and policyholders with excellence

Committed to our mission, vision, objectives, and our potential

Committed to be leaders in our fields of expertise, in the credit union movement and, most notably, to our employees

Committed to continuous learning and development—personally, and as a team

Committed to a culture founded on professionalism, competence, teamwork, empowerment, mutual respect and understanding, trust and service excellence

Committed to superior standards of honesty and fairness

Committed to open and honest interactive communication with each other and all people with whom we interact

Committed to recognizing opportunities and threats, through a constant awareness of the financial services industry and our marketplace, and capitalizing on that knowledge quickly and successfully

Committed to the "team"

CORPORATE DESCRIPTION

CUNA Mutual Insurance Society (CUNA Mutual) is a mutual life insurance company organized under the laws of the State of Wisconsin. The CUNA Mutual Insurance Group serves only credit unions and credit union members.

ADDRESS   5910 Mineral Point Rd.
Madison, WI 53705

INDUSTRY CATEGORY   Insurance

◆ ◆ ◆ ◆ ◆ ◆ ◆

Dana Corporation

STATEMENT | **Beyond 2000—Our Commitment to Growth**

1. The Dana Style Will Be Fully Implemented Throughout Dana's Globally Integrated Organization.
   - Dana people are our most important asset.
   - Dana's growth is dependent on "People Finding A Better Way" to improve continuously through concentration on:
     - idea generation (minimum of two ideas per person per month, 80% implemented),
     - education (minimum of 40 hours per person per year), and
     - cooperation among Dana people globally.

2. Dana Will Be The Leading Global Systems And Components Supplier To The Customers We Serve.
   - Dana will become the global leader by:
     - exceeding customers' expectations in everything we do,
     - being the leader in the development of innovative systems and services which make our customers more competitive in the market place,
     - focusing our people on providing world class technology, superior service, and customer care through the DQLA process, and
     - creating a customer support system making it easy to do business with Dana globally.
   - Dana will continue to provide innovative leasing services.
3. Dana Will Obtain 50% Of Sales From Highway Vehicle OEM Customers And 50% From Distribution, Off-Highway, And Industrial Markets.
   - Two-thirds of the growth will come from targeting new market segments, increasing our penetration of existing markets, and introduction of new products.
   - One-third of the growth will come through acquisitions.
4. Dana Will Obtain 50% Of Sales From Outside The United States.
   - Dana will continue to expand globally by—
     - supporting our customers' global activities with regional facilities,
     - emphasizing export activities,
     - focusing on growth sectors of international markets,
     - moving faster than our global competitors, and
     - sharing our technology and processes globally across SBUs.

5. Dana Will Be A Growth Company Providing Shareholders With Superior Investment Returns.
   - Through the accomplishment of the first four objectives, Dana will be positioned for continuous, profitable growth.
   - Dana's key financial goals are—
     - Sales growth ≥ 10% per year
     - Return on Sales ≥ 6% after-tax
     - Return on Shareholders' Equity ≥ 25% after-tax

CORPORATE DESCRIPTION

Dana is a global leader in the manufacturing and marketing of vehicular and industrial components.

ADDRESS   P.O. Box 1000
Toledo, OH 43697

INDUSTRY CATEGORY   Motor Vehicles and Related

◆　◆　◆　◆　◆　◆　◆

Deere & Company (John Deere)

STATEMENT | **GENUINE VALUE: OUR MISSION**

Who Are We?

John Deere has grown and prospered through a long-standing partnership with the world's most productive farmers. Today, John Deere is a global company with several equipment operations and complementary service businesses. These businesses are closely interrelated, providing the company with significant growth opportunities and other synergistic benefits.

Where Are We Going?

Deere is committed to providing Genuine Value to the company's stakeholders, including our customers, dealers, shareholders, employees and communities. In support of that commitment, Deere aspires to:

+ Grow and pursue leadership positions in each of our businesses.
+ Extend our preeminent leadership position in the agricultural equipment market worldwide.
+ Create new opportunities to leverage the John Deere brand globally.

How Will We Get There?

By pursuing the broader corporate goals of profitable growth and continuous improvement, each of the company's businesses is expected to:

+ Achieve world-class performance by attaining a strong competitive position in target markets.
+ Exceed customer expectations for quality and value.
+ Earn in excess of the cost of capital over a business cycle.

By growing profitably and continuously improving, each of the company's businesses will benefit from and contribute to John Deere's unique intangible assets:

+ Our distinguished brand.
+ Our heritage of integrity and teamwork.
+ Our advanced skills.
+ The special relationships that have long existed between the company and our employees, customers, dealers and other business partners around the world.

Each business will make a positive contribution to the corporation's objectives in the pursuit of creating Genuine Value for our stakeholders. Our "scorecard" includes:

+ Human Resources—Employee Satisfaction, Training
+ Customer Focus—Loyalty, Market Leadership
+ Business Processes—Productivity, Quality, Cost, Environment
+ Business Results—Return on Assets, Sales Growth.

© Deere & Company. Reprinted with permission of Deere & Company.

CORPORATE DESCRIPTION

John Deere is the world's leading producer of agricultural equipment and a major producer of industrial equipment for the construction, forestry, and public works markets, lawn and grounds care products for homeowners and commercial users, engines and other powertrain components, and replacement parts for its own products and those of other manufacturers. John Deere also provides financial services including credit, insurance, and managed health-care plans.

ADDRESS   1 John Deere Pl.
Moline, IL 61265

INDUSTRY CATEGORY   Manufacturing

◆ ◆ ◆ ◆ ◆ ◆ ◆

Delta Air Lines, Inc.

STATEMENT | **Vision for the Future**

Our Vision Is for Delta To Be the Worldwide Airline of Choice.
Worldwide .... We provide our customers access to the world and we will be an innovative, aggressive, ethical and successful competitor committed to profitable and superior customer service. Looking ahead, we will consider opportunities to expand through new routes and alliances.

Airline .... We will stay in the business we know best and where we are leaders—air transportation and related services. We believe air transportation will grow worldwide, and we will focus our time, attention and investment in building on our leadership position.

Of Choice .... We will be the airline of choice for customers, investors and Delta people. For experienced business and leisure travelers, we will provide value and a superior travel experience from the time a reservation is made to when baggage is claimed. For air shippers, we will provide service and value. For our stockholders, we will earn a consistent, superior financial return. For Delta people, we will offer challenging, rewarding, results-oriented work in an environment that respects and values their contribution.

CORPORATE DESCRIPTION

Delta Air Lines, Inc., has been engaged in the air transportation business since 1929. Based on calendar 1993 data, Delta is the third largest U.S. airline as measured by operating revenues and revenue passenger miles flown, and the largest U.S. airline as measured by passengers enplaned.

The Company provides scheduled air transportation over an extensive route network. At September 22, 1994, Delta served 153 domestic cities in 43 states, the District of Columbia, Puerto Rico, and the U.S. Virgin Islands, and 57 cities in 32 foreign countries. Service over most of Delta's routes is highly competitive. In addition to scheduled passenger service, Delta also provides air freight, mail and other related aviation services.

ADDRESS   1050 Delta Blvd.
Atlanta, GA 30320-6001

INDUSTRY CATEGORY   Transportation

◆   ◆   ◆   ◆   ◆   ◆   ◆

Deluxe Corporation

| **Vision**

Deluxe's vision is to partner for prosperity by pioneering information and payment solutions.

| **Envisioned Future**

Deluxe's envisioned future is that we will transform our company from a confederation of businesses to an organization that acts as a single company and is the recognized leader in providing information and payment solutions to customers throughout the world.

| **Mission**

Deluxe's mission is to provide integrated information, payment, and related services that create value for our customers throughout the world.

| **Core Values and Behaviors**

At Deluxe, we embrace the following values in all that we do and commit to modeling them with these behaviors.

Respect and Dignity for All
- Promoting diversity by valuing all colleagues for their unique qualities
- Actively seeking to know, understand, and include those who think, act, and are different from ourselves
- Actively seeking to interact and collaborate with others
- Demonstrating personal and professional courtesy in our interactions with others
- Accepting and offering constructive feedback
- Demonstrating and supporting a balance of work, family, and personal commitments

Openness, Trust, and Integrity
- Demonstrating honesty at all times
- Soliciting honest feedback from colleagues and respecting them for their candor

- Openly voicing opinions on important issues, then fully supporting the chosen direction
- Trusting that colleagues have the best interests of the company in mind in all that they do
- Demonstrating approachability and availability

Innovation
- Questioning how we can do things better, then seeking and offering alternative solutions
- Taking educated, well-intentioned risks
- Encouraging ourselves and others to challenge processes
- Working with others to overcome resistance to new ideas
- Encouraging ourselves and others to think creatively every day

Partnering for the Common Goal
- Being passionate about winning as part of one team with one scoreboard
- Being receptive to ideas that are different from our own
- Sharing ideas
- Actively developing and maintaining networks with people inside and outside Deluxe
- Executing the high standards we set for our work
- Becoming active and positive participants in all teams with which we are involved
- Purposefully developing our own skills

Recognition and Celebration
- Consciously looking for ways to recognize the efforts of others
- Recognizing and communicating to people we see supporting Deluxe values
- Recognizing and communicating team and individual accomplishments to all areas
- Having FUN

CORPORATE DESCRIPTION

Founded in 1915, Deluxe Corporation is a leading provider of integrated risk management, electronic transaction, and paper payment services to the financial services and retail industries.

ADDRESS   P.O. Box 64399
St. Paul, MN 55164-0399

INDUSTRY CATEGORY   Business Products

◆   ◆   ◆   ◆   ◆   ◆   ◆

Deposit Guaranty Corp.

STATEMENT | **Mission Statement**

The mission of Deposit Guaranty Corp. is to increase shareholder value by providing financial services in our areas of operation with balanced emphasis on customer sales and service, credit quality, operational efficiency, and profitability.

Amplification

"... financial services ...": our core business is providing basic banking services, gathering deposits and extending credit. In addition to traditional banking, Deposit Guaranty provides a broad range of financial services designed to meet more completely our customers' financial needs. Basic deposit and credit products are complimented [sic] by the asset management services of our Trust Division, full and discount brokerage services, a family of private label mutual funds, select insurance products, and cash management services. These ancillary products and services are designed to strengthen existing customer relationships, enhance our competitive advantages, and provide additional cross-selling opportunities. All of the products and services we provide must add profit on their own or through synergy with other products. The broader range of financial services will strengthen the value of the Deposit Guaranty franchise, as well as enhance and diversify our stream of earnings.

"... areas of operation ...": we are part of a regional banking organization serving markets in Mississippi and the Shreveport, LA, metropolitan area, and offer corporate and financial services in contiguous states and on a nationwide basis to companies with Mississippi and Ark-La-Tex operations. While we are not seeking to acquire for expansion's sake, when conditions are correct, we will consider acquiring other financial institutions. These conditions include acquisition candidates that have markets with favorable characteristics and acquisition prices which can increase our profits over time. Geographic proximity to where we operate, as well as an organizational culture that can mesh with ours are important considerations.

"... balanced emphasis ...": customer sales and service, credit quality, and operational efficiency are musts for profitability, and adequate profitability does not exist without excellent customer sales and service, excellent credit quality, and operational efficiency.

"... customer sales and service ...": excellent customer sales and service is vital to attracting and retaining customers, who are our reason to exist. Treating customers in an exceptional manner is the goal of Service Vision—"Win One for the Customer," both internal and external, results in winning one for all of us.

"... credit quality ...": low credit losses are essential to soundness and profitability. Making credit available to a borrower, when it is not sound to do so, results in harm to the customer and to the bank; making credit available on a sound basis will help a customer grow and help our bank. While some losses are part of doing business, we need to strive for low charge-offs.

"... profitability ...": adequate profits are essential to our growth and continued viability as a financial organization and are the necessary ingredient to reward our shareholders and have competitive wages, benefits and personal growth opportunities for our employees. We endeavor to pass a portion of our profits and efforts back into our communities to help the areas in which we operate develop economically and in the long term help our profitability because of a better market in which to operate.

Increasing profitability is a function of superior customer service, sound credit quality, and operational efficiency. Deposit Guaranty is committed to increasing shareholder value and profitability by effectively balancing the often competing needs of customer sales and service, credit quality and operating efficiency.

CORPORATE DESCRIPTION

Deposit Guaranty Corp. is a Jackson, Mississippi-based financial services company with over $5 billion in assets. Its primary subsidiaries are Deposit Guaranty National Bank, Mississippi's largest financial institution with 130 banking locations across the state, and Commercial National Bank, Louisiana's fifth largest bank with 12 branches in the Shreveport area.

Other subsidiaries include Deposit Guaranty Mortgage Company, one of the largest mortgage loan services in Mississippi; Deposit Guaranty Investments Inc., a full-service broker dealer subsidiary; and G & W Life Insurance Company, a 79 percent-owned subsidiary which provides credit life insurance.

ADDRESS   P.O. Box 730
Jackson, MS 39205

INDUSTRY CATEGORY   Banking

♦   ♦   ♦   ♦   ♦   ♦   ♦

Diamond Shamrock, Inc.

STATEMENT | **"Be the Best—Grow and Win"**

Our Vision

As a cohesive team we will grow and achieve superior financial results for our company.

We will consistently:
- Focus On Our Customers
- Continuously Improve Everything We Do

- Produce Quality Products And Service
- Out-Perform Competition
- Create Opportunities Out Of Change
- Value, Respect, And Develop Every Employee
- Encourage Each Employee's Participation And Ideas
- Be Ethical, Responsible, And Protective Of The Environment
- Be Safe, Have Fun, And Take Pride In Our Work

CORPORATE DESCRIPTION

Diamond Shamrock, Inc. is a highly focused, regional refiner and marketer of petroleum products. Its two efficient refineries in Texas have a combined throughput capacity of 205,000 barrels per day and operate at near capacity levels producing quality products such as gasoline, diesel, and jet fuel. Approximately 4,600 miles of crude oil and refined products pipelines bring crude oil into the refineries and connect these refineries to 14 products terminals throughout the company's Southwest markets. Annually, the company sells over two billion gallons of performance tested gasoline through nearly 2,000 branded outlets—776 company-owned Corner Stores in Texas, Colorado, Louisiana, and New Mexico, and 1,194 branded stations in eight states supplied by jobbers. Other businesses include petrochemical processing and natural gas liquids marketing and storage.

ADDRESS   P.O. Box 696000
San Antonio, TX 78269-6000

INDUSTRY CATEGORY   Oil and Gas

◆   ◆   ◆   ◆   ◆   ◆   ◆

Donnelly Corporation

Values

All companies have goals, plans and standards by which they measure their performance. Donnelly's corporate identity has always been shaped by the values that are listed in this document. As we continue to operate in a rapidly changing environment, it is essential that we clearly express and understand our values. This ensures that we accept personal responsibility for upholding them and that they guide our actions.

We invite you to join us in the exploration of issues that these values raise and in the work of making them a visible part of everyday life at Donnelly. While this may not be easy work, it is very exciting and rewarding. Let's make it happen!

Dwane Baumgardner
Chairman of the Board

We believe these elements to be essential in operating our business.

One

We serve our customers with excellence. Our existence depends on them.

Two

We respect people. They are important and we empower them.

Three

We are highly productive through participation, teamwork and accountability.

Four

We demonstrate integrity, high ethical standards, and respect for the community and environment in all of our actions.

Five

We are a manufacturing organization thriving on change, committed to continuous improvement, and achieving zero defects in all areas.

Six

We have strong leadership at all levels which is critical to our success.

Seven

We expand and strengthen synergistic core competencies.

Eight

We select products based on strong competitive advantage, high profitability, and global potential.

Nine

We grow profitably to achieve security and above average returns for employees and shareholders.

Ten

We support long-term cooperative relationships with excellent suppliers.

CORPORATE DESCRIPTION

Donnelly Corporation is a supplier to the global automotive industry. In North America, Europe, and Asia . . . nearly every major auto maker in the world receives products from Donnelly. The company operates from 19 facilities worldwide.

ADDRESS   414 E. 40th St.
Holland, MI 49423-5368

INDUSTRY CATEGORY   Motor Vehicles and Related

◆   ◆   ◆   ◆   ◆   ◆   ◆

The Dow Chemical Company

STATEMENT

[Excerpts from the company publication "Vision: and Strategy for the Nineties"]

| Vision

A premier global company . . . dedicated to growth . . . driven by quality performance and innovation . . . committed to maximizing our customers' success . . . always living our Core Values.

| Strategy

Technology

To realize our Vision, we will be the leader in chemistry-related technologies, which are the foundation for all of our businesses. It is the application of all technologies by every function to create real solutions to important customer problems that will create the growth our Vision demands.

We will search for and find additional technologies and products from both internal and external sources to enhance those already in place.

Strategic Business Mix

Our six Global Business Groups will provide the foundation for growth and diversification to pursue our Vision through the end of this century. We will continue to search for strategic acquisitions as a part of our commitment to growth. Top priority will be given to further expand value-added products, services and technologies.

Geographic Emphasis

The Areas, in concert with the Global Business Groups, will continuously prioritize geographic opportunities and devote resources only to those with satisfactory potential for profits and growth. In general, and in the long term, production should be placed in the market it supports.

Organization

We will continue to refine the concept of globally integrated businesses, operating in a matrix organization with geographic implementation of global business strategies, through functional centers of technical expertise. Emphasizing and sharpening our marketing efforts will improve our ability to identify and meet customer needs.

A lean organization with a minimum of managerial layers is central to our organizational style.

People

Our employees are the source of Dow's success. We treat them with respect, promote teamwork, and encourage personal freedom and growth. Excellence in performance is sought and rewarded.

We will foster an environment in which people look forward to change and are committed to improvement though a life-long pursuit of continuous personal development. We will emphasize respect for the individual through:

♦ Encouragement of entrepreneurism.
♦ Training and development programs.
♦ Decentralization of responsibility and authority.
♦ Liberation and utilization of talent and experience.
♦ Recognition of individual initiative in the achievement of team success.

Dow Core Values

If you can't do it better, why do it?
—H.H. Dow, Founder

Long-term profit growth is essential to ensure the prosperity and well-being of Dow employees, stockholders, and customers. How we achieve this objective is as important as the objective itself. Fundamental to our success are the core values we believe in and practice.
Employees are the source of Dow's success. We treat them with respect, promote teamwork, and encourage personal freedom and growth. Excellence in performance is sought and rewarded.

Customers will receive our strongest possible commitment to meet their needs with high quality products and superior service.

Our Products are based on continuing excellence and innovation in chemistry-related sciences and technology.

Our Conduct demonstrates a deep concern for ethics, citizenship, safety, health and the environment.

CORPORATE DESCRIPTION

Dow manufactures and supplies more than 2,000 products and services, including chemicals and performance products, plastics, hydrocarbons and energy, and consumer specialties—which include agricultural products, pharmaceuticals and consumer products. The company operates 183 manufacturing sites in 33 countries and employs about 55,400 people around the world.

ADDRESS   2030 Dow Center
                Midland, MI 48674

INDUSTRY CATEGORY   Chemicals

◆ ◆ ◆ ◆ ◆ ◆ ◆

Dreyer's Grand Ice Cream, Inc.

STATEMENT | **Mission**

To become the pre-eminent ice cream company in the United States by the year 2000.

CORPORATE DESCRIPTION

Dreyer's Grand Ice Cream, Inc. is the leading manufacturer, marketer and distributor of premium ice cream in the United States. The Company's principal product line is sold under the Dreyer's brand throughout the thirteen western states, Texas and certain markets in the Far East. An identical product line is sold throughout the remainder of the United States under the Edy's name. Taken together, Dreyer's and Edy's is the best-selling brand of packaged ice cream and related products in the country.

ADDRESS   5929 College Ave.
Oakland, CA 94618

INDUSTRY CATEGORY   Food/Beverage

◆　◆　◆　◆　◆　◆　◆

Duke Power Company

STATEMENT | **Our Shared Vision**

We will be the supplier of choice by our customers, the employer of choice by our co-workers and our communities, the investment of choice by our owners and the model of integrity and excellence for business and industry.

| **Our Mission**

We produce and supply electricity, provide related products and services and pursue opportunities that complement our business. We will continually improve our products and services to better meet our customers' needs and expectations, helping our customers, employees, owners and communities to prosper.

| **Our Guiding Principles**

We pursue excellence in all we do.
We strive continually to improve our products and services, our human and community relations, the safety of our operations and our financial performance.
Customers are our focus.
We anticipate, understand and meet our customers' changing needs and expectations.

Involved employees are our most important asset.
We give our best and work to create an environment that provides each of us the opportunity to reach our potential.
Financial success keeps us in business.
To prosper, both as employees and as a corporation, we maintain the financial strength of our company and provide a competitive return to our owners.
We are involved, responsible citizens.
We maintain our tradition of citizenship and service through actions that demonstrate our care for the people and environment around us.
Teamwork is our way of life.
We work in partnership with our co-workers, and with our customers, suppliers, owners and governments to achieve mutual goals. Trust and respect are the foundations of our team approach.
Integrity is never compromised.
Our actions and decisions reflect the highest ethical and professional standards.

CORPORATE DESCRIPTION

Headquartered in Charlotte, NC, Duke Power supplies electricity to more than 1.7 million residential, commercial and industrial customers in a 20,000-square-mile service area in North Carolina and South Carolina. Since its founding nearly 90 years ago, the Company has grown to become the nation's sixth-largest investor-owned electric utility as measured by kilowatt-hour sales.

ADDRESS   P.O. Box 1005
Charlotte, NC 28201-1005

INDUSTRY CATEGORY   Utility

◆　◆　◆　◆　◆　◆　◆

Eastern Enterprises

STATEMENT | **Eastern's Mission Statement**

Eastern's primary objective is to maximize total return to its share-holders, by investing in companies which provide their customers with quality products and services, and managing those businesses in a manner that achieves, over time, sustainable earnings growth and an above average return on invested capital.

CORPORATE DESCRIPTION

Eastern Enterprises is comprised of 3 business segments:

1) Boston Gas Company: New England's largest gas distribution company serving over 500,000 residential, commercial and industrial customers in Boston and 73 other cities and towns throughout eastern and central Massachusetts.

2) Midland Enterprises, Inc.: The nation's leading carrier of coal in the inland waterways.

3) WaterPro Supplies Corporation: The large U.S. distributor of components for repairing and expanding municipal water supply and wastewater collection systems.

ADDRESS   9 Riverside Rd.
Weston, MA 02193

INDUSTRY CATEGORY   Diversified

♦ ♦ ♦ ♦ ♦ ♦ ♦

Eaton Corporation

Producing the highest quality products at costs which make them economically practical in the most competitively priced markets.

To be achieved by our global commitment to:

+ Customer satisfaction
+ Profitable growth
+ Total quality leadership
+ Continuous productivity improvement
+ The Eaton Philosophy of excellence through people
+ Concern for our communities and environment, and
+ The highest standard of integrity

CORPORATE DESCRIPTION

Eaton manufactures a variety of components and controls for automobiles, trucks, appliances, military equipment, industrial products, hydraulics, and semiconductor equipment.

ADDRESS   Eaton Center
1111 Superior
Cleveland, OH 44114-2584

INDUSTRY CATEGORY   Manufacturing

◆ ◆ ◆ ◆ ◆ ◆ ◆

Ecolab Inc.

Our Mission, Philosophy and Standard of Performance

Our Mission. Our mission is to be the leading global innovator, developer and provider of cleaning, sanitation and maintenance products, systems and services. As a team, we will achieve aggressive growth and a fair return for our shareholders. We will accomplish this by exceeding the expectations of our customers while conserving resources and preserving the quality of the environment.

Our Shareholders. We are a growth company. We will provide our shareholders with a 15% annual growth in per share earnings while continually investing in product research and business development to assure a reliable future. Dividends will be consistent and recognize shareholders' needs for an adequate return and the company's need for growth capital. Our financial objectives also include a minimum 20% return on beginning of the year shareholders' equity and an "A" rated balance sheet. We intend to remain an independent company and chart our own course.

Recognizing that the quality of our shareholders' investment is built and measured over time, we will not sacrifice long-term growth in sales and earnings for short-term results.

To effectively maximize our shareholders' equity, we must have strong, positive relationships with our customers and our associates. Our objective is to have all associates be shareholders.

Our Employees. Our most important resource is our associates. We recognize and reward associates who actively demonstrate and support The Ecolab Culture and Quest for Excellence.

We are committed to creating a global environment that respects diversity and individuality. To best utilize and develop our associates' many talents, we invest in their education and training. We have constructive and open lines of communication, and establish goals with our associates. We encourage associates to participate in setting these goals and judging their own performance.

Our global workforce is a team of diverse, talented, action-oriented people who demonstrate spirit, pride, determination, commitment, passion and integrity. Our associates are enthusiastic, honest, open and hardworking, do their jobs well, and expect their co-workers to do likewise. We use the company's assets as carefully as if they were our own, suggest ways to be more productive, and help each other.

We encourage people to take initiative, go the extra mile, make the additional call! Above all, we want associates who accept responsibility and accountability for their own growth, behavior and performance.

We provide a clean and safe work environment. We care about each other and enjoy working together as a team. We learn from our mistakes and celebrate our victories. We hire the best qualified people. Associates are rewarded based on performance and teamwork. We encourage self-development and promotion from within.

Our Customers. Our customers are our business partners. We listen to them, respond quickly to their current needs and anticipate their future needs. We deliver quality services, products and systems that are safe and reliable. We are superior to our competitors, providing the highest value to our customers at a fair price.

We work closely with out customers, tell them the truth and earn their business every day. Superior service built this company and continues to be our central policy and philosophy. We are a vigorous, tough, ethical competitor.

Our Organization. We are a flexible, innovative, responsive and entrepreneurial organization. We structure our businesses around the needs of our customers and provide only those central services which are essential to our growth, the protection of our corporate assets, or provide significant advantages in terms of quality and cost. Performance is judged on the extent to which it promotes the overall good of the corporation over the separate interests of individual business units and functions.

Our business environment is constantly changing. We are committed to creative, innovative approaches that lead to breakthrough performance. We are always improving.

We favor simplicity; we take action. We expect results. We endorse substance over form, and quality over quantity. We believe in the free flow of candid, objective information, up, down, and across organizational lines. We observe uniform accounting practices and prompt disclosure of operating results, with no surprises. We insist on preparation and planning. We encourage over-achievement.

Our Society. We recognize the importance of service to society and will contribute positively to the communities in which we operate. Our business is conducted in accordance with the law and stated corporate and societal standards of conduct.

This statement is an expression of our mission and shared values, the achievement of which is an ongoing challenge and a never-ending process. It requires us to respond effectively to an ever-changing environment. It requires pragmatism and dreams, courage and confidence, trust and commitment. It is our Quest for Excellence.

The Ecolab Culture

"We have many different ideas and many different people throughout our organization. Yet we are one company, one team, with one culture."

—Al Schuman, president and chief executive officer, Ecolab

SPIRIT

Ecolab associates are the company's heart and soul. Hungry to succeed and passionate to achieve, we embrace the unknown, fearlessly taking risks, confident in our ability to deliver results. We are eager and ambitious. We tenaciously persevere, surmounting obstacles with grit and determination. Above all, we find joy in our work, and in serving the company and our customers.

PRIDE

Exceptional service, exceptional products . . . We delight in presenting premium quality in all we offer. No matter how big the project, or how small the request, we strive for excellence in our response, for we relish perfection. We cherish our company, and represent it with honor.

DETERMINATION

Ambitious and aggressive, driven and determined, enthusiastic and energetic, we cultivate the opportunity to compete. We thrive on challenges, viewing them as an invitation to success. A true team, we work together to routinely please our customers, surpass our record achievements, and drive our organization to greater success.

COMMITMENT

Like a family, we are united by an unspoken pledge, bound by our convictions. We prize dedication, and are moved to help each other and our customers. We accept nothing less than loyalty in our ranks. We are true to each other and to our cause.

PASSION

We wholeheartedly believe in our company; its goals and objectives are our mission, and we enthusiastically embrace them and relentlessly pursue them. More importantly, we truly believe in each other, care, protect and support each other.

INTEGRITY

Professional. Reliable. Trustworthy. Honest. Our corporate integrity is a critical asset and we are committed to upholding it worldwide. We set high standards, and we abide by them as we practice business fairly and behave ethically. We share our expectations with each other and strive to maintain a work place built on mutual values, trust and goodwill.

CORPORATE DESCRIPTION

Ecolab is the leading global developer of premium cleaning, sanitizing and maintenance products and services for the hospitality, institutional and industrial markets. Customers include hotels and restaurants, foodservice and healthcare facilities, dairy plants and farms, and food and beverage processors around the world.

ADDRESS   Ecolab Center
370 Wabasha St. N.
St. Paul, MN 55102-1390

INDUSTRY CATEGORY   Business Services

◆   ◆   ◆   ◆   ◆   ◆   ◆

Edwards (A.G. Edwards & Sons, Inc.)

STATEMENT | **Mission Statement**

Our purpose is to furnish services of value to our clients. We should act as their agents, putting their interests before our own.

We are confident that if we do our jobs well and give value for what we charge, not only will mutual trust and respect develop, but satisfaction and a fair reward will result.

Ethics Statement

The highest standard of ethical conduct is expected of A. G. Edwards personnel. When faced with possible conflicts of interests, we should give preference to the client and the firm over our personal interests. We should not, without management approval, use the firm or our positions in it for personal gain other than our direct compensation.

Operating Philosophies

During 1968 and '69, our top management team spent two days a month for 24 months developing a model of the firm we wanted to be and to which we were determined to commit our careers and our capital. We agreed that building this firm would take precedence over our concerns for our personal estates or positions.

We committed ourselves to delivering financial services of value to a market called the "mass, class market" through a network of retail branches acting as agent for the customer. We wanted to be customer-driven, and the agency relationship meant that our first allegiance had to be to the client. We should eliminate any profit centers or incentives that conflicted with the welfare or interest of the client. We realized that this plan would not allow us to manufacture our own financial products.

We recognize that the most important relationship in our business is a bond of trust between the client and the investment broker, and we should build and strengthen this relationship. If we are to be customer-driven, we must listen to our customers and be conscious of their interests in all our decisions.

Our growth should come naturally and involve only people of high character who share our philosophy of putting the customer first.

Only after we have found better-than-average quality and a philosophical fit should we then look toward viability.

Profit is not the purpose of our business and should not be sought for its own sake. Rather, it is a necessity if we are to be able to continue to deliver value to our clients, so we must be careful to do what we have chosen to do in a manner that is efficient and cost-effective. We should be more concerned with the client than with the competitor.

It is one of our corporate objectives to have fun. To enjoy what we are doing, we must like those with whom we work. In order to do this, we must respect each other and work together in mutual trust. To encourage trust, we must strive for completely open communication: management must not keep secrets and must not be defensive when criticized. We must foster an atmosphere that encourages fellow employees to speak candidly and without fear of reprisal. How else can we learn?

It is important for all of us to remember why we are here and to be careful to deliver value to our customers for what we charge them. We should try to do our jobs better each week and to have fun doing them.

Ken Edwards
December 1991

CORPORATE DESCRIPTION

A.G. Edwards, Inc. is a holding company whose subsidiaries provide securities and commodities brokerage, investment banking, trust, asset management, and insurance services. Its principal subsidiary, A.G. Edwards & Sons, Inc., is a St. Louis-based financial services company with more than 450 locations in 48 states and the District of Columbia. A.G. Edwards & Sons provides a full range of financial products and services to individual and institutional investors, and offers investment banking services to corporate, governmental and municipal clients.

ADDRESS   One North Jefferson
St. Louis, MO 63103-2287

INDUSTRY CATEGORY   Financial Investment Services

◆   ◆   ◆   ◆   ◆   ◆   ◆

Energen Corporation

STATEMENT | **Energen Statement of Principles**

We will conduct our business and earn a profit based on ethical standards and values which recognize:

- The dignity and worth of all individuals
- Commitment to excellence in performance
- Personal and business integrity and
- Courage of convictions and action.

CORPORATE DESCRIPTION

Energen is a diversified energy company based in Birmingham, Alabama. The Company has two major lines of business:
—Natural gas distribution through Alagasco
—Oil and gas exploration and production through Taurua Exploration

ADDRESS   2101 Sixth Ave. N.
Birmingham, AL 35203

INDUSTRY CATEGORY   Oil and Gas

◆   ◆   ◆   ◆   ◆   ◆   ◆

Ethyl Corporation

Our Vision

To Be At The Top of Customers' Lists of Suppliers

In the markets we serve, Ethyl will be at the top of existing and potential customers' lists of companies from which they will choose to do business.

To achieve this vision, we will operate according to the following values:

Respect for People

Achieving our vision depends entirely on the ability of Ethyl's people to contribute individually and collectively, to develop new skills, to work in an environment that fosters pride and to share in the contributions they make toward the success of the company. This success requires a culture that makes it possible for Ethyl people to achieve full potential. Such a culture is based on mutual trust and respect.

Unquestionable Integrity

Personal and corporate integrity are the foundations for all our activities. Integrity is a cherished possession we want never to lose.

Continually Improving Quality

Quality means satisfying customers' needs now and in the future. To do this, we must continually improve the quality of everything we make or do.

Our Partners—Customers and Suppliers

To be at the top of customers' lists, we must become their partners. This means we must share their business goals, champion their interests and link our resources to theirs in anticipation of their future needs. We need and will encourage the partnership of our suppliers in support of our customers' needs and goals as well.

Safety and Environment Responsibility

It is Ethyl's goal to provide workplaces for employees that are safe, healthy and environmentally sound. Likewise, our presence in communities will not adversely affect the safety, health or environment of our neighbors. Finally, we will participate in ongoing activities, like Responsible Care®, that improve the health, safety and environment of the world.

Good Citizenship

We intend to be good citizens wherever we have a presence throughout the world. Good citizens do more than simply comply with laws; they support causes that help to improve the community. We will support such causes as a corporation and encourage Ethyl people to take active roles in answering community needs.

Economic Viability

To realize this vision, Ethyl must be an economically viable and profitable organization. As we operate according to our vision and values, Ethyl will enjoy long-term growth with continually improving importance.

CORPORATE DESCRIPTION

Ethyl Corporation develops, manufactures and blends performance enhancing fuel and lubricant additives marketed worldwide to refiners and others who sell petroleum products for use in transportation and industrial equipment. Ethyl additives increase the value of gasoline, diesel and heating fuels as well as lubricants for engines, automatic transmissions, gears and hydraulic and industrial equipment.

Ethyl spun-off its chemicals business in February 1994. Ethyl Corporation Vision and Values was created to reflect the values of the newly focused corporation.

ADDRESS   330 S. Fourth St.
P.O. Box 2189
Richmond, VA 23217

INDUSTRY CATEGORY   Chemicals

♦   ♦   ♦   ♦   ♦   ♦   ♦

Exxon

STATEMENT | **Exxon Strategies**

The following strategies have and will continue to guide Exxon as we strive to meet shareholder and customer expectations:

- Identifying and implementing quality investment opportunities at a timely and appropriate pace, while maintaining a selective and disciplined approach
- Being the most efficient competitor in every aspect of our business
- Maintaining a high-quality portfolio of productive assets
- Developing and employing the best technology
- Ensuring safe, environmentally sound operations
- Continually improving an already high-quality work force
- Maintaining a strong financial position and ensuring that financial resources are employed wisely

CORPORATE DESCRIPTION

Exxon is engaged in all aspects of the worldwide oil and natural gas business—exploration, production, manufacturing, distribution, and marketing. Exxon is also a leading producer and marketer of petrochemicals and has interests in coal, minerals, and electric power generation.

ADDRESS   5959 Las Colinas Blvd.
Irving, TX 75039

INDUSTRY CATEGORY   Oil & Gas

◆　◆　◆　◆　◆　◆　◆

FDX Corporation (FedEx)

STATEMENT | **Corporate Mission and Values**

FDX will produce superior financial returns for its shareholders by providing transportation, high value-added logistics, and related information services through focused operating companies. Customer requirements will be met in the highest quality manner appropriate to each market segment served. FDX will strive to develop mutually rewarding relationships with its employees, partners, and suppliers. Safety will be the first consideration in all operations. Corporate activities will be conducted to the highest ethical and professional standards.

CORPORATE DESCRIPTION

Federal Express Corporation offers a wide range of customized services for the time-definite transportation and distribution of goods and documents throughout the world, using an extensive fleet of aircraft and vehicles.

ADDRESS 2005 Corporate Ave.
Memphis, TN 38132

INDUSTRY CATEGORY Package Delivery Service

◆ ◆ ◆ ◆ ◆ ◆ ◆

Federal-Mogul Corporation

STATEMENT | **Federal-Mogul Mission Statement**

Federal-Mogul's primary strategic focus is the manufacturing and distribution of products into the global vehicular and industrial aftermarket. The company is committed to providing these markets with world class quality products and adding value through the interdependence of our manufacturing and distribution operations.

We will also continue our history of support to the original equipment market. In fact, we will strive to be a leader in all OEM products in which the company participates.

Through this integrated approach, we will create sufficient value to be rewarded by our customers. This unique value created will result in profits for our investors, and help meet our commitment of providing job satisfaction and a pleasant work environment for all of our employees.

Our product development, manufacturing and distribution systems will be designed for flexibility, high quality and fast customer response. This will create Federal-Mogul's time-based competitive advantage of supplying low volume/high variety products.

Corporate Strategy

The elimination of time in dealing with the development, manufacturing, distribution and administrative needs of our customers is our major priority.

Guiding Principles

1. Quality
Complete customer satisfaction in products and services is crucial to our continued survival in a global environment.

2. Customer Response
Our customers are our reason for being. All our efforts must be directed towards providing them with the best products and services.

3. Continuous Improvement

We must never be satisfied with our performance. We must strive to provide the very best in products, services and value.

4. Respect for All Individuals

Employee involvement means trust and respect for each other as members of a team.

5. Ethical Conduct

Our integrity in the marketplace and with each other must never be compromised. We are committed to equal opportunities for all individuals.

CORPORATE DESCRIPTION

Federal-Mogul Corporation is a global distributor and manufacturer of a broad range of precision parts, primarily components for automobiles, light and heavy duty trucks, farm and construction vehicles, and industrial products.

ADDRESS 26555 Northwestern Hwy.
Southfield, MI 48034

INDUSTRY CATEGORY Manufacturing

◆ ◆ ◆ ◆ ◆ ◆ ◆

Federated Department Stores, Inc.

STATEMENT | **Corporate Philosophy**

Federated clearly recognizes that the customer is paramount, and that all actions and strategies must be directed toward providing an enhanced merchandise offering and better service to targeted consumers through dynamic department stores.

Aggressive implementation of the company's strategies, as well as careful and thorough planning, will provide Federated's department stores with a competitive edge.

Federated is committed to open and honest communications with employees, shareholders, vendors, analysts and the news media. The company will be pro-active in sharing information and in keeping these audiences up-to-date on important and material objectives.

Corporate Objectives

The corporate objectives of Federated Department Stores, Inc. are:

- ◆ To accelerate future sales growth;
- ◆ To continue to increase the company's profitability levels, defined as EBITDA (earnings before interest, taxes, depreciation and amortization) as a percent to sales and ROGI (return on gross investment). The company continues to be focused on reducing its cost structure;
- ◆ To identify strategic growth opportunities that are consistent with the company's business objectives;
- ◆ To continue to strengthen the company's balance sheet.

CORPORATE DESCRIPTION

Federated Department Stores, Inc. is the nation's largest operator of department stores, located in all major regions of the United States.

ADDRESS   7 W. Seventh St.
Cincinnati, OH 45202

INDUSTRY CATEGORY   Retail

◆　◆　◆　◆　◆　◆　◆

Ferro Corporation

STATEMENT | **Ferro's Corporate Mission**

Ferro is organized and managed to achieve steady growth in operating profits, enhancement of shareholder value, and dividend payments commensurate with earnings growth.

Operations are directed to meeting the needs of customers for high-performance specialty materials, engineered products and services worldwide. These businesses will have sufficient size, technical scope and market position to provide opportunities for current and future growth.

Because a company's reputation is one of its main valued assets, Ferro conducts its business on sound ethical principles, based upon integrity and fairness to all constituencies.

While the Company's ultimate responsibility is to its shareholders, Ferro also has a deep commitment to its employees, whose skills, attitudes and efforts are essential to the Company's continued success.

CORPORATE DESCRIPTION

Ferro Corporation is a leading worldwide producer of specialty materials for industry. These materials include specialty coatings, colors, ceramics, plastics and chemicals.

The Company's major markets encompass building and renovation, home appliances, household furnishings, transportation, industrial products, packaging and leisure applications. The Company's strong worldwide status is based upon its manufacturing presence in 22 countries and its marketing and customer service operations in over 100 nations.

ADDRESS   1000 Lakeside Ave.
Cleveland, OH 44114-1183

INDUSTRY CATEGORY   Industrial, Specialized

◆　◆　◆　◆　◆　◆　◆

First American Corporation

Our primary responsibility is to manage the company soundly, profitably and with adequate growth to serve the needs of our customers, our employees and our communities, thereby increasing the value of our SHAREHOLDERS' investment.

We believe that by providing our CUSTOMERS with convenient access to high-quality products, coupled with superior service, we can excel and be a leader in our priority markets: individual consumers and small to mid-sized businesses of Tennessee.

We view our EMPLOYEES as partners. We are committed to providing a fair and challenging workplace, one that respects and empowers the individual; encourages professional growth; and recognizes and rewards outstanding performance.

We take seriously our responsibility to our COMMUNITIES. We endeavor to foster their success by offering appropriate financial services to all economic segments and by actively demonstrating our role as a caring corporate citizen. We invest our capital in Tennessee and build strong relationships with our Tennessee suppliers.

CORPORATE DESCRIPTION

First American Corporation is a bank holding company which was incorporated under the laws of Tennessee in 1968. First American's largest subsidiary is First American National Bank. First American is also the parent of First American Trust Company, N.A. On the basis of total deposits and total assets, First American Corporation is the largest bank holding company headquartered in Nashville, Tennessee, and the second largest in Tennessee.

ADDRESS   First American Center
300 Union
Nashville, TN 37237

INDUSTRY CATEGORY   Banking

◆   ◆   ◆   ◆   ◆   ◆   ◆

First Interstate Bancorp

| **Mission Statement**

At First Interstate Bank, our mission is to provide superior value and exceptional service to our customers.

To accomplish this:

We believe in being a preferred employer.

We believe in the importance of maintaining superior asset quality.

We believe in actively supporting the communities we serve.

We believe in maintaining the highest levels of professional integrity and personal ethics.

We believe in rewarding our shareholders with returns that consistently meet their expectations.

As a result, we will be recognized as a leader in the financial services industry.

| **Values and Strategies**

Value

We provide superior value and exceptional service to our customers.

Strategy

We are building relationships with customers to become their primary financial services provider.

We provide a diverse range of financial products and services that meet a variety of customer needs. Our employees accurately assess our customers' financial requirements and recommend the appropriate products and services.

We differentiate ourselves from our competitors through quality service. We acknowledge the difficulty of maintaining and improving services levels while building a lower cost structure, but can manage this challenge.

First Interstate will be a banking company of common products marketed at the local level. We foster a strong sales and service culture that understands our local markets and works to expand our share of individual and business customers in all of our regions.

Value

We believe in being a preferred employer.

Strategy

We provide our employees with an environment that recognizes their value as individuals and as members of the team. We are a caring employer and treat all employees with respect, creating a climate of trust, pride, and positive empowerment.

We encourage teamwork, open, two-way communication and personal development to reinforce our commitment to our employees.

We seek to attract the highest quality individuals whose personal values and professional skills are consistent with our strategy of providing exceptional service to our customers.

Our employees are encouraged to accept accountability for personal development. The company provides educational opportunities that enhance individual and team effectiveness.

We are strongly committed to fair compensation and recognition which demonstrate to our employees our desire to reward their effort and commitment.

We encourage and reward teamwork within and between regions and the corporate staff.

Value

We believe in the importance of maintaining superior asset quality.

Strategy

Credit quality will be one of our highest priorities. Decisions will demonstrate adherence to the company's policies and guidelines.

We continuously improve our lending processes. We utilize standard credit policies and procedures across the corporation. We monitor and control concentrations of credit portfolio, and borrow risk. The skills of our leaders are enhanced through their participation in our Exemplary Credit Program.

Value

We believe in actively supporting the communities we serve.

Strategy

We invest financial and human support to improve the quality of life in our communities.

We affirm our responsibility to be a valued corporate citizen, sensitive to community needs and concerns. We actively encourage and support the involvement of all employees in volunteer organizations.

We strongly support the aims and objectives of the Community Reinvestment Act and seek to exceed regulatory requirements.

Value

We believe in maintaining the highest levels of professional integrity and personal ethics.

Strategy

We evaluate all of our decisions and actions against an ethical framework based on openness, honesty, and fairness.

We emphasize the importance of behavior that consistently reflects our values and mission. We are measured by the integrity and ethics we demonstrate in our relationships with internal and external customers.

Value

We believe in rewarding our shareholders with returns that consistently meet their expectations.

Strategy

We will achieve long-term, sustainable profitability by focusing on relationships and transactions that will produce predictable and consistent earnings streams.

We will deliver excellent financial results as measured by return on equity while maintaining a conservative balance sheet and strong-capital position.

We are committed to outstanding credit quality, proper revenue and expense management, and prudent fixed asset investments. We will enhance our revenue stream by increasing our share of core deposits, capitalizing on appropriate lending opportunities, continuing to expand noninterest income sources, and promoting the sales of alternative investment products that fit our customers' needs.

We recognize the importance of short- and long-term planning and accept accountability for achieving planned results.

Value
We will be recognized as a leader in the financial services industry.

Strategy
As we consistently adhere to our values and strategies and achieve our goals, we will demonstrate our leadership position in the industry.

We emphasize continuous improvement as we pursue quality in every aspect of our business.

CORPORATE DESCRIPTION

First Interstate is the 14th largest commercial banking company in the U.S. and the largest based in Southern California. Its 1,093 domestic offices in 13 western states serve individuals, small businesses, middle market companies and selected large corporations and financial institutions. First Interstate provides quality common financial products and services marketed at the local level to nearly five million households in over 500 western U.S. communities.

ADDRESS   633 W. 5th St.
Los Angeles, CA 90071

INDUSTRY CATEGORY   Banking

◆ ◆ ◆ ◆ ◆ ◆ ◆

First of America Bank Corporation

STATEMENT | **First of America Bank Corporation
Mission Statement**

We will compete in the financial services market by serving the needs of our customers first as we strive to maximize the value of our shareholders' investment. As we compete, our highest guiding values will remain CARING, LEADERSHIP, QUALITY, and PROFESSIONALISM.

CARING: We will guide our business activities by a sense of genuine caring as we serve our customers, fellow employees and our communities. We will treat our employees with fairness and provide them with opportunities for development to be their best. We will contribute to the economic vitality and quality of life in all of our communities.

LEADERSHIP: We will achieve or maintain a leading position within our markets and our industry, in market share, growth, return on investment, efficiency and innovative products and services.

QUALITY: We will remain committed to a superior level of quality in the development, design, sales and delivery of products and services to our individual, commercial, governmental and agricultural customers.

PROFESSIONALISM: We will conduct ourselves and our business in a way that creates confidence in First of America among customers, shareholders and our communities. We will apply expertise to serving the financial needs of our customers and maintain high ethical standards in all situations.

CORPORATE DESCRIPTION

First of America Bank Corporation, headquartered in Kalamazoo, Michigan, is one of the largest bank holding companies in the Midwest with assets over $23 billion. First of America has 611 offices in Michigan, Indiana, Illinois, and Florida that serve over 350 communities. The banks engage in commercial banking, retail banking and mortgage banking, and provide trusts and other financial services. Based on net income, profitability and size of franchise, First of America is ranked among the top 36 banking companies in the United States.

ADDRESS 211 S. Rose St.
Kalamazoo, MI 49007

INDUSTRY CATEGORY Banking

◆　◆　◆　◆　◆　◆　◆

First Tennessee National Corporation

STATEMENT | **Mission Statement**

Working together to create value and build loyalty one opportunity at a time.

CORPORATE DESCRIPTION

First Tennessee National Corporation is headquartered in Memphis, Tennessee, and is a nationwide, diversified financial services institution which provides banking and other financial services to its customers through various regional and national business lines.

ADDRESS   P.O. Box 84
Memphis, TN 38101-0084

INDUSTRY CATEGORY   Banking

◆　◆　◆　◆　◆　◆　◆

First Virginia Banks, Inc.

STATEMENT

[*Author's note:* The following appears to be addressed to the company's employees]

| The First Virginia Creed

Our goal is to provide friendly and professional service. We must continually strive to make our customers feel welcome. As an individual, you can accomplish this goal by greeting customers by name whenever possible, and by always thanking them for banking with us. And, when customers have questions, you should attempt to answer them as quickly and as accurately as possible. Collectively, we must carefully evaluate the needs of all customers and be sure to provide them with all the financial services they need.

Finally, we must realize that, individually and as a whole, we are responsible for creating the atmosphere that will make customers feel at home. Our fundamental responsibility is to consider how our attitudes and actions will affect customer opinion and satisfaction. Along with being fiscally responsible and earning an acceptable return for our stockholders, providing friendly, helpful service is a fundamental part of our business philosophy.

(Signed)
Barry J. Fitzpatrick
Chairman, President, and Chief Executive Officer

CORPORATE DESCRIPTION

First Virginia Banks, Inc. is the oldest bank holding company headquartered in Virginia. It is a multistate organization with banking companies in Virginia, Maryland and East Tennessee and nonbanking offices throughout the mid-Atlantic and Southeastern states.

ADDRESS   One First Virginia Plaza
6400 Arlington Blvd.
Falls Church, VA 22042-2336

INDUSTRY CATEGORY   Banking

◆ ◆ ◆ ◆ ◆ ◆ ◆

Flagstar Companies, Inc.

STATEMENT | **Mission 2000**

[*Author's note:* The following statements are excerpted from the "Chairman's Letter," which appeared in the company's 1992 Annual Report and was written by Chairman and Chief Executive Officer Jerome J. Richardson.]

To be the best food service company in the world by the year 2000. Mission 2000 is the process we are using to achieve this goal.

As part of Mission 2000, we are measuring our success in the following key areas:

- **Competition.** Increasing customer traffic more rapidly than our competition.
- **Employment.** Achieving measurable reductions in employee turnover, improving productivity and maximizing customer satisfaction.
- **Citizenship.** Monitoring the commitment of employee knowledge and time, corporate contributions and in-kind gifts to priority needs in the communities we serve, as well as progress toward specific goals in the hiring and achievement of women and minorities and the development of business relationships with firms owned by women and minorities.
- **Shareholder value.** Achieving an investment grade rating on our debt securities and a 2:1 long-term debt to equity ratio, and annual improvements in operating income of 10 percent or more.

CORPORATE DESCRIPTION

Flagstar Companies, Inc. through its wholly owned subsidiary, Flagstar Corporation, is one of the largest food service enterprises in the United States, operating (directly and through franchises) more than 2,400 moderately priced restaurants. These restaurants are Denny's, Hardee's, Quincy's Family Steakhouse, and El Pollo Loco.

ADDRESS   203 E. Main St.
Spartanburg, SC 29319

INDUSTRY CATEGORY   Food/Beverage

♦   ♦   ♦   ♦   ♦   ♦   ♦

Fleming Companies, Inc.

STATEMENT | **Fleming's Mission**

is to . . .

Become a World-Class Marketing and Distribution Company
Our primary focus will be on the efficient and effective marketing and distribution of food and related products. We are committed to achieving sound growth, outstanding business results and a superior return for our shareholders.

We will seek to expand our business both domestically and in global markets, and will make selective investments in retail niche operations and excellent wholesale operations to further augment a world-class marketing and distribution system.

Position the Customers We Serve to Win at Retail
State-of-the-art services must be offered to the retailers we serve. Major investments in technology will be made to create a competitive edge in distribution and retailing. We must provide the cost-effective support necessary to assure the long-term success of our retailers because our success is directly related to theirs.

Always Remember that Individuals Make the Difference
We will strive to attract, motivate and retain the most talented people in our industry. Innovation and risk taking will be encouraged at every level. We will maintain a highly productive environment based on teamwork, individual initiative, mutual trust and respect for our fellow associates. Our business will be conducted according to the highest ethical standards.

Maintain a Clear Vision of Our Future Direction
To accomplish our objectives, we recognize the importance of setting priorities and executing plans consistent with our strategic goals. This requires strong leadership and the pursuit of excellence in every aspect of our business.

CORPORATE DESCRIPTION

Fleming supplies food and related products to more than 4,800 stores in 36 states, the Caribbean, Mexico, and other Central and South American countries.

ADDRESS   P.O. Box 26647
6301 Waterford Blvd.
Oklahoma City, OK 73126

INDUSTRY CATEGORY   Food/Beverage

◆　◆　◆　◆　◆　◆　◆

Flowserve Corporation

STATEMENT | **Our Mission**

Consistently improve efficiency and reliability in flow management
Help build productive economies
Provide superior return to our shareholders

CORPORATE DESCRIPTION

Flowserve Corporation was formed in July 1997 by the merger of BW/IP, Inc. and Durco International Inc. Flowserve is one of the world's leading providers of industrial flow management services. The company produces engineered pumps for the process industries, precision mechanical seals, automated and manual quarter-turn valves, control valves and valve actuators, and a range of related flow management services.

ADDRESS   222 West Las Colinas Blvd.
Suite 1500
Irving, TX 75039

INDUSTRY CATEGORY   Industrial, Specialized

◆　◆　◆　◆　◆　◆　◆

Ford Motor Company

| **Mission**

Ford Motor Company is a worldwide leader in automotive and financial products and services. Our mission is to improve continually our products and services to meet our customers' needs, allowing us to prosper as a business and to provide a reasonable return for our stockholders, the owners of our business.

| **Values**

How we accomplish our mission is as important as the mission itself. Fundamental to success for the Company are these basic values:

People—Our people are the source of our strength. They provide our corporate intelligence and determine our reputation and vitality. Involvement and teamwork are our core human values.

Products—Our products are the end result of our efforts, and they should be the best in serving customers worldwide. As our products are viewed, so are we viewed.

Profits—Profits are the ultimate measure of how efficiently we provide customers with the best products for their needs. Profits are required to survive and grow.

| **Guiding Principles**

Quality comes first—To achieve customer satisfaction, the quality of our products and services must be our number one priority.

Customers are the focus of everything we do—Our work must be done with our customers in mind, providing better products and services than our competition.

Continuous improvement is essential to our success—We must strive for excellence in everything we do: in our products, in their safety and value—and in our services, our human relations, our competitiveness, and our profitability.

Employee involvement is our way of life—We are a team. We must treat each other with trust and respect.

Dealers and suppliers are our partners—The Company must maintain mutually beneficial relationships with dealers, suppliers, and our other business associates.

Integrity is never compromised—The conduct of our Company worldwide must be pursued in a manner that is socially responsible and commands respect for its integrity and for its positive contributions to society. Our doors are open to men and women alike without discrimination and without regard to ethnic origin or personal beliefs.

CORPORATE DESCRIPTION

Ford Motor Company is a worldwide leader in automotive and financial products and services.

ADDRESS   The American Road
P.O. Box 1899
Dearborn, MI 48121

INDUSTRY CATEGORY   Motor Vehicles and Related

◆   ◆   ◆   ◆   ◆   ◆   ◆

Foremost Farms USA

STATEMENT | **OUR VISION**

Foremost Farms USA strives to be the leader in serving local, regional, national and international dairy and related markets for the benefit of member-owners.

| **MISSION**

The mission of Foremost Farms USA Cooperative is to provide dairy farmers with a financially sound organization that efficiently assembles, processes and markets milk and related dairy products to customers in a manner that generates fair and equitable returns for past, present and future member-owners.

KEY SUCCESS FACTORS

The key factors in successfully achieving our mission include meeting the needs of our member-owners, customers, employees, milk haulers and distributors, while operating our multiple-plant system efficiently, marketing products effectively and maintaining our cooperative's financial integrity.

CORPORATE DESCRIPTION

Foremost Farms USA Cooperative is principally engaged in the processing, manufacturing and marketing of dairy products and chilled juices for sale primarily to food industry companies, wholesalers and retailers within the United States. Foremost Farms USA is a non-stock cooperative.

ADDRESS   P.O. Box 111
Baraboo, WI 53913

INDUSTRY CATEGORY   Food/Beverage

◆　◆　◆　◆　◆　◆　◆

Forest Oil Corporation

STATEMENT | **Mission Statement**

To enhance shareholder value through application of the company's existing technical expertise and operating capabilities by making selected oil and gas investments whose business risk characteristics and return potentials are consistent with the financial risk capacity of the corporation.

CORPORATE DESCRIPTION

Forest Oil Corporation is one of the oldest independent energy companies in the U.S. Forest explores for, develops and markets natural gas and crude oil in North America.

ADDRESS   1600 Broadway
Suite 2200
Denver, CO 80202

INDUSTRY CATEGORY   Oil and Gas

◆ ◆ ◆ ◆ ◆ ◆ ◆

Fortune Brands, Inc.

STATEMENT | **Corporate Vision**

To be recognized as one of the most successful consumer products companies in the world.

CORPORATE DESCRIPTION

Fortune Brands is a consumer products company. Its operating companies have powerhouse brands with leading positions in the home and office, golf and distilled spirits categories. Some of these brands include Jim Beam, Cobra, Master Lock, Moen, Titleist and Swingline.

ADDRESS   1700 E. Putnam Ave.
Old Greenwich, CT 06870

INDUSTRY CATEGORY   Consumer Goods and Services

◆ ◆ ◆ ◆ ◆ ◆ ◆

FPL Group, Inc.

STATEMENT

We will be the preferred provider of safe, reliable, and cost-effective products and services that satisfy the electricity-related needs of all customer segments.

CORPORATE DESCRIPTION

FPL Group is one of the country's largest providers of electricity-related services. Its principal subsidiary, Florida Power & Light Company, serves millions of people along the eastern seaboard and the southern portion of Florida. Other operations include FPL Energy, a leader in producing electricity from clean and renewable fuels.

ADDRESS   P.O. Box 14000
June Beach, FL 33408

INDUSTRY CATEGORY   Utility

◆   ◆   ◆   ◆   ◆   ◆   ◆

Fuller (H.B. Fuller Company)

STATEMENT | **The Company's Mission**

The H.B. Fuller corporate mission is to be a leading and profitable worldwide formulator, manufacturer and marketer of quality specialty chemicals, emphasizing service to customers and managed in accordance with a strategic plan. H.B. Fuller Company is committed to its responsibilities, in order of priority, to its customers, employees, stockholders and communities. H.B. Fuller will conduct business legally and ethically, support the activities of its employees in their communities and be a responsible corporate citizen.

CORPORATE DESCRIPTION

H.B. Fuller Company is a 107-year-old worldwide manufacturer and marketer of adhesives, sealants, coatings, paints and other specialty chemicals. These are used in a wide range of industries, including packaging, woodworking, automotive, aerospace, graphic arts, appliances, filtration, windows, nonwoven/hygienic, sporting goods, shoes and ceramic tile.

ADDRESS 2400 Energy Park Dr.
Saint Paul, MN 55108-1591

INDUSTRY CATEGORY Manufacturing

◆ ◆ ◆ ◆ ◆ ◆ ◆

Gannett Company, Inc.

STATEMENT | **Gannett's Basic Game Plan**

Strategic Vision
- Create and expand quality products through innovation.
- Make acquisitions in news, information and communications and related fields that make strategic and economic sense.

Operating Principle
- Provide effective leadership and efficient management.
- Achieve a positive return on new and acquired products and properties in a reasonable period of time, while recognizing those with high growth potential may take more time.
- Increase profitability and increase return on equity and investment over the long term.
- Enhance the quality and editorial integrity of our products, recognizing that quality products ultimately lead to higher profits.

- Guarantee respect for and fairness in dealing with employees.
- Offer a diverse environment where opportunity is based on merit.
- Show commitment and service to communities where we do business.
- Deliver customer satisfaction.
- Dispose of assets that have limited or no potential or where an offer has been made that the Board of Directors believes is in the best interest of the shareholders.
- In all activities, we show respect for the First Amendment and our responsibility to it.

CORPORATE DESCRIPTION

Gannett is a multi-billion-dollar media and information company whose assets include *USA Today,* daily and weekly newspapers, specialty publications, television, cable in Top 25 or growth markets, online news, information and advertising.

ADDRESS   1100 Wilson Blvd.
Arlington, VA 22234

INDUSTRY CATEGORY   Media

◆　◆　◆　◆　◆　◆　◆

General American Life Insurance Company

STATEMENT | **Mission**

Our mission is to provide life insurance, health insurance, retirement plans, and related financial services to individuals and groups of employees as well as reinsurance to other insurance companies.

| **Objective**

Our objective is to do a superior job of meeting the needs of an ever increasing number of clients and to do so by outperforming our competitors in products, services, marketing, administration, and financial results.

CORPORATE DESCRIPTION

General American is among the nation's 50 largest insurance companies. A mutual company, it is owned by its policyholders.

ADDRESS   P.O. Box 396
St. Louis, MO 63166

INDUSTRY CATEGORY   Insurance

◆ ◆ ◆ ◆ ◆ ◆ ◆

General Electric Company

STATEMENT | **GE Values**

GE Leaders ... Always with Unyielding Integrity:

- Have a Passion for Excellence and Hate Bureaucracy
- Are Open to Ideas from Anywhere ... and Committed to Work-Out
- Live Quality ... and Drive Cost and Speed for Competitive Advantage
- Have the Self-Confidence to Involve Everyone and Behave in a Boundaryless Fashion
- Create a Clear, Simple, Reality-Based Vision ... and Communicate It to All Constituencies
- Have Enormous Energy and the Ability to Energize Others
- Stretch ... Set Aggressive Goals ... Reward Progress ... Yet Understand Accountability and Commitment
- See Change as Opportunity ... Not Threat
- Have Global Brains ... and Build Diverse and Global Teams

CORPORATE DESCRIPTION

GE is a diversified technology, manufacturing and service company with a commitment to achieving worldwide leadership in each of its 13 major businesses: aerospace, aircraft engines, broadcasting (NBC), electrical distribution equipment, electric motors, financial services, industrial and power systems, information services, lighting, locomotives, major appliances, medical systems and plastics.

ADDRESS   3135 Easton Turnpike
Fairfield, CT 06431

INDUSTRY CATEGORY   Diversified

♦   ♦   ♦   ♦   ♦   ♦   ♦

General Mills, Inc.

STATEMENT | **General Mills**
The Company of Champions
Statement of Corporate Values

Consumers

Consumers choose General Mills because we offer competitively superior products and services.

Employees

Employees choose General Mills because we reward innovation and superior performance and release their power to lead.

Investors

Investors choose General Mills because we consistently deliver financial results in the top 10 percent of all major companies.

Our heritage and commitment to outstanding accomplishment has made General Mills "The Company of Champions." Each of us at General Mills must strive to exemplify the values that distinguish us as a unique and special company.

Products and Services

We will provide competitively superior products and services to our customers and consumers. This superiority will be measured by rigorous, comparative testing versus the best competitive offerings and by growth in market share.

Providing championship products and services is a never-ending job requiring continuous improvement ahead of competition.

People and Organization

General Mills' people will be the best in our industries—people who are winners, ever striving to exceed their past accomplishments. Exceptional performance is the result of these people working together in small and fluid teams on those issues where success will clearly widen our competitive advantage.

We value diversity and will create workplaces where people with diverse skills, perspectives, and backgrounds can exercise leadership and help those around them release their full power and potential.

We will minimize organizational levels and have broad spans of responsibility. We will drive out bureaucracy and parochialism. We will trust each other and have the self-confidence to challenge and accept challenge.

Innovation

Innovation is the principal driver of growth. Innovation requires a bias for action. To be first among our competitors, we must constantly challenge the status quo and be willing to experiment. The anticipation and creation of change, both in established businesses and in new products and services, is essential for competitive advantage.

We recognize that change—and risk—are inherent to innovation. Our motivation system will strongly reward successful risk-taking, while not penalizing an innovative idea that did not work.

Speed

We will be the fastest moving and most productive competitor. We will set specific goals to improve our speed and productivity each year compared to our own past performance and to the competition.

Commitment

Our commitment to our shareholders is to deliver financial results that place us in the top 10 percent of all major companies. This can only be accomplished with the personal commitment of each of us.

The persistency to bounce back from disappointments, the intensity to pursue the exceptionally difficult, and the reliability to deliver promised results are all part of our commitment to our shareholders, to each other, and to our pride in "The Company of Champions." This commitment is demonstrated by substantial and increasing levels of employee stock ownership.

Citizenship

We will have significant positive impact on our communities. We will focus on specific projects where our efforts will make a difference in direct philanthropy, in our corporate investment in nonprofit ventures, and through our own personal involvement in civic and community affairs.

CORPORATE DESCRIPTION

General Mills manufactures a variety of breakfast cereals. The consumer food group includes Betty Crocker Desserts, Bisquick, Helper Dinner Mixes, Yoplait Yogurt, Fruit Snacks, Gorton's Frozen Seafood and Pop Secret Popcorn. Restaurant operations include Red Lobster and The Olive Garden. General Mills also manufactures and markets food products in foreign countries.

ADDRESS   P.O. Box 1113
Minneapolis, MN 55440

INDUSTRY CATEGORY   Food/Beverage

◆ ◆ ◆ ◆ ◆ ◆ ◆

General Motors Acceptance Corporation (GMAC)

STATEMENT | **The GMAC Mission**

We are dedicated to providing financial services to GM dealers and their customers in such form and of such quality as to **enhance** the marketing of GM cars and trucks, **enable** our employees to share in General Motors Acceptance Corporation's success and **provide** our shareholder, General Motors, with superior return on investment.

CORPORATE DESCRIPTION

General Motors Acceptance Corporation (GMAC) is the finance and insurance subsidiary of General Motors.

ADDRESS   3044 W. Grand Blvd.
Detroit, MI 48202

INDUSTRY CATEGORY   Financial Investment Services

◆ ◆ ◆ ◆ ◆ ◆ ◆

General Motors Corporation

| **Our Vision: Industry Leadership through Customer Enthusiasm**

Our vision is for GM to be the world leader in transportation products and services. We'll know we've achieved the vision when we have the most satisfied and enthusiastic customers in all market segments where we compete. Customer enthusiasm in the marketplace is what ultimately translates into leadership in sales, earnings, and returns on investment and assets.

And we will build customer enthusiasm by focusing our people and our processes on teamwork and continuous improvement in all areas of the business.

CORPORATE DESCRIPTION

General Motors Corporation is best known as the world's large full-line vehicle manufacturer. It makes and sells cars, trucks, and locomotives worldwide. GM's other substantial business interests include GM Hughes Electronics Corporation, involved in automotive electronics, commercial technologies, telecommunications and space, and defense electronics; Electronic Data Systems Corporation, applying information technologies around the globe; and General Motors Acceptance Corporation and its subsidiaries, providing financing and insurance to GM customers and dealers.

ADDRESS   3044 W. Grand Blvd.
Detroit, MI 48202

INDUSTRY CATEGORY   Motor Vehicles and Related

◆   ◆   ◆   ◆   ◆   ◆   ◆

General Public Utilities Corporation

STATEMENT | **Purpose**

People providing people with energy to meet today's needs and realize tomorrow's dreams.

| **Mission**

To be a premier supplier of energy and energy-related services through the skills of our employees and the excellence of our customer service.

| **GPU System's Values**

RESPECT
- Be a good listener; encourage diverse opinions and be willing to accept them
- Recognize the achievements of others
- Don't prejudge another person's qualities or intentions
- Respect confidences
- Recognize each individual's human dignity and value

HONESTY & OPENNESS
- Be forthright and never use information as a source of power
- Strive for clarity, avoid "slippery" words
- Focus on issues, not personalities
- Carry no hidden agendas
- Be willing to admit your own mistakes and be tolerant of others' mistakes

TEAMWORK
- Acknowledge all co-workers in the GPU System companies as valuable team members
- Practice solidarity by respecting and supporting team decisions
- Encourage initiative and participation
- Demand excellence from yourself and seek it from others
- Be accountable to the team

INTEGRITY & TRUST
- Act and speak ethically
- Show confidence in the character and truthfulness of others
- Keep commitments
- Be accountable for your own actions and expect accountability of others as well
- Accept responsibility for your own mistakes and give credit to others for their accomplishments

COMMITMENT
- Seek opportunities for positive and appropriate change
- Be clear in describing what needs to be change and why and how that change can be accomplished
- Challenge and change inappropriate policies
- Recognize that taking and accepting reasonable risks is necessary business conduct
- Lead by example
- Demonstrate a sense of urgency in all that we do.

CORPORATE DESCRIPTION

GPU is a Pennsylvania corporation and was organized in 1946 as a holding company registered under the Public Utility Holding Company Act of 1935. GPU does not operate any utility properties directly, but owns all the outstanding common stock of three electric utilities serving customers in New Jersey—Jersey Central Power & Light Company (JCP&L)—and Pennsylvania—Metropolitan Edison Company (Met-Ed) and Pennsylvania Electric Company (Penelec). The business of these subsidiaries consists predominantly of the generation, transmission, distribution and sale of electricity. GPU also owns all of the common stock of GPU Service Corporation (GPUSC), a service company; GPU Nuclear Corporation (GPUN), which operates and maintains nuclear units of the subsidiaries; and Energy Initiatives, Inc. (EI) and EI Power, Inc. (EI Power), which develop and operate non-utility generating facilities.

ADDRESS   100 Interpace Pkwy.
Parsippany, NJ 07054-1149

INDUSTRY CATEGORY   Utility

◆　◆　◆　◆　◆　◆　◆

Georgia Gulf

STATEMENT | **Mission**

Georgia Gulf will continue to be an efficient, integrated manufacturer and marketer of quality chemical and plastic products to users worldwide and will be dedicated to continuous improvement of the processes, products and services required to meet our customers' changing needs. We will strive to earn a superior long-term return for our shareholders while providing meaningful work for our employees and always operating with the highest regard for environmental protection, safety and the overall well-being of the communities in which we operate.

(September 1994)

| **Guiding Principles**

All applicable laws and regulations will be adhered to with special emphasis on meeting or exceeding environmental and safety standards.

Relationships with customers, stockholders, employees, suppliers and the communities in which we operate will be conducted in a fair, open and ethical manner. Never ending process improvement will be practiced in order to provide quality products and services which meet the needs of our customers.

Equal opportunity for advancement will be provided to all employees in an atmosphere of open communication, trust, respect and support.

Competitive compensation and benefits, including incentive and equity programs based upon company profitability and long-term growth, recognizing both team work and individual achievements, will be offered to all employees.

(May 1994)

CORPORATE DESCRIPTION

Georgia Gulf is an efficient, integrated manufacturer and marketer of quality chemical and plastic products.

ADDRESS   400 Perimeter Center Terrace
                 Ste. 595
                 Atlanta, GA 30346

INDUSTRY CATEGORY   Chemicals

◆   ◆   ◆   ◆   ◆   ◆   ◆

Geraghty & Miller, Inc.

STATEMENT | **Company Mission Statement**

Creating Environmental Value

From day-to-day activities through long-term planning, Geraghty & Miller is guided by this simple and clear mission. The creation of *environmental value* for clients, the Company, its employees, and its stockholders is achieved by adhering to a set of principles which, taken together, define *environmental value*.

◆ Anticipate and Respond to Client Needs.
◆ Cost Effective Solutions.
◆ Broad Range of Applied Expertise.
◆ Dynamic and Seamless National and International Network of People and Skills.
◆ Staff Driven by Personal Integrity, Trust, Communication and Cooperation.
◆ Staff Empowered to Meet Client Needs.
◆ Quality Processes to Produce Quality Results.
◆ Maintenance of Financial Integrity of Projects and the Firm.
◆ Maximizing Employee and Stockholder Benefits by Maximizing Product Value.
◆ Improvement of Environmental Quality.

CORPORATE DESCRIPTION

Geraghty & Miller, Inc. is a full-service environmental company that provides a wide spectrum of consulting, engineering, hydrocarbon and remediation services. The Company enjoys a preeminent reputation in the development, management, and protection of ground-water resources and the correction of soil and ground-water contamination.

ADDRESS   1099 18th St.
Ste. 2950
Denver, CO 80202

INDUSTRY CATEGORY   Environmental Engineering

◆ ◆ ◆ ◆ ◆ ◆ ◆

Gibson Greetings, Inc.

STATEMENT | **Our Mission**

Our mission is to provide the highest quality products that communicate personal expression; to support our retailers' business objectives through innovation, responsiveness and productivity; and to achieve the goals of our shareholders and our associates.

Our Values
Who We Are and What We Stand For:

- ◆ We are a TEAM committed to achieving our mission.
- ◆ We strive to be the best in everything we do.
- ◆ We seek open communication and feedback by listening and responding to our customers, our shareholders and our associates.

- We adhere to a stringent code of honor and integrity.
- We trust, respect, and care for each other.
- We mutually establish clear accountability and goals.
- We seek to attack the problem and not the person.
- We encourage our associates to become prudent risk takers, to grow, to contribute, and to accomplish.
- We take satisfaction from winning and having fun in the process.

© Gibson Greetings, Inc.
Reprinted with Permission of Gibson Greetings, Inc.
Cincinnati, Ohio 45237
All Rights Reserved

CORPORATE DESCRIPTION

Gibson Greetings, Inc. produces greeting cards, gift wrap and related social expression items.

ADDRESS   2100 Section Rd.
Cincinnati, OH 45237

INDUSTRY CATEGORY   Retail

♦ ♦ ♦ ♦ ♦ ♦ ♦

The Gillette Company

Our mission is to achieve or enhance clear leadership, worldwide, in the existing or new core consumer product categories in which we choose to compete.

Current core categories are:

+ Male grooming products, including blades and razors, electric shavers, shaving preparations, and deodorants and antiperspirants.
+ Female grooming products, including wet shaving, hair removal and hair care appliances, deodorants and antiperspirants.
+ Alkaline and specialty batteries and cells.
+ Writing instruments and correction products.
+ Certain areas of the oral care market, including toothbrushes, interdental devices and oral care appliances.
+ Selected areas of the high-quality small household appliance business, including coffeemakers and food preparation products.

To achieve this mission, we will also compete in supporting product areas that enhance the Company's ability to achieve or hold the leadership position in core categories.

| Values

In pursuing our mission, we will live by the following values:

People—We will attract, motivate and retain high-performing people in all areas of our business. We are committed to competitive, performance-based compensation, benefits, training and personal growth based on equal career opportunity and merit. We expect integrity, civility, openness, support for others and commitment to the highest standards of achievement. We value innovation, employee involvement, change, organizational flexibility and personal mobility. We recognize, value and are committed to the benefits in the diversity of people, ideas and cultures.

Customer Focus—We will invest in and master the key technologies vital to category success. We will offer consumers products of the highest levels of performance for value. We will provide quality service to our customers, both internal and external, by treating them as partners, by listening, understanding their needs, responding fairly and living up to our commitments. We will be a valued customer to our suppliers, treating them fairly and with respect. We will provide these quality values consistent with improving our productivity.

Good Citizenship—We will comply with applicable laws and regulations at all governmental levels wherever we do business. We will contribute to the communities in which we operate and address social issues responsibly. Our products will be safe to make and to use. We will conserve natural resources and we will continue to invest in a better environment.

We believe that commitment to this mission and to these values will enable the Company to provide a superior return to our shareholders.

(Courtesy, The Gillette Company)

CORPORATE DESCRIPTION

Founded in 1901, The Gillette Company is the world leader in male grooming, a category that includes blades, razors and shaving preparations. Gillette also holds the number one position worldwide in selected female grooming products, such as wet shaving products and hair epilation devices. The Company is the world's top seller of writing instruments and correction products, toothbrushes and oral care appliances. In addition, the Company is the world leader in alkaline batteries.

Gillette manufacturing operations are conducted at 62 facilities in 25 countries, and products are distributed through wholesalers, retailers and agents in over 200 countries and territories.

ADDRESS   Prudential Tower Bldg.
Boston, MA 02199

INDUSTRY CATEGORY   Consumer Goods and Services

◆　◆　◆　◆　◆　◆　◆

Goodyear Tire & Rubber Company

STATEMENT

OUR MISSION is constant improvement in products and services to meet our customers' needs. This is the only means to business success for Goodyear and prosperity for its investors and employees. QUALITY IS THE KEY TO CUSTOMER SATISFACTION.

Guiding Principles

CUSTOMER SATISFACTION—Everything we do is directed to the satisfaction of present and future customers. Quality is defined by the current expectations, as well as by future needs and desires of our customers.

PROCESS IMPROVEMENT—Results are achieved through the management of processes. All processes—and the resulting products and services—can be improved, forever. The improvements may take the form of revolutionary changes, innovations or the accumulation of many small steps. The improvements may involve such areas as quality, cost, delivery or time.

PEOPLE—We value the commitment, knowledge and creativity of the men and women of Goodyear. Everyone has the ability to contribute to our mission of constant improvement. Cooperation and respect among individuals and departments are fundamental to success.

ACTION BASED ON FACTS—Sound business decisions are based on sound data and rigorous analysis. Facts are reviewed in an atmosphere without blame. Understanding and use of data collection and analysis is vital in all areas.

CORPORATE DESCRIPTION

Goodyear's principal business is the development, manufacture, distribution, marketing and sale of tires for most applications throughout the world. In addition to being a leading tire manufacturer, the company manufactures and sells several lines of rubber products for the transportation industry and various industrial and consumer markets and numerous rubber-related chemicals for various applications. Goodyear also provides automotive repair and other services.

ADDRESS   1144 E. Market St.
                Akron, OH 44316-0001

INDUSTRY CATEGORY   Motor Vehicles and Related

◆ ◆ ◆ ◆ ◆ ◆ ◆

Grace (W.R. Grace & Co.)

STATEMENT | **Mission**

Grace's mission is to maximize long-term value to shareholders while balancing value to other stakeholders—our employees, customers, suppliers and communities.

CORPORATE DESCRIPTION

Grace is the world's largest specialty chemical company and holds a leadership position in specialized health care.

ADDRESS   One Town Center Rd.
                Boca Raton, FL 35486-1010

INDUSTRY CATEGORY   Chemicals

◆ ◆ ◆ ◆ ◆ ◆ ◆

Haemonetics Corporation

STATEMENT | **Mission**

♦ Enhance the safety and quality of the world's blood supply
♦ Increase the availability of blood components from a shrinking donor population

Haemonetics Quality Statement

Quality is . . . conformance to our customer requirements with an absolute, measurable yes or no.

CORPORATE DESCRIPTION

Haemonetics pioneered, and is the world leader in the design, manufacture, and marketing of blood processing equipment and related disposables.

ADDRESS   400 Wood Rd.
P.O. Box 9114
Braintree, MA 02184-9114

INDUSTRY CATEGORY   Medical Products and Services

◆   ◆   ◆   ◆   ◆   ◆   ◆

Hanna (M.A. Hanna Company)

STATEMENT | **Mission**

M.A. Hanna's mission is to create an international specialty chemicals company that:

Builds and maintains leadership in its markets by delivering superior value to its customers, as measured by customer service and responsiveness, product quality, product offering, technology and product development capability;

Attracts and retains qualified and productive associates by providing a challenging work environment, decision-making authority consistent with responsibility, continuous training, competitive compensation and opportunities to share in the financial success of the business through pay-for-performance and stock ownership;

Develops long-term partnerships with its suppliers and customers because of its unparalleled market access, market knowledge and value-added capabilities;

Commands respect as a corporate citizen by enforcing high ethical, legal, social and safety standards and preserving and protecting the environment;

And rewards investors with a consistently superior return on investments.

CORPORATE DESCRIPTION

M.A. Hanna Company is a leading international specialty chemicals company whose products and services extend to a wide range of markets in the polymers industry.

ADDRESS   200 Public Square
Ste. 36-5000
Cleveland, OH 44114-2304

INDUSTRY CATEGORY   Chemicals

◆　◆　◆　◆　◆　◆　◆

Harrah's Entertainment, Inc.

STATEMENT | **Vision Statement**

Our Vision at Harrah's Entertainment, Inc. is to offer exciting environments and to be legendary at creating smiles, laughter and lasting memories with every guest we entertain.

CORPORATE DESCRIPTION

Harrah's Entertainment, Inc. is the most recognized brand name in the casino entertainment industry, with facilities across the United States.

ADDRESS   1023 Cherry Rd.
Memphis, TN 38117

INDUSTRY CATEGORY   Hotel, Hospitality, and Entertainment

◆　◆　◆　◆　◆　◆　◆

Harsco Corporation

STATEMENT | **New Mission Statement**

The Mission of Harsco Corporation is to achieve consistent, superior financial returns from operations complemented by targeted and prudent growth in markets and technologies familiar to the Company. Enhanced shareholder value will be obtained by developing and maintaining lead industry positions in the markets served through the delivery of products and services that provide the best value to the customer.

CORPORATE DESCRIPTION

Harsco, a diversified industrial manufacturing and service company, conducts its business through 10 Divisions and has 16 varied classes of products and services. Its operations fall into three Operating Groups: Metal Reclamation and Mill Services; Infrastructure, Construction and Transportation; and Process Industry Products. Harsco has over 175 major facilities in 30 countries, including the United States. Harsco also holds a 40% ownership in United Defense, L.P., a $1.0 billion joint venture with FMC Corporation, which principally manufactures ground combat planes for the U.S. and international governments.

ADDRESS   P.O. Box 8888
                Camp Hill, PA 17001-8888

INDUSTRY CATEGORY   Manufacturing

◆ ◆ ◆ ◆ ◆ ◆ ◆

Haworth Inc.

Our global vision is to be world class in the eyes of our customers at creating well-designed, effective, and exciting work environments.

OUR PRINCIPLES

Customer Satisfaction

To completely satisfy our customers is our primary mission. We listen to our customers and understand their changing needs. We achieve their satisfaction by quickly translating these needs into products and services that are world class and that emphasize quality, design, innovation, and value. We know that our success is built on satisfied customers. We believe that our customers are best served through a strong dealer network. Haworth dealers aggressively represent us and offer a range of complimentary professional services to our customers. Our dealers collaborate with us to forge customer-satisfying teams. Our dealers are also our customers, and we are committed to their satisfaction.

The People of Haworth

Haworth members are the most important resource of our company, and we depend on the talents of all Haworth members. Because we value differences and trust people, we try to create work environments that encourage the contributions of every member. Our members endorse the practice of continuous improvement, believing it offers the best path to pride in their work, greater job security, customer satisfaction, and success for our company. Our corporate culture offers a participative environment that supports teams and individuals. Haworth encourages member development and achievement through recognition, rewards, and opportunities for career growth.

Dedication to Quality

In order to achieve total customer satisfaction, Haworth methods of operation are shaped by our dedication to quality. Corporate-wide quality initiatives result in superior products and services for our customers. At Haworth we combine intelligence with hard work to eliminate wasted time, effort, and materials. Our philosophy of continuous improvement is embraced by suppliers and dealers. They share our commitment to total customer satisfaction. With them, we create a seamless flow of high quality products and services to the end user. Our philosophy includes the preservation of our environment and the protection of resources. Our pursuit of quality extends to our communities, where we build for the future by investing in the quality of life.

CORPORATE DESCRIPTION

Haworth is the second-largest manufacturer of office furniture and seating products in the world. The company remains privately held and family run after 50 years. Haworth has manufacturing facilities and sales offices located throughout North America, South America, Europe, and Asia/Pacific.

ADDRESS   One Haworth Center
Holland, MI 49423

INDUSTRY CATEGORY   Manufacturing

◆ ◆ ◆ ◆ ◆ ◆ ◆

Hershey Foods Corporation

STATEMENT | **Mission Statement**

Our mission is to be a focused food company in North America and selected international markets and a leader in every aspect of our business. Our goal is to enhance our number one position in the North America confectionery market, be the leader in U.S. pasta and chocolate-related grocery products, and to build leadership positions in selected international markets.

This mission will be accomplished through emphasis on vision and organization/teamwork as follows:

Vision

♦ Dramatically accelerate growth in North America chocolate/confectionery business, with particular emphasis in U.S.
♦ Grow the Hershey Pasta and Grocery Group business to improve cash flows, returns and economic value.
♦ Build growing, profitable, economic value-adding confectionery businesses in selected markets outside North America.
♦ Capitalize on value-added business opportunities within the broader sweet snack category which leverage our business capabilities.

Organization/Teamwork

The growth vision and business goals will be achieved by developing and leveraging the skills and knowledge of our people as a unified Hershey Foods team. A seamless organizational structure will provide low-cost business capabilities as guided by the QTE process, a clear focus on customer satisfaction as its #1 priority, and a commitment to integrity, personal leadership and team work.

(Please note: On December 15, 1998, Hershey Foods Corporation announced the sale of its Pasta division. As the sale is completed, the above mission statement is subject to change.)

CORPORATE DESCRIPTION

Hershey Foods Corporation, which celebrated its centennial in 1994, is a leading North American producer of chocolate and confectionary products and has international interests in Germany, Italy, The Netherlands, Belgium, Mexico and the Far East.

ADDRESS 100 Crystal A Drive
Hershey, PA 17033

INDUSTRY CATEGORY Food/Beverage

♦   ♦   ♦   ♦   ♦   ♦   ♦

Hewlett-Packard Company

The organizational framework for our objectives

The achievements of an organization are the result of the combined efforts of each individual in the organization working toward common objectives. These objectives should be realistic, should be clearly understood by everyone in the organization and should reflect the organization's basic character and personality.

At Hewlett-Packard, we have five underlying organizational values that guide us as we work toward our common objectives.

♦ **We have trust and respect for individuals.** We approach each situation with the understanding that people want to do a good job and will do so, given the proper tools and support. We attract highly capable, innovative people and recognize their efforts and contributions to the company. HP people contribute enthusiastically and share in the success that they make possible.

♦ **We focus on a high level of achievement and contribution.** Our customers expect HP products and services to be of the highest quality and to provide lasting value. To achieve this, all HP people, but especially managers, must be leaders who generate enthusiasm and respond with extra effort to meet customer needs. Techniques and management practices which are effective today may be outdated in the future. For us to remain at the forefront in all our activities, people should always be looking for new and better ways to do their work.

♦ **We conduct our business with uncompromising integrity.** We expect HP people to be open and honest in their dealings to earn the trust and loyalty of others. People at every level are expected to adhere to the highest standards of business ethics and must understand that anything less is totally unacceptable. As a practical matter, ethical conduct cannot be assured by written HP policies and codes; it must be an integral part of the organization, a deeply ingrained tradition that is passed from one generation of employees to another.

♦ **We achieve our common objectives through team work.** We recognize that it is only through effective cooperation within and among organizations that we can achieve our goals. Our commitment is to work as a worldwide team to fulfill the expectations of our customers, shareholders and others who depend on us. The benefits and obligations of doing business are shared among all HP people.

♦ **We encourage flexibility and innovation.** We create a work environment which supports the diversity of our people and their ideas. We strive for overall objectives which are clearly stated and agreed upon, and allow people flexibility in working toward goals in ways which they help determine are best for the organization. HP people should personally accept responsibility and be encouraged to upgrade their skills and capabilities through ongoing training and development. This is especially important in a technical business where the rate of progress is rapid and where people are expected to adapt to change.

The Hewlett-Packard objectives which follow were initially published in 1957. Since then they have been modified from time to time, reflecting the changing nature of our business and social environment. This version represents the latest updating of our organization framework and objectives. We hope you will find this informative and will look to these objectives and underlying values to guide your activities as part of the HP team.

(Signed)
Dave Packard
Chairman of the Board

(Signed)
Bill Hewlett
Director Emeritus

(Signed)
John Young
President and Chief Executive Officer

Profit

To achieve sufficient profit to finance our company growth and to provide the resources we need to achieve our other corporate objectives. . . .

Customers

To provide products and services of the highest quality and the greatest possible value to our customers, thereby gaining and holding their respect and loyalty. . . .

Fields of Interest

To participate in those fields of interest that build upon our technology and customer base, that offer opportunities for continuing growth, and that enable us to make a needed and profitable contribution. . . .

Growth

To let our growth be limited only by our profit and our ability to develop and produce innovative products that satisfy real customer needs. . . .

Our People

To help HP people share in the company's success which they make possible; to provide employment security based on their performance; to ensure them a safe and pleasant work environment; to recognize their individual achievements; and to help them gain a sense of satisfaction and accomplishment from their work. . . .

Management

To foster initiative and creativity by allowing the individual great freedom of action in attaining well-defined objectives. . . .

Citizenship

To honor our obligations to society by being an economic, intellectual and social asset to each nation and each community in which we operate. . . .

CORPORATE DESCRIPTION

Hewlett-Packard designs, manufactures and services electronic products and systems for measurement, computation and communication.

ADDRESS   P.O. Box 1301
Palo Alto, CA 94303-0890

INDUSTRY CATEGORY   High Technology

◆   ◆   ◆   ◆   ◆   ◆   ◆

Hibernia Corporation

STATEMENT | **Purpose Statement**

Hibernia's purpose is to make it possible for people to achieve their financial goals and realize their dreams.

| **Mission Statement**

By 1999, we will be recognized by our customers, employees and shareholders as the best financial services company in each of our markets.

TEN COMMANDMENTS

1. Make service matter
2. Act empowered, like an owner
3. Make smart, quick, common-sense decisions
4. Accept prudent risk; price accordingly; sell ethically and aggressively
5. Encourage continuous improvement
6. Listen carefully, then communicate openly and in a timely manner
7. Create an environment where people can excel, be rewarded for it and have fun
8. Win in the marketplace as a team
9. Treat others with respect
10. Invest to prepare ourselves and Hibernia for long-term success

CORPORATE DESCRIPTION

Hibernia is the largest publicly traded national bank headquartered in Louisiana, Texas, Arkansas, Oklahoma or Mississippi.

ADDRESS P.O. Box 61540
New Orleans, LA 70161

INDUSTRY CATEGORY Banking

◆ ◆ ◆ ◆ ◆ ◆ ◆

Hoechst Celanese Corporation

STATEMENT | **Mission**

We are a large, international company based in the United States. We operate a broad spectrum of chemistry-related businesses within the worldwide Hoechst organization.

We will be the recognized leader in our target markets.

We will be the preferred employer in our industry.

We recognize that people are our most valuable asset.

We will be the partner of choice for customers, suppliers, and other creators of innovative concepts.

We will be a major contributor to and take full advantage of the strong technological base of the Hoechst Group.

We will continually increase the long-term value of our company.

We operate in a decentralized manner, allowing each business to develop within our Values.

| **Vision**

Hoechst Celanese will leverage core competencies to grow market value faster than any of the five largest chemical companies in North America. We will be a publicly traded company with values-based leadership, strategically managing a balanced portfolio of businesses to achieve consistent excellent performance.

CORPORATE DESCRIPTION

Hoechst Celanese Corporation is a subsidiary of Hoechst AG of Germany, with leading positions in chemicals, fibers, advanced materials and technologies, and the life sciences.

Products include commodity and specialty chemicals; textiles and technical fibers; polyester resins and films; engineering and high performance plastics; branded prescription, generic and bulk pharmaceuticals; crop protection and animal health products.

ADDRESS   Route 202-206
                P.O. Box 2500
                Somerville, NJ 08876-1258

INDUSTRY CATEGORY   Chemicals

◆   ◆   ◆   ◆   ◆   ◆   ◆

HON Industries, Inc.

STATEMENT | **Our Vision**

HON INDUSTRIES and its members are dedicated to achieving excellence through the pursuit of a philosophy, strategies, and day-to-day actions aimed at achieving rapid continuous improvement. We continuously strive to develop a culture where members, customers, suppliers, shareholders, and the public experience fairness and respect in their relations with the company.

Achieving excellence depends on individual and collective integrity and the relentless pursuit of the following long-standing beliefs:
HON INDUSTRIES SHALL BE PROFITABLE.
The Company pursues mutually profitable partnerships with customers and suppliers. Only when the company achieves an adequate profit can the other elements of this Vision be realized.
HON INDUSTRIES SHALL BE ECONOMICALLY SOUND.
The company safeguards and grows the shareholders' equity by attaining superior financial performance and maintaining a strong

balance sheet. This allows us greater flexibility to respond in a continuously changing market and business environment.

HON INDUSTRIES SHALL PURSUE SOUND GROWTH.

The company pursues profitable growth in order to continue providing increased job and financial opportunities for members, customers, suppliers, shareholders, and the public.

HON INDUSTRIES SHALL BE A SUPPLIER OF QUALITY PRODUCTS AND SERVICES.

The company provides reliable products and services of high quality and value to our end-users which exceed our customers' expectations and allow the distributor and the company to make a fair profit.

HON INDUSTRIES SHALL BE A GOOD PLACE TO WORK.

The company pursues a participative environment and culture that nurture the active involvement of each member, and that attract and retain the most capable people who work safely, are motivated, and are devoted to making the company and themselves jointly prosper.

HON INDUSTRIES SHALL BE A RESPONSIBLE CORPORATE CITIZEN.

The company and its members actively participate in the civic, cultural, educational, environmental, and governmental affairs of our society. The company follows, and requires all members to follow, ethical and legal business practices.

When the company is appreciated by its members, favored by its customers, supported by its suppliers, respected by the public, and admired by its shareholders, this Vision is fulfilled.

CORPORATE DESCRIPTION

HON Industries, Inc. is a manufacturer and marketer of office furniture, office products, and home building products.

ADDRESS   414 E. Third St.
P.O. Box 1109
Muscatine, IA 52761-7109

INDUSTRY CATEGORY   Business Products

◆　◆　◆　◆　◆　◆　◆

Honeywell

| **Our Vision**

To grow profitably by delighting customers and achieving undisputed leadership in control.

| **Our Mission**

To create value for shareowners through our leadership in advanced control solutions that help customers worldwide achieve their goals.

| **Our Values**

- INTEGRITY and the highest ethical standards
- MUTUAL RESPECT and trust in our working relationships
- INNOVATION and encouragement to challenge the status quo
- COMMUNICATION that is open, consistent and two-way
- TEAMWORK and meeting our commitments to one another
- CONTINUOUS IMPROVEMENT, development and learning in all we do
- DIVERSITY of people, cultures and ideas
- PERFORMANCE with recognition for results

CORPORATE DESCRIPTION

Honeywell provides the benefits of control—through products, system solutions and services—to customers worldwide in the home and building, industrial, and space and aviation markets.

ADDRESS   P.O. Box 524
Minneapolis, MN 55440

INDUSTRY CATEGORY   Scientific, Photo, and Control Equipment

♦　♦　♦　♦　♦　♦　♦

Hormel Foods Corporation

STATEMENT | **Company Mission**

To be a leader in the food field with highly differentiated quality products that attain optimum share of market while meeting established profit objectives.

| **Quality Policy**

We will supply defect-free products and services which conform to clearly defined requirements to meet the needs of our customers, employees and others we serve.

The five principles of quality management form the foundation of this policy. They are:

♦ The Definition of Quality is Conformance to Customer Requirements
♦ The System of Quality is Prevention and Continuous Improvement
♦ The Performance Standard is Zero Defects
♦ The Measurement of Quality is the Price of Nonconformance
♦ All Work is a Process

© Hormel Foods Corporation 1994

| **Company Values**

Our mission will be accomplished by focusing on values relating to our consumers, customers, employees, shareholders, suppliers and the communities we serve.

Consumers—We strive to:

♦ anticipate, listen and respond to consumer desires for innovative new products.
♦ develop loyal consumers through continuous improvement of product quality and consistency.
♦ be a trustworthy provider of wholesome, nutritious and good tasting food products of excellent value.

Trade Customers—We strive to:

- provide service that is innovative, responsive, reliable, courteous and professional.
- develop partnerships with our customers to assure mutual success.
- provide quality products supported by innovative and effective marketing programs.

Employees—We seek to provide an environment in which:

- all employees trust and respect one another.
- teamwork and positive attitudes are commonplace.
- all ideas are valued, respected and recognized.
- continuous improvement, innovation and prevention are a way of life.
- everyone strives to satisfy customers at all times.

Shareholders—We are committed to:

- long-term profitability and growth.
- providing optimum economic value for our shareholders.
- a satisfactory return on assets employed.
- making sound economic decisions based on thorough risk and return assessments.

Suppliers—We develop mutually beneficial supplier relationships built on:

- trust and respect.
- optimization of total value through innovation, technology and process involvement.
- quality, price and service.

Communities—We serve our communities by:

- operating modern, clean, safe and efficient facilities which add value to the community.
- our active participation and leadership in community affairs.
- leading and supporting community and national efforts to improve the environment.

© Hormel Foods Corporation 1994

CORPORATE DESCRIPTION

Having served the needs of generations of consumers for more than a century, Hormel Foods Corporation continues to successfully build upon its role as one of the leading processors and marketers of branded, value-added meat and food products. Hormel Foods competes nationally and internationally.

Hormel Foods and its family of subsidiaries manufacture, market and distribute thousands of processed food products which are known and respected by consumers, retail grocers, foodservice operators and industrial customers.

A majority of the Company's products are sold under the Hormel brandmark. The company also has at least 26 other well-established brandmarks.

ADDRESS   1 Hormel Place
Austin, MN 55912

INDUSTRY CATEGORY   Food/Beverage

◆   ◆   ◆   ◆   ◆   ◆   ◆

Household International, Inc.

STATEMENT | **Mission Statement**

The business objectives of Household International are established within the framework of our corporate mission:

"We will be a premier financial services organization meeting the needs of individuals and companies through consumer banking, consumer finance, commercial finance, insurance, investments and related services.

"We will treat our customers with dignity and respect as we deliver the best service in the industry. We will develop and maintain long-term relationships with our customers by offering a broad line of high quality products and services which meet their needs. We will be vigorous, innovative and a leading participant in the markets we serve.

"We view our employees as our greatest resource and will provide every opportunity for them to achieve their hopes, goals and career aspirations. We will encourage our employees to be involved in the civic affairs of their communities.

"We will be exemplary corporate citizens, always conducting ourselves in an ethical and honest manner.

"We will accomplish these goals while providing our shareholders with a superior return on their investments."

CORPORATE DESCRIPTION

Household International is the nation's largest and oldest consumer finance company.

ADDRESS   2700 Sanders Rd.
Prospect Heights, IL 60070

INDUSTRY CATEGORY   Financial Investment Services

◆　◆　◆　◆　◆　◆　◆

Houston Industries Incorporated

STATEMENT | **Mission Statement**

The mission of Houston Industries Incorporated is to maximize shareholder value and satisfy its customers' needs, while providing its employees a rewarding and productive work environment and conducting its affairs responsibly in the community.

Houston Industries will accomplish this mission by creating a corporate vision of successful growth, by carefully managing its assets and by integrating its businesses through effective planning and allocation of resources.

CORPORATE DESCRIPTION

Houston Industries Incorporated is a diversified holding company involved in the electric utility, cable television and non-regulated power businesses.

ADDRESS   P.O. Box 4567
Houston, TX 77210

INDUSTRY CATEGORY   Utility

◆　◆　◆　◆　◆　◆　◆

Huntington Bancshares Incorporated

STATEMENT | **Mission Statement**

The mission of Huntington Bancshares Incorporated is to meet the financial services needs of individuals and businesses. We seek dominant position in the markets where we choose to compete by providing high quality, differentiated products, and legendary customer service. Our thrust for business development is to penetrate existing markets, deliver products and services to new geographic markets, and strategically manage our business mix to achieve superior results.

CORPORATE DESCRIPTION

Huntington Bancshares Incorporated is an $18 billion regional bank holding company headquartered in Columbus, Ohio. The company's banking subsidiaries operate 352 offices in Ohio, Florida, Illinois, Indiana, Kentucky, Michigan, Pennsylvania, and West Virginia. In addition, mortgage, trust, investment banking and automobile finance subsidiaries manage 89 offices in the eight states mentioned as well as Connecticut, Delaware, Maryland, Massachusetts, New Jersey, North Carolina, Rhode Island and Virginia.

ADDRESS   41 S. High St.
Columbus, OH 43287

INDUSTRY CATEGORY   Banking

◆　◆　◆　◆　◆　◆　◆

IBM
(International Business Machines Corporation)

STATEMENT | **IBM Missions**

We have two fundamental missions:

- We strive to lead in the creation, development and manufacture of the most advanced information technologies.
- We translate advanced technologies into value for our customers as the world's largest information services company. Our professionals worldwide provide expertise within specific industries, consulting services, systems integration and solution development and technical support.

Reproduced by permission of IBM. © 1999 International Business Machines Corporation

CORPORATE DESCRIPTION

IBM creates, develops, manufactures and sells advanced information technologies, including computer systems, software, networking systems, storage devices and microelectronics.

ADDRESS   New Orchard Road
Armonk, NY 10504

INDUSTRY CATEGORY   High Technology

◆ ◆ ◆ ◆ ◆ ◆ ◆

ICN Pharmaceuticals, Inc.

| **The ICN Mission**
Our Goals

♦ **Quality Products**

To make health care products that improve the quality of life for mankind

♦ **Financially Strong**

To deliver a strong and consistent financial performance that provides a fair return to our investors

♦ **Global Leader**

To become one of the largest and most successful health care companies in the world

♦ **Customer-Driven**

To deliver friendly professional service fully responsive to the needs of our customers

♦ **Good Employer**

To sustain a working environment that attracts, retains and develops committed employees who take pride in the success of the company

♦ **Good Neighbor**

To be a good global citizen responsive to the needs of our communities and constituencies

To achieve these goals, we must:

- ♦ Deliver friendly, professional service consistently through well-trained and motivated employees
- ♦ Search continuously for improvement through innovation and the use of technology
- ♦ Employ planning and decision-making processes that provide clear direction and sense of purpose
- ♦ Foster a leadership style throughout the organization which encourages respect for individuals, teamwork and close identification with customers
- ♦ Strive constantly to achieve agreed standards of quality at competitive cost levels

CORPORATE DESCRIPTION

ICN Pharmaceuticals, Inc. is the parent company for SPI Pharmaceuticals, Inc., which manufactures, markets, and distributes over 600 pharmaceutical products in over 60 countries throughout the world, serving the U.S., Eastern and Western Europe, Canada, Mexico and the Far East. Major products include a variety of prescription and nonprescription pharmaceutical products, including antivirals, antibiotics, dermatologicals, cardiovasculars, analgesics, antirheumatics, central nervous system compounds and vision care lines. SPI products are marketed under the ICN tradename.

ADDRESS   ICN Plaza
3300 Hyland Ave.
Costa Mesa, CA 92626

INDUSTRY CATEGORY   Pharmaceutical/Biotechnology

◆ ◆ ◆ ◆ ◆ ◆ ◆

Illinova Corporation

STATEMENT | **Vision**

Our vision is to meet customers' energy and related service needs better than any other. We will be the best.

CORPORATE DESCRIPTION

Illinova Corporation, headquartered in Decatur, Illinois, is an energy services holding company with annual revenues of $2.5 billion.

Illinois Power Company, an Illinova subsidiary, is an electric and natural gas utility. Illinois Power has net electric generating capability of approximately 4,100 megawatts and serves about 650,000 customers over a 15,000-square-mile area of Illinois.

Illinova's independent power subsidiary, Illinova Generating Company, invests in, develops, and operates energy-related projects and facilities throughout the world. A third subsidiary, Illinova Energy

Partners, markets energy, including natural gas, and energy-related services to customers in the United States and Canada.

ADDRESS   500 S. 27th St.
               Decatur, IL 62521

INDUSTRY CATEGORY   Utility

◆   ◆   ◆   ◆   ◆   ◆   ◆

IMC Global

STATEMENT |

Five Strategic Goals For Becoming The World's Most Successful Crop Nutrients And Animal Feed Ingredients Supplier

[From "Pursuing the Vision" company publication]

Growing The Company

We must grow the company by increasing sales and earnings, with the emphasis on earnings, through opening new markets, serving our existing markets more efficiently, and becoming the world's leading low-cost producer.

Becoming A Truly Global Company

The biggest opportunities for real, sustained growth lie in the emerging global markets. We must be there in strength—the right people at the right time with the right services and products to serve the world.

Cost Leadership & Continuous Improvement

We must become the lowest-cost producer and maintain that position. By taking bold, innovative steps. By better matching of supply to demand. By a constant vigilance that looks for methods to create more from less.

Exceptional Customer Service & Support

We must deliver the world's finest customer service and support. With exceptional ideas, ingenious services and world-class products that, better than ever before, help our customers meet their growing needs.

Creating A High Performance Culture

We must be recognized in image and practice as a company that values its people and their values. A company that prepares its people for the responsibilities of today and tomorrow. A company that rewards hard work, innovative thinking, problem-solving and performance. A company where you want to come to work ... every day.

CORPORATE DESCRIPTION

IMC Global is one of the world's leading producers and marketers of phosphate and potash crop nutrients and animal feed ingredients. The company is also one of the nation's leading distributors of crop nutrients, including nitrogen, and related products through its Farmarket® and Rainbow® networks. Additionally, it sells potash and other products to industrial users.

ADDRESS   2100 Sanders Rd.
Northbrook, IL 60062

INDUSTRY CATEGORY   Agriculture

♦   ♦   ♦   ♦   ♦   ♦   ♦

Ingersoll-Rand Company

STATEMENT | **Our Vision**

Customers respond to our excellence in serving them by making Ingersoll-Rand Company their supplier and partner of choice.

| **Our Mission**

Create an environment conducive for all of our people working productively together to make the changes needed to attain leadership in customer service, quality and financial returns. Focus on attaining leadership in all the businesses we commit to.

Ignite the desire within all of us to make the changes to accomplish the mission. Develop an organization actively executing major change followed by continuous improvement. Reach out—make possible the impossible.

| **Our Guiding Principles**

At Ingersoll-Rand we will:

- acknowledge that our company and our people are capable of great things
- create an atmosphere where all ideas can be expressed freely
- cultivate an environment of mutual trust, honesty and respect
- communicate with each other openly and frequently
- define what constitutes good job performance
- provide employees the opportunity to take pride in their work
- encourage greater individual responsibility
- minimize supervision and bureaucracy
- exercise teamwork across businesses, functions and departments
- value swift action over lengthy deliberation
- encourage all employees to be agents of change
- prefer change over failure to seek change
- set goals beyond our reach but within our stretch
- implement radical change, followed by continuous improvement
- achieve excellence

CORPORATE DESCRIPTION

Ingersoll-Rand is a multinational manufacturer of primarily nonelectrical industrial machinery and equipment. The company's principal lines of business are air compressors, architectural hardware products, automotive parts and components, construction equipment, golf cars and utility vehicles, pumps, tools and transport temperature control systems. The company's broad product line has applications in numerous industries including automotive, construction, mining, utilities, housing, recreational and transportation, as well as the general industrial market.

ADDRESS   200 Chestnut Ridge Rd.
Woodcliff Lake, NJ 07675

INDUSTRY CATEGORY   Manufacturing

◆　◆　◆　◆　◆　◆　◆

Inland Paperboard & Packaging, Inc.

STATEMENT | **Mission**

To be the preferred supplier of containerboard and corrugated by delivering the highest value in products and services to our customers. We will accomplish this by fully involving our people in the process of continuous improvement through quality and the elimination of waste. We believe that the pursuit of continuous improvement will earn our shareholders a sustained high rate of return on investment and provide our people with safe and rewarding employment.

CORPORATE DESCRIPTION

Inland is a subsidiary and business unit of Temple-Inland, a Diboll, Texas-based holding company with major interests in paper, packaging, building products and financial services.

ADDRESS   4030 Vincennes Rd.
Indianapolis, IN 46268

INDUSTRY CATEGORY   Manufacturing

◆　◆　◆　◆　◆　◆　◆

Inland Steel Industries

To be a market-oriented, quality-driven management company focused on distribution of industrial materials and production of high quality steel products and other engineered materials.

Market oriented: Inland Steel Industries will served selected customer groups in the industrial materials market and will focus on improving the long-term competitive position of its customers. Inland will achieve competitive advantage by strategically positioning its businesses in targeted segments of the industrial materials market.

The Inland business units pursue competitive advantage based upon superior knowledge of their customers' products, markets and economics. They seek to improve the competitive position of their customers by providing superior products and services.

Quality-driven: Inland is committed to continuous improvement in the quality of all of its products and services provided to customers, internal as well as external. All line and staff operations will measure quality by how well they anticipate and satisfy customer needs.

Management company: Inland competes as an interrelated group of businesses designed to increase shareholder value by sustained superior profitability. It is not a loose holding of independent businesses. Each business receives competitive benefits through sharing of financial resources, information, technology, plant and equipment, personnel, know-how, and markets with related business units. Inland provides strategic direction to its businesses units; creates strategic alliances; stimulates change; performs the financial functions; sets the standards for and evaluates performance; allocates resources; directs and coordinates the interactivities among units; and defines the specific mix of businesses at any point in time.

Distribution of industrial materials: Inland has an excellent foundation of experience in servicing the industrial market with its existing distribution businesses. The distribution segment concentrates on customers who require just-in-time delivery, processing and broad product selection, and who value service. Inland will grow this business group through internal development and acquisition of new businesses. While currently focused on steel, aluminum, and plastic products, Inland will seek profitable opportunities in distribution of other industrial materials.

Production of high quality steel products: Inland's business focus in manufacturing is on carbon steel. Its vision for the steel segment is to produce efficiently sophisticated sheet and bar products, fully competitive with the best producers in the world. The principal steel market focus is the automotive, appliance, electric motor and office furniture segments of the industrial materials market. Our steel businesses will serve customers who are leaders in their markets, that need sophisticated products made to exacting standards, and who value technical service and long-term relationships.

. . . and other engineered materials: The Company believes that the industrial market offers excellent opportunities to expand into manufacturing and processing of other engineered materials in concert with or separate from carbon steel.

CORPORATE DESCRIPTION

Inland Steel Industries, Inc. is a holding company whose businesses are leaders in value-added steel and material distribution. It owns Inland Steel Company, the fifth largest integrated steel producer in the United States, and Inland Materials Distribution Group, Inc., the nation's largest metal distribution network.

ADDRESS   30 W. Monroe St.
Chicago, IL 60603

INDUSTRY CATEGORY   Manufacturing

♦   ♦   ♦   ♦   ♦   ♦   ♦

International Game Technology

IGT is in business to provide for the needs of our customers, our employees and our shareholders, while recognizing our responsibility to the communities in which we operate.

- ◆ IGT is committed to providing our customers with quality products at a competitive price which, together with excellent service and support, will assist them in maximizing their profitability.
- ◆ IGT is committed to providing our employees with a stable and rewarding work environment, the opportunity to grow to the extent of their talents, and the opportunity to share in the success of the company which they make possible.
- ◆ IGT is committed to providing our shareholders with an above average return on their investment, since our ability to serve the needs of our customers and employees is made possible only through their support.
- ◆ IGT is committed to being a responsible corporate citizen in the communities in which we operate, and encourages our employees to individually be an asset to the community in which they live.

CORPORATE DESCRIPTION

International Game Technology (IGT) is a world leader in the design, development and manufacture of microprocessor-based slot machines, video gaming machines and software systems.

ADDRESS   9295 Prototype Dr.
P.O. Box 10580
Reno, NV 89510-0580

INDUSTRY CATEGORY   Hotel, Hospitality, and Entertainment

◆　◆　◆　◆　◆　◆　◆

Johnson Controls, Inc.

Johnson Controls Vision

Our Creed

We believe in the free enterprise system. We shall constantly treat our customers, employees, shareholders, suppliers and the community with honesty, dignity, fairness and respect. We will conduct our business with the highest ethical standards.

Our Mission

Continually exceed our customers' increasing expectations.

What We Value

INTEGRITY: Honesty and fairness are essential to the way we do business and how we interact with people. We are a company that keeps its promises. We do what we say we will do, and we will conduct ourselves in accordance with our code of ethics.

CUSTOMER SATISFACTION: Customer satisfaction is the source of employee, shareholder, supplier and community benefits. We will exceed customer expectations through continuous improvement in quality, service, productivity and time compression.

OUR EMPLOYEES: The diversity and involvement of our people is the foundation of our strength. We are committed to their fair and effective selection, development, motivation and recognition. We will provide employees with the tools, training and support to achieve excellence in customer satisfaction.

SAFETY AND THE ENVIRONMENT: Our products, services and workplaces reflect our belief that what is good for the environment and the safety and health of all people is good for Johnson Controls.

Objectives

CUSTOMER SATISFACTION: We will exceed customer expectations through continuous improvement in quality, service, productivity and time compression.

TECHNOLOGY: We will apply world-class technology to our products, processes and services.

GROWTH: We will seek growth by building upon our existing businesses.

MARKET LEADERSHIP: We will only operate in markets where we are, or have the opportunity to become, the recognized leader.

SHAREHOLDER VALUE: We will exceed the after-tax, median return on shareholders' equity of the Standard & Poor's Industrials.

CORPORATE DESCRIPTION

Johnson Controls is a global market leader in facility services and control systems, automotive seating systems, plastic packaging, and automotive batteries.

ADDRESS   5757 N. Green Bay Ave.
P.O. Box 991
Milwaukee, WI 53201-0591

INDUSTRY CATEGORY   Business Services

◆ ◆ ◆ ◆ ◆ ◆ ◆

Johnson & Johnson

STATEMENT | **Our Credo**

We believe our first responsibility is to the doctors, nurses and patients, to mothers and fathers and all others who use our products and services.

In meeting their needs everything we do must be of the highest quality.

We must constantly strive to reduce our costs in order to maintain reasonable prices.

Customers' orders must be serviced promptly and accurately.

Our suppliers and distributors must have an opportunity to make a fair profit.

We are responsible to our employees, the men and women who work with us throughout the world.

Everyone must be considered as an individual.

We must respect their dignity and recognize their merit.

They must have a sense of security in their jobs.

Compensation must be fair and adequate, and working conditions clean, orderly and safe.

We must be mindful of ways to help our employees fulfill their family responsibilities.

Employees must feel free to make suggestions and complaints.

There must be equal opportunity for employment, development and advancement for those qualified.

We must provide competent management, and their actions must be just and ethical.

We are responsible to the communities in which we live and work
and to the world community as well.

We must be good citizens—support good works and charities and bear our fair share of taxes.

We must encourage civic improvements and better health and education.

We must maintain in good order the property we are privileged to use, protecting the environment and natural resources.

Our final responsibility is to our stockholders.

Business must make a sound profit.

We must experiment with new ideas.

Research must be carried on, innovative programs developed and mistakes paid for.

New equipment must be purchased, new facilities provided and new products launched.

Reserves must be created to provide for adverse times.

When we operate according to these principles, the stockholders should realize a fair return.

CORPORATE DESCRIPTION

Johnson & Johnson is the world's most comprehensive and broadly based manufacturer of health care products, as well as a provider of related services, for the consumer, pharmaceutical and professional markets.

ADDRESS   One Johnson & Johnson Plaza
New Brunswick, NJ 08933

INDUSTRY CATEGORY   Health Care

♦   ♦   ♦   ♦   ♦   ♦   ♦

Johnson Wax (S.C. Johnson & Sons, Inc.)

STATEMENT | **This We Believe**
Our Guiding Principles

Our company has been guided by certain basic principles since its founding in 1886.

These principles were first summarized in 1927 by H.F. Johnson, Jr., in his Christmas Profit Sharing speech:

"The goodwill of the people is the only enduring thing in any business. It is the sole substance. . . . The rest is shadow!"

In 1976, we formally stated these basic principles in **"This We Believe."** Since then, our statement of corporate philosophy has been translated and communicated around the world—not only within the worldwide company, but also to key external audiences. It has served us well by providing all employees with a common statement of the basic principles which guide the company in all the different cultures where we operate. It has also provided people outside the company with an understanding of our fundamental beliefs. It communicates the kind of company we are.

Now, more than twenty years after **"This We Believe"** was developed and following the celebration of our 100th anniversary, it is appropriate to restate, clarify and reaffirm our commitment to uphold these principles, because our company, like most others in these highly volatile times, has had to adjust its business strategies worldwide. This restatement and clarification is important to assure that our corporate policies and the actions of our managers and other employees continue to be fully supportive of our beliefs.

"**This We Believe**" states our beliefs in relation to the five groups of people to whom we are responsible and whose trust we have to earn:

Employees

We believe that the fundamental vitality and strength of our world-wide company lies in our people.

Consumers and Users

We believe in earning the enduring goodwill of consumers and users of our products and services.

General Public

We believe in being a responsible leader within the free market economy.

Neighbors and Hosts

We believe in contributing to the well-being of the countries and communities where we conduct business.

World Community

We believe in improving international understanding.

These beliefs are real and we will strive to live up to them. Our commitment to them is evident in our actions to date.

The sincerity of our beliefs encourages us to act with integrity at all times, to respect the dignity of each person as an individual human being, to assume moral and social responsibilities early as a matter of conscience, to make an extra effort to use our skills and resources where they are most needed, and to strive for excellence in everything we do.

Our way of safeguarding these beliefs is to remain a privately held company. Our way of reinforcing them is to make profits through growth and development, profits which allow us to do more for all the people on whom we depend.

We believe that the fundamental vitality and strength of our worldwide company lies in our people, and we commit ourselves to:

♦ **Maintain good relations among all employees around the world based on a sense of participation, mutual respect, and an understanding of common objectives, by:**

—Creating a climate whereby all employees freely air their concerns and express opinions with the assurance that these will be fairly considered.

—Attentively responding to employees' suggestions and problems.

—Fostering open, two-way communications between management and employees.

—Providing employees with opportunities to participate in the process of decision-making.

—Encouraging employees at all levels and in all disciplines to work as a team.

—Respecting the dignity and rights of privacy of every employee.

♦ **Manage our business in such a way that we can provide security for regular employees and retirees, by:**

—Pursuing a long-term policy of planned, orderly growth.

—Retaining regular employees, if at all possible, as conditions change. However, this may not always be possible, particularly where major restructuring or reorganization is required to maintain competitiveness.

—Retraining employees who have acceptable performance records and are in positions no longer needed, providing suitable jobs are available.

♦ **Maintain a high level of effectiveness within the organization, by:**

—Establishing clear standards of job performance.

—Ensuring that the performance of all employees meets required levels by giving appropriate recognition to those whose performance is good and by terminating those whose performance, despite their managers' efforts to help, continues below company standards.

- Provide equal opportunities in employment and advancement, by

  —Hiring and promoting employees without discrimination, using qualifications, performance, and experience as the principal criteria.

- Remunerate employees at levels that fully reward their performance and recognize their contribution to the success of their company, by:

  —Maintaining base pay and benefit programs both of which are fully competitive with those prevailing within the relevant marketplaces.

  —Maintaining, in addition to our fully competitive pay and benefit programs, our long-standing tradition of sharing profits with employees.

- Protect the health and safety of all employees, by:

  —Providing a clean and safe work environment.

  —Providing appropriate safety training and occupational health services.

- Develop the skills and abilities of our people, by:

  —Providing on-the-job training and professional development programs.

  —Helping employees qualify for opportunities in the company through educational and development programs.

- Creative environments which are conducive to self-expression and personal well-being, by:

  —Fostering and supporting leisure-time programs for employees and retirees.

  —Developing job-enrichment programs.

  —Maintaining the long tradition of high quality and good design in our office and plants.

- Encourage initiative, innovation, and entrepreneurism among all employees, thereby providing opportunities for greater job satisfaction while also helping the worldwide company achieve its objectives.

We believe in earning the enduring goodwill of consumers and users of our products and services, and we commit ourselves to:

- **Provide useful products and services throughout the world, by:**

  —Monitoring closely the changing wants and needs of consumers and users.

  —Developing and maintaining high standards of quality.

  —Developing new products and services which are recognized by consumers and users as being significantly superior overall to major competition.

  —Maintaining close and effective business relations with the trade to ensure that our products and services are readily available to consumers and users.

  —Continuing our research and development commitment to provide a strong technology base for innovative and superior products and services.

- **Develop and market products which are environmentally sound and which do not endanger the health and safety of consumers and users, by:**

  —Meeting all regulatory requirements or exceeding them where worldwide company standards are higher.

  —Providing clear and adequate directions for safe use, together with cautionary statements and/or symbols.

  —Incorporating protection against misuse where this is appropriate.

  —Researching new technologies for products which favor an improved environment.

- **Maintain and develop comprehensive education and service programs for consumers and users, by:**

  —Disseminating information to consumers and users which promotes full understanding of the correct use of our products and services.

  —Handling all inquiries, complaints, and service needs for consumers and users quickly, thoroughly, and fairly.

We believe in being a responsible leader in the free market economy, and we commit ourselves to:

- **Ensure the future vitality of the worldwide company, by:**
  —Earning sufficient profits to provide new investment for planned growth and progress.
  —Maintaining a worldwide organization of highly competent, motivated, and dedicated employees.
- **Conduct our business in a fair and ethical manner, by:**
  —Not engaging in unfair business practices.
  —Treating our suppliers and customers both fairly and reasonably, according to sound commercial practices.
  —Packaging and labeling our products so that consumers and users can make informed value judgments.
  —Maintaining the highest advertising standards of integrity and good taste.
  —Not engaging in bribery.
- **Share the profits of each local company with those who have contributed to its success, by:**
  —Rewarding employees through a profit sharing program.
  —Allocating a share of the profits to enhance the well-being of communities where we operate.
  —Developing better products and services for the benefit of consumers and users.
  —Providing to shareholders a reasonable return on their investment.
- **Provide the general public with information about our activities so that they have a better understanding of our worldwide company.**

We believe in contributing to the well-being of the countries and communities where we conduct business, and we commit ourselves to:

- **Seek actively the counsel and independent judgment of citizens of each country where we conduct business to provide guidance to local and corporate management, by:**
  —Selecting independent directors to serve on the board of each of our companies worldwide.

—Retaining distinguished associates and consultants to assist us in conducting our business according to the highest professional standards.

♦ **Contribute to the economic well-being of every country and community where we conduct business, by:**
—Ensuring that new investment fits constructively into the economic development of each host country and local community.
—Encouraging the use of local suppliers and services offering competitive quality and prices.

♦ **Contribute to the social development of every country and community where we conduct business, by:**
—Providing training programs for the development of skills.
—Staffing and managing with nationals from those countries wherever practicable.
—Involving ourselves in social, cultural, and educational projects which enhance the quality of life.

♦ **Be a good corporate citizen, by:**
—Complying with and maintaining a due regard for the laws, regulations, and traditions of each country where we conduct business.

We believe in improving international understanding, and we commit ourselves to:

♦ **Act with responsible practices in international trade and investment, by:**
—Retaining earnings necessary for reinvestment in our local companies and remitting dividends on a consistent basis.
—Making royalty, licensing, and service agreements which are fair and reasonable and which do not result in any hidden transfer of profits.
—Limiting foreign exchange transactions to normal business requirements and for the protection of our assets.

- **Promote the exchange of ideas and techniques, by:**
  —Encouraging the rapid diffusion of new technology to our local companies and licensees, while protecting our ownership rights and investment in such technology.
  —Organizing worldwide and regional meetings for the dissemination and exchange of information.
  —Providing support and assistance, especially in technical and professional fields, to develop skills throughout the organization.
  —Following a balanced approach between transferring people to new jobs to gain experience and leaving people on the job long enough to make positive contributions in their assignments.

CORPORATE DESCRIPTION

S.C. Johnson Wax is one of the world's leading manufacturers of chemical specialty products for home, personal care and insect control. It is also a leading supplier of products and services for commercial, industrial and institutional facilities. In the area of financial services, the corporation has interests in venture capital and insurance.

ADDRESS　　1525 Howe St.
Racine, WI 53404

INDUSTRY CATEGORY　　Consumer Goods and Services

◆　◆　◆　◆　◆　◆　◆

Jostens, Inc.

Jostens provides products and services that help people celebrate achievement, reward performance, recognize service and commemorate experiences.

We provide these achievement and affiliation products in partnership with the diverse organizations people belong to throughout their lives. As a partner, we are committed to delivering value and quality that exceed the needs of the people and organizations we serve. Jostens is a team of employees and independent business partners. Our aim is to be the world leader in providing achievement and affiliation products and to constantly deliver exceptional performance.

CORPORATE DESCRIPTION

Jostens' products and services include yearbooks, class rings, graduation products, student photography packages, technology-based educational products and services, customized sales and service awards, sports awards, and customized products for university alumni.

ADDRESS   5501 Norman Center Dr.
Minneapolis, MN 55437

INDUSTRY CATEGORY   Consumer Goods and Services

♦ ♦ ♦ ♦ ♦ ♦ ♦

Kansas City Life Insurance Company

| **Purpose**
of Kansas City Life Insurance Company

Kansas City Life Insurance Company exists to provide present and future financial security to people, thereby assuring them a dignity and a quality of life that they and their beneficiaries might otherwise not enjoy, and

To sustain Kansas City Life's own growth and prosperity through good management and reasonable profit, thus enabling the Company to continue to serve people for as long as their needs exist.

Business Philosophies
of Kansas City Life Insurance Company

The People Who are Kansas City Life Believe That:

Life Insurance is unequaled as a means of providing guaranteed financial protection to people, and Kansas City Life strives to promote and sell life insurance fairly and at a reasonable cost to meet the real needs of people.

The highest order of integrity and business ethics must be practiced in every transaction, and the protection of funds entrusted to the Company by policyowners for their future financial security is a basic responsibility of each person who makes up the Company.

Every Kansas City Life customer, whether policyowner, beneficiary, or loan customer, deserves the finest service and consideration from every Kansas City Life associate.

Kansas City Life stockholders are entitled to earn as good a return on their investments as the Company can produce, and they expect the management to conduct the Company's business in a manner that will be in the stockholders' best interest.

Kansas City Life recognizes that its own people are the primary reason for its continuing success, and these people always will be fairly compensated and advanced for their contributions to the Company's success. The Company and its general agencies are interdependent; both must succeed in order for each to grow and prosper.

Kansas City Life must be a good corporate citizen, participating in civic, community and business affairs with both money and personal involvement. The Company is and should continue to strive to be a highly regarded leader in the national life insurance business, participating in and supporting the activities of the industry as a whole. As such a leader, Kansas City Life should serve as an example of a company that will operate as honestly and efficiently without stringent governmental regulation as it would with such regulation.

Kansas City Life is a company concerned with and dedicated to improving the quality of human life.

CORPORATE DESCRIPTION

Kansas City Life Insurance Company markets individual life, annuity and group products through approximately 145 career general agencies.

The Kansas City Life corporate group includes Kansas City Life and two major subsidiaries—Old American Insurance Company and Sunset Life Insurance Company of America.

ADDRESS   3520 Broadway
Kansas City, MO 64111

INDUSTRY CATEGORY   Insurance

◆   ◆   ◆   ◆   ◆   ◆   ◆

Kansas City Power & Light Company

STATEMENT | **Mission Statement**

To be the regional energy supplier of choice.

CORPORATE DESCRIPTION

Kansas City Power & Light Company is a medium-size electric utility and the corporate successor to one of the world's first electric companies, generating electricity since 1882. Headquartered in downtown Kansas City, Missouri, the Company generates and distributes electricity to over 419,000 customers in a 4,700-square-mile area located in 23 counties in western Missouri and eastern Kansas. Customers include 368,000 residences, 49,000 commercial firms, and over 2,000 industrials, municipalities and other electric utilities.

ADDRESS   P.O. Box 418679
Kansas City, MO 64141-9679

INDUSTRY CATEGORY   Utility

◆ ◆ ◆ ◆ ◆ ◆ ◆

Kaufman and Broad Home Corporation

STATEMENT | **Kaufman and Broad Mission**

"We build homes to meet people's dreams."

Objectives

We are fiercely determined to continue to succeed. We intend to provide the best quality housing for our customers, a superior return to our shareholders, and a chance for every employee to make a difference and share in our success.

Vision

We strive to be the leading home builder in each market in which we operate. We intend to lead the way in home building well into the 21st century.

Core Values

It is our intention to deliver a quality product ... 100% of the time.

We believe the true test of quality is customer satisfaction.

There are no good excuses.

We treat each customer specially and each situation individually.

We strive to be at the cutting edge of product development and innovative design.

We reward innovation and encourage reasonable and prudent risk taking.

We don't just build homes, we build neighborhoods.

This business is built around people. We want self-directed winners who have high personal integrity.

This is a team business where we depend on one another. We expect each person to make a contribution.

All people at Kaufman and Broad have clout. We all work for the same ultimate boss, our customers.

Our subcontractors and suppliers are our partners. We demand a lot from them, especially high quality work. We expect to work and prosper together.

We respect the dignity of those with whom we deal. We always try to be fair.

While we are committed to steady growth and improved earnings, we will not over-emphasize short-term results.

We view land as a raw material for use in the building process, not as a speculative investment.

We believe in long-range planning. It is nonsense to say you can't plan the future in this business.

Our company's success is built on conservative financial policies, a strong capital base and superior earnings capacity. We believe a sustained level of solid profitability is critical to our future.

Autonomous regions are the cornerstone of our operational success. We have pioneered a divisional structure that links entrepreneurial executives with a lean headquarters group.

We are constantly striving to conduct our business in a way that will enable us to prosper in both good and lean times.

CORPORATE DESCRIPTION

Kaufman and Broad Home Corporation is the West's largest home builder and one of the largest builders in metropolitan Paris, France.

ADDRESS   10990 Wilshire Boulevard
Los Angeles, CA 90024

INDUSTRY CATEGORY   Construction

◆ ◆ ◆ ◆ ◆ ◆ ◆

Kaydon Corporation

STATEMENT | **Strategy**

Kaydon's strategy is to function as an extension of our customers' businesses through a commitment to identify and provide engineered solutions to design problems. We seek to blend technical innovation with cost-effective manufacturing and outstanding service.

We will strive to develop growth opportunities by expanding our range of technical capabilities through both internal developments and selected acquisitions. This will permit us to pursue our strategy of custom technical solutions beyond our current products into expanded product and market areas.

CORPORATE DESCRIPTION

Kaydon designs, manufactures and sells custom-engineered products for a broad and diverse customer base. Kaydon's principal products include antifriction bearings, bearing systems, filters, filter housings, high-performance rings, sealing rings, specialty retaining rings, shaft seals and slip-rings. These products are used in a variety of industrial applications.

ADDRESS   315 E. Eisenhower Pkwy.
Suite 300
Ann Arbor, MI 48108

INDUSTRY CATEGORY   Manufacturing

◆　◆　◆　◆　◆　◆　◆

Kellogg's (Kellogg Company)

STATEMENT | **Kellogg Company Philosophy**

"We are a company of dedicated people making quality products for a healthier world." W.K. Kellogg

| **Our Mission**

Kellogg is a global company committed to building long-term growth in volume and profit and to enhancing its worldwide leadership position by providing nutritious food products of superior value.

| **Our Working Environment**

The challenge of an increasingly competitive global marketplace requires an environment within our Company which encourages personal initiative and enables Kellogg people to contribute to their full potential. This environment must promote a free exchange of information, the generation of new ideas and the continued accumulation of knowledge.

To meet this challenge, we will:

- Exhibit a high level of personal integrity and fairness which respects the individual and our cultural diversity.
- Demonstrate leadership which encourages teamwork, open communication and mutual trust.
- Approach our work with a focus on results, a sense of urgency and a healthy dissatisfaction with the status quo.

Our Shared Values

Profit and Growth: Profitable growth is our primary purpose. We are committed to consistent, long-term growth in earnings and to superior returns for our shareholders. We want to be, and be recognized as, a growth company.

To meet this commitment, we will:

- Grow and expand our core businesses.
- Strengthen our global leadership in ready-to-eat cereal.
- Provide nutritious products of superior quality and value.
- Excel in the introduction of products that meet consumer needs.
- Consider acquisition opportunities consistent with our growth and profit objectives.

People: Kellogg people are our Company's greatest competitive advantage. Each and every individual will be given the opportunity to contribute to and share in the company's success. We are committed to helping Kellogg people reach their full potential and to recognizing their achievements.

To meet this commitment, we will:

- Attract, select and retain top quality people.
- Provide training, development and growth opportunities.
- Promote from within whenever possible.
- Provide an environment in which people can excel based on shared values, open communications and shared learning.
- Recognize achievement and reward performance.
- Provide equal opportunity and respect the cultural diversity of Kellogg people.

Consumer Satisfaction and Quality: The consumer is the ultimate judge of our success. Kellogg people, together with our suppliers and trade partners, will provide consumers with products and services of superior value. We are committed to excellence in everything we do.

To meet this commitment, we will:

- Strive for excellence as defined by our internal and external customers.
- Pursue partnerships with our customers, suppliers and Kellogg people to achieve common goals.
- Promote continuous and measurable improvement to increase our competitive advantage and leadership position.
- Build responsibility for quality into every function in our organization.

Integrity and Ethics: Integrity is the cornerstone of our business practice. We will conduct our affairs in a manner consistent with the highest ethical standards.

To meet this commitment, we will:

- Engage in fair and honest business practices.
- Show respect for each other, our consumers, customers, suppliers, shareholders and the communities in which we operate.
- Communicate in an honest, factual and accurate manner.

Social Responsibility: Social responsibility is an integral part of our heritage. We are committed to be, and be recognized as, an economic, intellectual and social asset in each community, region and country in which we operate.

To meet this commitment, we will:

- Produce quality products and market them in a responsible manner.
- Encourage Kellogg people to participate in community programs and invest company resources, human and financial, in organizations that benefit the people in our communities.
- Ensure our facilities, working environments and employment practices reflect good citizenship.
- Conduct our business in a manner which protects the environment and demonstrates good stewardship of our world's natural resources.

CORPORATE DESCRIPTION

Kellogg Company is the world's leading producer of ready-to-eat cereal and a leading producer of grain-based convenience foods, including toaster pastries, frozen waffles, cereal bars, and bagels.

ADDRESS   One Kellogg Sq.
Battle Creek, MI 49016-3599

INDUSTRY CATEGORY   Food/Beverage

◆ ◆ ◆ ◆ ◆ ◆ ◆

Kellwood Company

STATEMENT | **Kellwood's Mission**

To strengthen our ability to be a leading marketer, merchandiser and manufacturer of value-oriented products in each of our portfolios of soft goods companies.

To maintain a strong customer focus by building partnerships with retailers, providing them with a distinctive merchandising mix of branded and private label programs that add value and improve profitability.

To encourage and support our employees, for it is through their high standards, creativity and commitment, that our Company will prosper.

To achieve long-term growth of profits and return on shareowner investment through sound financial management practices and operating disciplines.

CORPORATE DESCRIPTION

Headquartered in St. Louis, Missouri, Kellwood Company is a multi-divisional marketer, merchandiser and manufacturer of primarily women's apparel. The company is the seventh largest publicly held apparel company in the United States. Known for its wide range of products and price points, the company's business units produce both branded and private label merchandise for more than 18,000 retailers.

Their broad customer base ranges from department and specialty stores to discount chains and catalogs.

ADDRESS   600 Kellwood Pkwy.
Chesterfield, MO 63017

INDUSTRY CATEGORY   Consumer Goods and Services

◆   ◆   ◆   ◆   ◆   ◆   ◆

Kelly Services, Inc.

STATEMENT | **VISION**

To be the world's best staffing services company and to be recognized as the best.

MISSION

To serve our customers, employees, shareholders and society by providing a broad range of staffing services and products.
   To achieve our Mission:

> We will develop innovative staffing services which meet the needs of our customers and contribute to their success.
> We will foster an environment which stimulates professional excellence and encourages contribution by all employees.
> We will provide our shareholders a fair return on their investment.
> We will demonstrate good corporate citizenship through the ethical conduct of our business.

SHARED VALUES

Integrity, Honesty and Ethical Behavior
Commitment to Quality and Customer Satisfaction
Dedication to Service and Personal Responsiveness
Professional Excellence and High Performance
Innovation, Creativity and Open-Mindedness

Employee Participation, Contribution and Teamwork
Diversity, Individual Dignity and Mutual Respect
Growth, Profitability and Industry Leadership

QUALITY POLICY

We are committed to quality and to the processes, measurement and continuous improvement which are the foundations of quality management.

Quality is a basic business principle for Kelly Services.

Quality means providing our internal and external customers innovative services and products that meet or exceed their expectations.

Quality improvement is the job of every Kelly Services employee.

CORPORATE DESCRIPTION

Kelly Services, Inc. is a leading global provider of staffing services. Kelly® provides employees with a wide range of skills, ranging from office and information technology, to legal and scientific. Kelly offers human resource solutions that include temporary staffing, outsourcing, staff leasing, vendor on-site and full-time placement. Kelly Assisted Living® Services provides in-home care for people who need assistance with their daily living activities.

ADDRESS   999 West Big Beaver Rd.
Troy, MI 48084

INDUSTRY CATEGORY   Business Services

♦   ♦   ♦   ♦   ♦   ♦   ♦

Kemper Corporation

STATEMENT | **Mission Statement**

Kemper Corporation is a financial services company that gathers, manages and protects the assets of individual, corporate and institutional clients. Our mission is to generate attractive returns and long-term appreciation for our clients and stockholders by developing and distributing high-quality products and services and operating in a highly professional and ethical manner.

CORPORATE DESCRIPTION

Kemper Corporation, with $14.8 billion in consolidated assets at year-end, is a financial services organization with businesses in asset management, life insurance, risk management services, securities brokerage, reinsurance and property-casualty insurance.

ADDRESS   One Kemper Dr.
Long Grove, IL 60049-0001

INDUSTRY CATEGORY   Insurance

◆　◆　◆　◆　◆　◆　◆

Kent Electronics Corporation

STATEMENT | **Corporate Objective**

To become the best national specialty electronics distribution company with sales offices and distribution centers in the major U.S. markets and to establish K*TEC as one of the largest multi-plant specialty electronic custom contract manufacturers.

CORPORATE DESCRIPTION

Kent Electronics is a national specialty electronics distributor and a multi-plant custom contract manufacturer. Kent distributes electronic connectors, wire and cable, passive and electromechanical products to original equipment manufacturers and industrial users and provides local area network (LAN) interconnect wiring products to the voice and data communication aftermarket. The Company is a custom contract manufacturer of electronic interconnect assemblies, other subassemblies and custom battery power packs.

ADDRESS   7433 Harwin Dr.
Houston, TX 77036

INDUSTRY CATEGORY   Electronics

◆　◆　◆　◆　◆　◆　◆

Keyport Life Insurance Company

STATEMENT | **Mission Statement**

Helping People Create Their Own Future . . . a Certain Future.

CORPORATE DESCRIPTION

Keyport is a specialty life insurance company providing retirement savings products including Fixed Rate Annuities and Variable Annuities. Its ultimate parent company is Liberty Mutual Insurance Company.

ADDRESS   125 High St.
Boston, MA 02110-2712

INDUSTRY CATEGORY   Insurance

◆　◆　◆　◆　◆　◆　◆

Kmart

STATEMENT | **Our Mission**

Kmart will become the discount store of choice for middle-income families with children by satisfying their routine and seasonal shopping needs as well as or better than the competition.

CORPORATE DESCRIPTION

Kmart Corporation is one of the nation's largest discount retailers and one of the world's largest mass merchandise retailers. Operating traditional Kmart and Big Kmart stores as well as Super Kmart Centers, Kmart Corporation offers convenient shopping in all 50 states in the United States as well as in Puerto Rico, Guam and the U.S. Virgin Islands.

ADDRESS 3100 W. Big Beaver Rd.
Troy, MI 48084

INDUSTRY CATEGORY Retail

◆ ◆ ◆ ◆ ◆ ◆ ◆

Knight-Ridder, Inc.

A Statement of Knight-Ridder Values

Knight-Ridder is one of the world's leading publishing and information companies. Our enterprise is both a business and a public trust, built on the highest standards of ethics and integrity. We are rooted in our founders' conviction that high-quality newspapers—fair, independent, probing, relevant and compassionate—are indispensable to our free society.

Our moral obligation is to excel in all that we do. We recognize that change is inevitable. We welcome change and intend to benefit from it. Our values, though, do not change. We intend that the name of Knight-Ridder shall be forever synonymous with the best in newspaper publishing, the delivery of business and professional information, and all other activities in which we choose to participate.

The Knight-Ridder Promise

No individual or single group can assure Knight-Ridder's continued success. All who care about this company and count upon its healthy future are dependent on one another. Therefore, we make these promises . . .

To Our Customers . . .

We promise to put you first. Unless we satisfy you, we cannot succeed. We are committed to meeting your needs and expectations—and exceeding them whenever possible. You can count on our honesty and fairness, our professionalism, our responsiveness, our courtesy, our dedication to quality, and our passion to serve you well.

To Our Employees . . .

We promise to help you achieve your full potential. We promise personal respect, fair pay, a clean and safe workplace. We promise equal opportunity for reward and advancement. We promise a role in a great enterprise that is central to our society—and recognition and appreciation for a job well done.

To Our Shareholders ...

We promise to work hard, in all parts of our company, to make your investment in Knight-Ridder an attractive one. We are committed to seeing that your money is invested in operations with sound economic prospects. We are committed to consistent growth in profits and a fair return on investment—not just when the economy is robust.

To Our Communities ...

We promise to be good citizens, to contribute to the quality of life and civic betterment of the communities that sustain us. We will do that through searching and sensitive journalism that fully meets our public-service obligations, through ethical and enlightened business practices, through civic participation and financial support.

To Our Society ...

We know that ours is not just another business, but one that requires special fidelity to the principles of democracy. We promise to be faithful to those principles and act always in vigorous support of a free press, freedom of speech and a free flow of information around the globe.

All these commitments are part of The Knight-Ridder Promise ... a promise for our people and for our future.

CORPORATE DESCRIPTION

Knight-Ridder, Inc. is an international information and communications company engaged in newspaper publishing, business news and information services, electronic retrieval services, news, graphics and photo services, cable television and newsprint manufacturing. Knight-Ridder's various information services reach more than 100 million people in 135 countries.

ADDRESS   One Herald Plaza
Miami, FL 33131-1693

INDUSTRY CATEGORY   Media

◆　◆　◆　◆　◆　◆　◆

The Kroger Co.

OUR MISSION is to be a leader in the distribution and merchandising of food, health, personal care, and related consumable products and services. In achieving this objective, we will satisfy our responsibilities to shareowners, employees, customers, suppliers, and the communities we serve.

We will conduct our business to produce financial returns that reward investment by shareowners and allow the Company to grow. Investments in retailing, distribution and food processing will be continually evaluated for their contribution to our corporate return objectives.

We will constantly strive to satisfy consumer needs better than the best of our competitors. Operating procedures will reflect our belief that the organizational levels closest to the consumer are best positioned to respond to changing consumer needs.

We will treat our employees fairly and with respect, openness and honesty. We will solicit and respond to their ideas and reward meaningful contributions to our success.

We value America's diversity and will strive to reflect that diversity in our work force, the companies with whom we do business, and the customers we serve. As a company, we will convey respect and dignity to each individual.

We will encourage our employees to be active, responsible citizens and will allocate resources for activities that enhance the quality of life for our customers, our employees and the communities we serve.

(Signed)
Joseph A. Pichler
Chairman and Chief Executive Officer

CORPORATE DESCRIPTION

The Kroger Company was founded in 1883 and incorporated in 1902. As of December 31, 1993 the Company was the largest grocery retailer in the United States based on annual sales. The Company also manufactures and processes food for sale by its supermarkets.

ADDRESS   1014 Vine St.
Cincinnati, OH 45202-1100

INDUSTRY CATEGORY   Food/Beverage

◆ ◆ ◆ ◆ ◆ ◆ ◆

Lafarge Corporation

STATEMENT | **Mission**

To be the best North American company in the cement, construction materials and waste conversion business.

| **Principles**

To be responsive to the needs of our:
Shareholders—giving them a competitive return on their investment through long-term earnings growth and financial strength;
Customers—contributing to their success by providing them with quality products and service on a competitive basis;
Employees—ensuring their fair treatment and helping them develop their skills and dedication;
Communities—being a good corporate citizen through community involvement and sound environmental practices.

CORPORATE DESCRIPTION

Lafarge Corporation was organized in April 1983, bringing together Canada Cement Lafarge, Ltd., Canada's largest cement producer, and General Portland Inc., the second-largest cement company in the United States. Lafarge also produces other construction materials.

ADDRESS   11130 Sunrise Valley Dr.
Reston, VA 20910

INDUSTRY CATEGORY   Construction

◆ ◆ ◆ ◆ ◆ ◆ ◆

Landstar Systems, Inc.

STATEMENT | **Mission Statement**

To be the leading provider of safe, specialized transportation services through a network of employees, agents, drivers and owner-operators who deliver safe, specialized services to a broad range of customers throughout North America.

CORPORATE DESCRIPTION

Landstar System, Inc., a transportation services company, operates the third largest truckload carrier business in North America.

ADDRESS   First Shelton Place
1000 Bridgeport Ave.
Shelton, CT 06484

INDUSTRY CATEGORY   Transportation

◆ ◆ ◆ ◆ ◆ ◆ ◆

Levi Strauss & Co.

STATEMENT | **Mission Statement**

The mission of the Company is to sustain responsible commercial success as a global marketing company of branded casual apparel. We must balance goals of superior profitability and return on investment, leadership market positions, and superior products and service. We will conduct our business ethically and demonstrate leadership in satisfying our responsibilities to our communities and to society. Our work environment will be safe and productive and characterized by fair treatment, teamwork, open communications, personal accountability and opportunities for growth and development.

CORPORATE DESCRIPTION

Levi Strauss & Co. is one of the world's largest brand-name apparel marketers, with 1998 sales of $6.0 billion. The company manufactures and markets branded jeans and casual sportswear under the Levis®, Dockers® and Slates® brands, and employs approximately 30,000 people worldwide.

ADDRESS   Levi's Plaza
P.O. Box 7215
San Francisco, CA 94120-7215

INDUSTRY CATEGORY   Consumer Goods and Services

♦   ♦   ♦   ♦   ♦   ♦   ♦

Lincoln National Corporation

| **Lincoln National Corporation Vision**

Lincoln National Corporation will be a high performing financial services company achieving benchmark service, growth and profit.

Mission

Lincoln National Corporation exists to satisfy the financial security needs of individuals and businesses. In so doing, LNC must create superior value for shareholders, offer quality products and services to customers, provide satisfying jobs for employees and be a responsible citizen in the communities in which it operates.

Goals

To win in the 1990's, LNC will maximize long-term shareholder value through superior operating performance and returns, as measured by:

15% annual return on equity; and

9% annual growth in book value.

Corporate Strategy

To establish LNC as the benchmark competitor in each of its businesses and markets through superior execution of core business activities and skills.

Each of LNC's businesses will be a top-tier performer in its respective segment of the financial services industry.

LNC will become the benchmark in each of business [sic] creating long-term value for our shareholders by:

- ◆ focusing resources and leveraging skills in only those areas where LNC can create substantial value and earn a superior return;
- ◆ demonstrating a commitment to excellence in customer services through an understanding of the needs and expectations of our customers;
- ◆ expanding opportunities for employees and maximizing employee satisfaction; and

- maintaining and enhancing the security of LNC capital foundation through superior investment results and management of key risks.

Strategic Imperatives

Top-tier Performance
Value Creation
Risk Management

CORPORATE DESCRIPTION

Lincoln National Corporation owns and operates financial services businesses with emphasis on annuities, life insurance, property-casualty insurance and life-health reinsurance.

ADDRESS   200 E. Berry St.
Fort Wayne, IN 46802

INDUSTRY CATEGORY   Insurance

◆   ◆   ◆   ◆   ◆   ◆   ◆

Litton Industries

STATEMENT | **The Mission of Litton Industries**

The mission of Litton Industries is to be a preeminent supplier in aerospace, defense and related commercial markets.

We accomplish this by placing a high priority on customer satisfaction, our growth and enhanced shareholder value.

Our growth is achieved by:
- Acquiring additional entities that complement strengths of the Litton family of companies,
- Integrating the long term business interests and resources of all our divisions,
- Expanding the competencies of the respective divisions and of our employees.

We succeed by demonstrating the highest possible regard for our employees, our customers, our suppliers and our communities.

CORPORATE DESCRIPTION

Litton is an aerospace, defense and commercial electronics company with technological and market leadership in its principal businesses. The company offers advanced electronic, defense and information systems and is a primary builder of large surface combatant ships for the U.S. Navy. Litton is also an international supplier of connectors, multilayer circuit boards, laser crystals, solder materials and other equipment used primarily in the telecommunications, industrial and computer markets.

ADDRESS   21240 Burbank Blvd.
Woodland Hills, CA 91367

INDUSTRY CATEGORY   Electronics

◆　◆　◆　◆　◆　◆　◆

Lockheed Martin

STATEMENT | **Mission Success at Lockheed Martin**

Our Purpose

To achieve Mission Success by attaining total customer satisfaction and meeting all our commitments.

Our Values

Ethics
Excellence
"Can-Do"
Integrity
People
Teamwork

Our Vision

For Lockheed Martin to be the world's leading technology and systems enterprise, providing best value to our customers, growth opportunities to our employees and superior returns to our shareholders.

Our Future

From the depths of the oceans to the far reaches of space, Lockheed Martin will continue to write new chapters in the chronicle of technological advances. We will enjoy success in the highly competitive global marketplace. Success will depend on the intensity with which we pursue our work and excellence in everything we do. We are proud of our heritage, confident of our present, and excited about our future.

Our Value Statements

Ethics

We will be well-informed in the regulations, rules, and compliance issues that apply to our businesses around the world. We will apply this knowledge to our conduct as responsible employees of Lockheed Martin, and will adhere to the highest standards of ethical conduct in all that we do.

Excellence

The pursuit of superior performance infuses every Lockheed Martin activity. We excel at meeting challenging commitments even as we achieve total customer satisfaction. We demonstrate leadership by advancing new technologies, innovative manufacturing techniques, enhanced customer service, inspired management, and the application of best practices throughout our organization. Each of us leads through our individual contributions to Lockheed Martin's core purpose.

"Can-Do"

We demonstrate individual leadership through a positive approach to every task, a "can-do" spirit, and a restless determination to continually improve upon our personal bests. We aggressively pursue new business, determined to add value for our customers with ingenuity, determination and a positive attitude. We utilize our ability to combine strength with speed in responding enthusiastically to every new opportunity and every new challenge.

Integrity

Each of us brings to the workplace personal values which guide us to meet our commitments to customers, suppliers, colleagues, and others with whom we interact. We embrace truthfulness and trust, and will treat everyone with dignity and respect—as we wish to be treated ourselves.

People

Outstanding people make Lockheed Martin unique. Success in rapidly changing markets requires that we continuously learn and grow as individuals and as an organization. We embrace lifelong learning through individual initiative, combined with company-sponsored education and development programs, as well as challenging work and growth opportunities.

Teamwork

We multiply the creativity, talents, and contributions of both individuals and businesses by focusing on team goals. Our teams assume collective accountability for their actions, share trust and leadership, embrace diversity, and accept responsibility for prudent risk-taking. Each of us succeeds individually ... when we as a team achieve success.

CORPORATE DESCRIPTION

Lockheed Martin is a global, diversified technology enterprise principally engaged in the research, design, development, manufacture, and integration of advanced technology systems, products, and services. The Corporation's fundamental businesses span space and telecommunications, electronics, information and services, aeronautics, energy, and systems integration.

ADDRESS   6801 Rockledge Dr.
                  Bethesda, MD 20817

INDUSTRY CATEGORY   Aerospace

◆　◆　◆　◆　◆　◆　◆

Lowe's Companies, Inc.

Lowe's is in the business of providing the products to help our customers build, improve and enjoy their homes. Our goal is to out-service the competition and be our customer's 1st Choice Store for these products.

CORPORATE DESCRIPTION

Lowe's Companies, Inc. is one of America's top forty retailers serving the do-it-yourself home improvement, home decor, home electronics, and home construction markets.

Lowe's more than 320 stores serve customers in 21 states located mainly in the South Atlantic and South Central regions.

ADDRESS   P.O. Box 1111
North Wilkesboro, NC 28656

INDUSTRY CATEGORY   Retail

♦ ♦ ♦ ♦ ♦ ♦ ♦

LSI Logic Corporation

STATEMENT | **Mission Statement**

LSI Logic's mission is to offer competitive advantages to our customers worldwide by providing them with the capability required for the rapid design and volume production of electronic systems.

CORPORATE DESCRIPTION

LSI Logic is a Fortune 500 designer and manufacturer of high-performance semiconductors. LSI Logic's ASIC (application-specific integrated circuit) technology and CoreWare approach to system-level integration enable customers to create electronic systems on a chip to increase performance and lower costs. The company operates leading-edge manufacturing facilities to produce submicron chips in volume.

LSI Logic has close working relationships with customers in fast-growing vertical markets, including digital video, telecommunications, networking, personal computers, workstations and servers. Using electronic design automation tools, LSI Logic's semiconductors are tailored to the unique requirements of customers in these markets.

ADDRESS   790 Sycamore Dr.
Milpitas, CA 95035

INDUSTRY CATEGORY   High Technology

♦   ♦   ♦   ♦   ♦   ♦   ♦

Lucent Technologies Inc.

STATEMENT | **Our Mission**

To provide our customers with the world's best and most innovative communications systems, products, technologies and customer support.

Powered by excellent people and technology, we will be a customer-driven, high performance company that delivers superior, sustained shareholder value.

| **Our Values**

1 an obsession with serving our customers
2 a commitment to business excellence
    speed
    innovation
    quality
3 a deep respect for the contributions of each person to the success of the team
    mutual respect & teamwork

personal accountability

integrity & candor

4 a strong sense of social responsibility

CORPORATE DESCRIPTION

Lucent Technologies Inc. is one of the world's leading designers, developers and manufacturers of communications systems, software and products. These integrated systems and software applications enable network operators and business enterprises to connect, route, manage and store information between and within locations. Lucent is a global market leader in the sales of public communications systems, and is a supplier of systems and software to the world's largest networks. Lucent is also a global leader in the sale of business communications systems and microelectronic components for communications systems and computer manufacturers. Lucent was formed from the systems and technology units that were formerly part of AT&T Corp., including the research and development capabilities of Bell Laboratories.

ADDRESS   600 Mountain Ave.

Murray Hill, NJ 07974-0636

INDUSTRY CATEGORY   Communications and Telecommunications

◆   ◆   ◆   ◆   ◆   ◆   ◆

Lyondell Petrochemical Company

Lyondell Petrochemical Company Values for Excellence

Lyondell Petrochemical Company purchases feedstocks and supplies, manufactures and markets refined petroleum products, petrochemicals and polymers.

Our goal is to be the best in every business in which we participate while providing consistent high quality products and services that meet and fully satisfy our customers' requirements and needs. We will provide these products and services at the lowest cost while maximizing value for our shareholders.

We will accomplish our goal through:

- Empowerment of all Lyondell employees
- Partner relationships with our customers and suppliers
- Innovation
- Integrity
- Continued improvement of our safety, health and environmental performance
- Total quality management
- High equal opportunity standards

We will succeed because maximizing every Lyondell employee's potential and clearly identifying our values will bring out the best of our resources—both people and processes.

CORPORATE DESCRIPTION

Lyondell Petrochemical Company is one of the nation's largest and most efficient petrochemical producers and refiners, with manufacturing facilities in Houston, Channelview and Pasadena, Texas and corporate headquarters in downtown Houston. Lyondell's products are primarily basic chemicals or refined products that are used to produce a multitude of consumer goods. Fibers for clothing, ingredients in paint, medicines, carpet, recording tape, trash bags, even automobile components are made from products produced by Lyondell. In addition, Lyondell has an approximately 90% interest in Lyondell-Citgo Refining Company Ltd., which operates the nation's eighth largest refinery.

ADDRESS 1221 McKinney
Ste. 1600
Houston, TX 77010

INDUSTRY CATEGORY Chemicals

◆ ◆ ◆ ◆ ◆ ◆ ◆

Maritz Inc.

STATEMENT | **Our Mission**

Our mission is to help our clients improve their performance in critical areas, such as sales, marketing, quality, customer satisfaction and cost reduction, by influencing the behavior of our clients' customers, employees and channel partners.

Emphasizing excellence and value, we will create, develop and implement the best possible action plans for our clients through a unique combination of our worldwide resources that includes marketing services, employee involvement processes and travel services. We will offer these services worldwide through our operating companies and their associates, either separately or in combination.

| **Our Vision**

We will strive to be acknowledged as the best global organization in the world at helping clients improve performance. While recognizing cultural differences, we will strive to standardize our applications, processes and services to the highest quality levels, and be the recognized leader in each line of business we pursue.

Through leadership in effective local and global human resources practices, facilities, information technology and business processes, we will strive to be recognized as the best place to work, and the best company with whom to associate.

We will pursue international growth and the globalization of services for each line of business. We will accomplish this through the establishment of our operating companies and new associations with the best companies in each country.

We and our associates will refer clients to one another, and share our expertise, experience and the financial benefits in an equitable manner.

Our Heritage

Above all, we value client service, people, diversity, teamwork, innovation, sales, profits, working hard, having fun, community service and ethical standards of business conduct.

To aid us in fulfilling our mission and vision, we will remain privately held and financially strong.

CORPORATE DESCRIPTION

The Maritz family of companies is the largest source of integrated performance improvement, travel and marketing research anywhere in the world.

ADDRESS   1375 N. Highway Dr.
St. Louis County, MO 63099

INDUSTRY CATEGORY   Business Services

◆　◆　◆　◆　◆　◆　◆

Marriott International, Inc.

STATEMENT | **Marriott Vision**

Marriott International's vision is to be the world's leading provider of hospitality services. To achieve this vision, our business goals center around preference, growth and profitability.

CORPORATE DESCRIPTION

Marriott International Inc. is a leading worldwide hospitality company, with over 1,700 operating units in the United States and 53 other countries and territories. Major businesses include hotels operated and franchised under the Marriott, Ritz-Carlton, Courtyard, Residence Inn, Fairfield, TownePlace Suites, SpringHill Suites, Renaissance, and Ramada International brands; vacation club (time-share) resorts; senior living communities and services; and food service distribution.

ADDRESS   One Marriott Dr.
Washington, DC 20058

INDUSTRY CATEGORY   Hotel, Hospitality, and Entertainment

◆   ◆   ◆   ◆   ◆   ◆   ◆

Maxus Energy Corporation

STATEMENT | **Vision Statement**

Our aim is to be a successful exploration and production company, generating and pursuing profitable and repeatable investment opportunities with primary emphasis on the areas where we now produce.

July 1994

CORPORATE DESCRIPTION

Maxus Energy Corporation, with headquarters in Dallas, Texas, is one of the largest independent oil and gas exploration and production companies in the world.

ADDRESS   717 N. Harwood St.
Dallas, TX 75201

INDUSTRY CATEGORY   Oil and Gas

◆   ◆   ◆   ◆   ◆   ◆   ◆

MBIA Inc.

Our goal is to be the best and most respected provider of products and services which enhance the efficiency of public finance while selectively expanding our credit enhancement products to other financial obligations.

◆ ◆ ◆

Our Business—We will make what we do best—enhancing the efficiency of public finance—our blueprint for a successful future. We will continue to build this strong viable business while prudently expanding into new areas where we are able to utilize our existing skills or better serve the changing needs of our traditional customer base.

◆ ◆ ◆

Our Bondholders—We will provide our securities' holders with a guarantee of unquestioned strength. We will do this by maintaining the most stringent underwriting standards in the industry, by providing the most comprehensive surveillance of our insured credits and by maintaining the financial strength necessary to comfortably meet all of our commitments.

◆ ◆ ◆

Our Customers—We will provide our customers with innovative value-added solutions and a level of service that is second-to-none.

◆ ◆ ◆

Our Shareholders—We will achieve strong, sustainable and predictable growth in earnings and in the value of our Company.

◆ ◆ ◆

Our Employees—We will set high expectations for ourselves and for our business. We will strive to build a culture that is open and treats all fairly. We will create an environment which encourages individual decision-making and working together as a team in the interest of serving our clients and shareholders. We will give of our time, skills and capital to make our community a better place for us all to live and work.

CORPORATE DESCRIPTION

MBIA Inc., through its wholly owned subsidiary, Municipal Bond Investors Assurance Corporation, is the leading insurer of municipal bonds, including new issues and bonds traded in the secondary market. The company also guarantees asset-backed transactions and high-quality obligations offered by qualified financial institutions. In addition, MBIA provides investment management products and services for school districts, municipalities and bond insurers. MBIA Securities Corporation provides fixed-income investment management and trading services for MBIA's municipal cash-management subsidiaries. MBIA Corporation and its French subsidiary, MBIA Assurance S.A., have a claims-paying rating of Triple-A from Moody's Investors Service, Inc. and Standard & Poor's.

ADDRESS   113 King St.
Armonk, NY 10504

INDUSTRY CATEGORY   Financial Investment Services

◆　◆　◆　◆　◆　◆　◆

MBNA Corporation

STATEMENT | **MBNA Is A Company Of People Committed To:**

- Providing the Customer with the finest products backed by consistently top-quality service.
- Delivering these products and services efficiently, thus ensuring fair prices to the Customer and a sound investment for the stockholder.
- Treating the Customer as we expect to be treated—putting the Customer first every day—and meaning it.
- Being leaders in innovation, quality, efficiency, and Customer satisfaction. Being known for doing the little things and the big things well.
- Expecting and accepting from ourselves nothing short of the best. Remembering that each of us, the people of MBNA, makes the unassailable difference.

CORPORATE DESCRIPTION

MBNA Corporation's primary subsidiary is MBNA America Bank, N.A., a national bank with its principal office in Delaware. It is one of the nation's largest lenders through bank credit cards. All of the company's services are delivered through the mail and by telephone.

ADDRESS   400 Christiana Rd.
Newark, DE 19713

INDUSTRY CATEGORY   Banking

◆   ◆   ◆   ◆   ◆   ◆   ◆

MCI Communications Corporation

STATEMENT | **MCI Mission Statement**

MCI provides the full range of basic and advanced telecommunications services domestically and internationally. We are the second largest long distance carrier in the U.S. and the fifth largest carrier of international traffic in the world.

Our key mission through network MCI, our strategic vision, is to continue to grow domestic market share profitably, expend our global capabilities, and take full advantage of emerging technologies to become a leader and meet our customers' needs in the coming world of multimedia.

MCI's strengths in the marketplace are its people, its responsiveness to customers' needs, the development of innovative products based on MCI's flexible, intelligent network platform—integrating the most advanced technologies from the world's leading suppliers.

CORPORATE DESCRIPTION

MCI is a leading Information Age telecommunications company; a global company with broad international presence. It is the second largest long-distance carrier in the U.S. and the fifth largest carrier of international traffic in the world.

ADDRESS   1801 Pennsylvania Ave., N.W.
Washington, DC 20006

INDUSTRY CATEGORY   Communications and Telecommunications

♦   ♦   ♦   ♦   ♦   ♦   ♦

Medtronic, Inc.

| **Medtronic Mission Statement**

Mission

- To contribute to human welfare by application of biomedical engineering in the research, design, manufacture, and sale of instruments or appliances that alleviate pain, restore health, and extend life.

- To direct our growth in the areas of biomedical engineering where we display maximum strength and ability; to gather people and facilities that tend to augment these areas; to continuously build on these areas through education and knowledge assimilation; to avoid participation in areas where we cannot make unique and worthy contributions.

- To strive without reserve for the greatest possible reliability and quality in our products; to be the unsurpassed standard of comparison and to be recognized as a company of dedication, honesty, integrity, and service.

- To make a fair profit on current operations to meet our obligations, sustain our growth, and reach our goals.

- To recognize the personal worth of employees by providing an employment framework that allows personal satisfaction in work accomplished, security, advancement opportunities, and means to share in the company's success.

- To maintain good citizenship as a company.

CORPORATE DESCRIPTION

Medtronic, Inc. is a leader in producing therapeutic medical devices to improve the cardiovascular and neurological health of patients around the world.

ADDRESS   7000 Central Ave. N.E.
Minneapolis, MN 55432

INDUSTRY CATEGORY   Scientific, Photo, and Control Equipment

◆ ◆ ◆ ◆ ◆ ◆ ◆

Merck & Co., Inc.

The Mission of Merck is to provide society with superior products and services—innovations and solutions that improve the quality of life and satisfy customer needs—to provide employees with meaningful work and advancement opportunities and investors with a superior rate of return.

| **OUR VALUES**

I

Our business is preserving and improving human life. All of our actions must be measured by our success in achieving this goal. We value above all our ability to serve everyone who can benefit from the appropriate use of our products and services, thereby providing lasting consumer satisfaction.

2

We are committed to the highest standards of ethics and integrity. We are responsible to our customers, to Merck employees and their families, to the environments we inhabit, and to the societies we serve worldwide. In discharging our responsibilities, we do not take professional or ethical shortcuts. Our interactions with all segments of society must reflect the high standards we profess.

3

We are dedicated to the highest level of scientific excellence and commit our research to improving human and animal health and the quality of life. We strive to identify the most critical needs of consumers and customers, and we devote our resources to meeting those needs.

4

We expect profits, but only from work that satisfies customer needs and benefits humanity. Our ability to meet our responsibilities depends on maintaining a financial position that invites investment in leading-edge research and that makes possible effective delivery of research results.

5

We recognize that the ability to excel—to most competitively meet society's and customers' needs—depends on the integrity, knowledge, imagination, skill, diversity and teamwork of employees, and we value these qualities most highly. To this end, we strive to create an environment of mutual respect, encouragement and teamwork—a working environment that rewards commitment and performance and is responsive to the needs of employees and their families.

CORPORATE DESCRIPTION
Merck & Co., Inc. is the world's largest pharmaceutical company.

ADDRESS   One Merck Dr.
P.O. Box 100
Whitehouse Station, NJ 08889-0100

INDUSTRY CATEGORY   Pharmaceutical/Biotechnology

◆　◆　◆　◆　◆　◆　◆

Meridian Bancorp, Inc.

STATEMENT | **Statement of Purpose**

Meridian will be a strong, profitable, growth-oriented, diversified provider of financial services that strives aggressively to achieve maximum shareholder and franchise value.

| **Our Vision**

Our Vision is Meridian's statement of core values that defines the company's culture and the Meridian way of thinking.

At Meridian, individuals make the difference. Success depends upon a strong customer focus, quality service and continuous improvement by employees who show integrity, caring and initiative.

Our business goes beyond simply meeting customer needs. As a premier provider of financial services, we work together to identify and surpass the expectations of our internal and external customers.

We work together to reach across titles, job responsibilities and organizational structure in order to share information and expertise. Teamwork brings the best of Meridian to our customers.

How we serve our customers is crucial. Each of us enhances relationships with those we serve by being prompt, accurate, professional and by adding a personal touch.

When problems arise, we turn them into opportunities to provide exceptional service. We act decisively, using sound business judgment, creativity and integrity.

We always look for ways to improve. We encourage innovative thinking to find new sources of income, to control costs, to enhance service quality and to work more efficiently. Improving the quality of our lives as employees is essential to Meridian's success. We are dedicated to providing new approaches that help employees enjoy a balance between commitment to work and life away from work.

The increasing diversity of our workforce in terms of race, gender and cultural background adds richness to our lives. We value diversity, and we encourage an environment where each individual can make a difference in the success of our Company.

Our efforts to enhance the success of our customers, our organization and ourselves depend upon our ability to initiate change and make it work for us. While the forces of change have never been stronger, our opportunities have never been greater.

CORPORATE DESCRIPTION

Meridian Bancorp, Inc. is a bank and financial services holding company headquartered in Reading, Pennsylvania.

ADDRESS   10 N. 5th St.
P.O. Box 1102
Reading, PA 19603

INDUSTRY CATEGORY   Banking

◆ ◆ ◆ ◆ ◆ ◆ ◆

Merrill Lynch & Co., Inc.

Client Focus

Our clients are the driving force behind what we do.

Our company's founder, Charles E. Merrill, declared that the client's interests must come first. Today, client focus is just as imperative as it was in Mr. Merrill's day. In our increasingly competitive industry, success rests not on our ability to sell a certain product or service, but on the degree to which clients value Merrill Lynch as their trusted advisor.

To achieve this stature, it will not be enough merely to meet our clients' expectations. We must constantly strive to exceed them.

Respect For The Individual

We respect the dignity of each individual, whether an employee, shareholder, client or member of the general public.

We strive to be a lean, decisive and aggressive organization, but on a personal level to treat each individual with dignity, consideration and respect. This means sharing the credit when credit is due, avoiding public criticism of one another, and encouraging an atmosphere in which openness, cooperation and mutual consultation are the norms. It means following the Golden Rule.

As a company, we will seek, nurture and reward the highest-caliber employees, regardless of race, national origin, religion, gender, age or physical ability. We will encourage this diversity amongst ourselves, realizing it to be an important competitive advantage in the rapidly emerging global marketplace.

Teamwork

We strive for seamless integration of services. In our clients' eyes, there is only one Merrill Lynch.

It is great teams that win, not loose affiliations of all-stars. Therefore, we expect real teamwork throughout our company, and we reward people for it. We are committed to an honest sharing of both risks and rewards with one another, so that when clients achieve their goals, everyone at Merrill Lynch benefits.

Our people and resources are unmatched in our industry, yet they are not enough to guarantee continued success. In order to be our clients' trusted adviser, we must take pride in working as a team—at all levels and across all boundaries—bringing all of the diverse skills and resources of Merrill Lynch to bear in solving client problems.

Responsible Citizenship

As the company that brought Wall Street to Main Street and the world, we seek to improve the quality of life in the communities where our employees live and work.

Responsible citizenship means that we are committed to giving something back to the communities in which we earn our livelihood. We encourage employee volunteerism and community involvement. Both as a corporation and as individuals, we support education, the cultural arts, the environment and community services in the U.S. and around the world.

And, we advocate public policies—such as open global markets and enhanced incentives for savings and investment—that promote long-term economic growth and opportunity around the world.

Integrity

No one's personal bottom line is more important than the reputation of our firm.

Our most important corporate asset is the great Merrill Lynch "tradition of trust"—our company's long-standing reputation for integrity in the marketplace.

As beneficiaries of this great tradition, we will be tolerant of ordinary mistakes made in the course of business; we will not tolerate lapses in ethics or integrity.

While "R.O.I." does not appear in our financial statements, Merrill Lynch enjoys a return on integrity we will protect, whatever the cost, as the bedrock of our prosperity and our pride.

CORPORATE DESCRIPTION

Merrill Lynch & Co., Inc. is a holding company that, through its subsidiaries and affiliates, provides investment, financing, advisory, insurance, and related services on a global basis.

ADDRESS   World Financial Center
North Tower
New York, NY 10281

INDUSTRY CATEGORY   Financial Investment Sservices

♦ ♦ ♦ ♦ ♦ ♦ ♦

Meyer (Fred Meyer, Inc.)

STATEMENT | **Our Philosophy**

At Fred Meyer we are governed by the beliefs that:
- Customers are essential, for without them we would have no business. Customers shop most where they believe their wants and needs will be satisfied best.
- Satisfactory profits are essential, for without profits our business can neither grow nor satisfy the wants and needs of our Customers, employees, suppliers, shareholders or the community.
- Skilled, capable, dedicated employees are essential, for the overall success of our business is determined by the combined ideas, work and effort of all Fred Meyer employees.

Based on these beliefs, we are committed to:
- Serving Customers so well that after shopping with us they are satisfied and want to shop with us again.
- Operating our business efficiently and effectively, so we earn a satisfactory profit today and in the future.

- Providing an environment that encourages employees to develop their abilities, use their full potential and share ideas that further the success of the business, so they gain a sense of pride in their accomplishments and confidence in their capabilities.

We believe that by following this philosophy we will satisfy Customers and earn their patronage, provide for the profitable growth of our company, and enrich the lives of Fred Meyer employees and their families.

CORPORATE DESCRIPTION

Fred Meyer, Inc., a Delaware corporation, and its subsidiaries operate a chain of 123 retail stores offering a wide range of food, apparel, fine jewelry, and products for the home, with emphasis on necessities and items of everyday use. The stores are located in Oregon, Washington, Utah, Alaska, Idaho, Northern California, and Montana and include 94 free-standing, multidepartment stores and 29 specialty stores.

ADDRESS   P.O. Box 42121
Portland, OR 97242-0121

INDUSTRY CATEGORY   Retail

◆　◆　◆　◆　◆　◆　◆

Microsoft Corporation

STATEMENT | **Vision**

A computer on every desk and in every home.

[*Author's note:* Microsoft's 1993 Annual Report includes an explanation of their Vision, as follows.]

We are single-minded in our commitment to this vision. And we have maintained that singular focus ever since our company was founded in 1975.

This vision has created a revolution that's changed how people around the world do business. We believe that our own success, in large measure, has resulted directly from the effective use of our technology.

This vision is also shaping the future.

While we know that great possibilities lie ahead for us, we also know that the future will make great demands on us. At the same time we commit ourselves to delivering outstanding products today, we are also committing ourselves to creating the infrastructure that will define the information systems of the next 25 years and beyond. In addition, our hope is to make computer technology as indispensable at home as the telephone, and as widespread as the television.

To accomplish these objectives, we hire bright, talented people who share our enthusiasm for technology and our goal of making it easier for people to do more with personal computing.

Ultimately, our dream is to put the power of computers—in business and at home—into people's hands so they can access, integrate, and use information more easily than ever before; what we call Information At Your Fingertips.

It's a dream we believe is within our reach, and within our capabilities.

CORPORATE DESCRIPTION

Microsoft develops, manufactures, markets, licenses, and supports a wide range of software products, including operating systems for personal computers (PCs), office machines, and personal information devices; applications programs; and languages; as well as personal computer books, hardware, and multimedia products.

ADDRESS   One Microsoft Way
Redmond, WA 98052-6399

INDUSTRY CATEGORY   High Technology

◆   ◆   ◆   ◆   ◆   ◆   ◆

Mid-America Dairymen, Inc.

STATEMENT | **Mission Statement of Mid-America Dairymen, Inc.**

The mission of Mid-America Dairymen is to provide each member market security by providing a market for all the milk he or she desires to produce and marketing that milk in the form and market channels providing maximum returns consistent with long term stability.

CORPORATE DESCRIPTION

Mid-America Dairymen, Inc. is a dairy marketing cooperative, governed by the 13,000 farm families who belong to the cooperative.

ADDRESS   3253 E. Chestnut Expwy.
Springfield, MO 65802

INDUSTRY CATEGORY   Food/Beverage

◆   ◆   ◆   ◆   ◆   ◆   ◆

Minnesota Mining and Manufacturing Company (3M)

STATEMENT | **Statement of 3M Corporate Values**

We are committed to:

—Satisfying our **customers** with superior quality and value,

—Providing **investors** with an attractive return through sustained, high-quality growth,

—Respecting our **social and physical environment,**

—Being a company that **employees** are proud to be a part of.

Satisfying our customers with superior quality and value—

♦ Providing the highest quality products and services consistent with our customers' requirements and preferences.

♦ Making every aspect of every transaction a satisfying experience for our customers.

♦ Finding innovative ways to make life easier and better for our customers.

Providing investors an attractive return through sustained, high-quality growth—

Our goals are:

♦ Growth in earnings per share averaging 10 percent a year or better,

♦ A return on capital employed of 27 percent or better,

♦ A return of shareholders' equity of between 20 and 25 percent,

♦ At least 30 percent of our sales each year from products new in the last four years.

Respecting our social and physical environment—

♦ Complying with all laws and meeting or exceeding regulations,

♦ Keeping customers, employees, investors and the public informed about our operations,

♦ Developing products and processes that have a minimal impact on the environment,

♦ Staying attuned to the changing needs and preferences of our customers, employees and society,

- Uncompromising honesty and integrity in every aspect of our operations.

Being a company that employees are proud to be a part of—
- Respecting the dignity and worth of individuals,
- Encouraging individual initiative and innovation in an atmosphere characterized by flexibility, cooperation and trust,
- Challenging individual capabilities,
- Valuing human diversity and providing equal opportunity for development.

CORPORATE DESCRIPTION

3M is a worldwide manufacturer serving industrial, commercial, health care and consumer markets. 3M develops, manufactures and markets products through three business sectors: Industrial and Consumer; Information, Imaging and Electronic; and Life Sciences.

ADDRESS   3M Center
St. Paul, MN 55144-1000

INDUSTRY CATEGORY   Scientific, Photo, and Control Equipment

♦ ♦ ♦ ♦ ♦ ♦ ♦

Mondavi (Robert Mondavi Winery)

STATEMENT | **OUR VISION**

We will be the preeminent fine wine producer in the world.

| **OUR MISSION**

By strongly adhering to our values and management philosophy, we will:

- Produce and market top quality wines providing exceptional value across the premium wine segment for our worldwide customers, and,
- Manage for the long-term to build value for our shareholders and stakeholders.

| **OUR VALUES**

To achieve our vision of being the preeminent fine wine producer in the world, we believe it essential to:

- **Listen to our customers** for opportunities to add value
- **Continually mold and refine** the preferences of our wine consumers
- Consider all employees **ambassadors** of the company who have a critical role in its operation
- Have an **uncompromising passion for excellence and improvement**
- Encourage **creativity and innovation**
- Demand **absolute integrity** in our internal and external business relationships, based on mutual trust and respect, and,
- Create a **family-oriented, small-company environment.**

| **OUR MANAGEMENT PHILOSOPHY**

To achieve our vision of being the preeminent fine wine producer in the world, we will:

- Understand and exceed our external and internal customer expectations
- Add value in **everything** we do

- Treat **everyone** as a valued member of the team
- Recognize outstanding contribution
- Actively solicit ideas and feedback to improve our processes and performance
- Provide information and education so that everyone can be an effective **ambassador** of the company
- Develop the skills of our people
- Be open to change
- Lead by example
- Accept responsibility for our performance
- Communicate openly
- Celebrate success, and,
- Provide a safe, healthy and fun work environment.

CORPORATE DESCRIPTION

Robert Mondavi Winery makes fine table wines sold around the world. The company produces wine sold under a variety of brands including Robert Mondavi Winery, Woodbridge by Robert Mondavi, and Opus One in partnership with the Rothchild family of France.

ADDRESS   7801 St. Helena Highway
Oakville, CA 94562

INDUSTRY CATEGORY   Food/Beverage

◆　◆　◆　◆　◆　◆　◆

Montana Power Company

STATEMENT | **Objectives**

Corporate: The Montana Power Company and its subsidiaries produce and sell energy and related services and products, at competitive prices, in an environmentally compatible, safe, and reliable manner.

Utility: To create value for the company's customers, employees, shareholders, and our communities, primarily by providing electricity, natural gas, and related services.

Entech: To develop and market energy, technology and related products and services in Montana and other areas, while providing a reasonable profit to our investors.

Independent Power Group: To develop, acquire, operate, purchase, and manage facilities and resources to provide energy services to customers at reasonable prices which provide the Corporation's shareholders with an attractive profit.

CORPORATE DESCRIPTION

Montana Power Co. has three operating divisions: the Utility Division, Entech Inc., and the Independent Power Group (IPG).

Entech Inc. is the administrative arm for MPC's diversified enterprises in coal mining, oil, and natural gas and technology.

IPG is a wholesale and independent power operation, engaged in cogeneration investments and the marketing of energy.

ADDRESS   40 E. Broadway
Butte, MT 59701-9394

INDUSTRY CATEGORY   Utility

◆　◆　◆　◆　◆　◆　◆

Nalco Chemical Company

| **Nalco Philosophy of Operations "Building Value"**

For Customers

Nalco seeks to improve the profitability and process performance of our customers' operations and to assure a return on their investment with us. We are on-site problem-solvers and we bring technically innovative solutions to our customers' dynamic systems. Our goal is customer satisfaction in all that we do.

For Employees

Our employees are the strength behind our customer focus. We strive to add value through our quality process and through an environment of opportunity, challenge, trust and reward so that employees may effectively satisfy our customers, contribute to our goals and enjoy personal growth and fulfillment. We will treat each other with respect and dignity. All employees should be able to work in an environment that is safe, healthy, free from discrimination and fair in all aspects of work, pay, benefits and career opportunities.

For Shareholders

Nalco is committed to a strategy of leadership, focusing on markets, strengths and financial goals that will build shareholder value and provide continuous growth. We expect to make a reasonable profit so that we can reward our shareholders and employees, invest in our future and enrich the communities in which we operate.

For Communities

We will obey the law, act ethically and with integrity, be responsible with respect to the environment and be active and interested in civic and community affairs. Safety, product stewardship and Responsible Care® are essential ingredients of our value-building commitment.

Nalco employees are expected to uphold these commitments in all aspects of their work. We strive to conduct our business so that everyone who comes in contact with Nalco enjoys the same considerations and fair treatment.

* Responsible Care is a registered trademark of the Chemical Manufacturers Association.

CORPORATE DESCRIPTION

Nalco Chemical Company is the world's largest producer of specialty chemicals and services for water and industrial process treatment.

ADDRESS   One Nalco Center
Naperville, IL 60563-1198

INDUSTRY CATEGORY   Chemicals

◆ ◆ ◆ ◆ ◆ ◆ ◆

National Semiconductor

STATEMENT | **Our Mission and Beliefs**

Our mission is to excel in serving chosen markets by delivering semiconductor-intensive products and services of the highest quality and value, thereby providing a competitive advantage to our customers worldwide.

TO ACCOMPLISH OUR MISSION, WE BELIEVE WE MUST:

◆ Maintain our integrity and fairness with each other, our customers and suppliers, our investors and the communities in which we live and work.

◆ Exhibit respect for our fellow employees, our environment, and a healthy balance between our work and family.

◆ Enhance our capabilities and skills throughout our careers.

◆ Be curious, imaginative, and courageous in challenging our current thinking.

- Create innovative solutions using our technological strengths.
- Grow our expertise by learning through teamwork.
- Make continuous improvement a way of life.
- Strive for excellence in all our efforts.
- Reward our shareholders with reasonable profits as a result of exceeding our customers' expectations.

CORPORATE DESCRIPTION

National Semiconductor is the fourth largest U.S. semiconductor manufacturer and 12th largest worldwide. National Semiconductor designs, manufactures, and markets high-performance semiconductor products and is a global leader in mixed analog-and-digital technologies. Major market segments are analog-intensive markets, communications-intensive markets, and markets for personal systems.

ADDRESS 2000 Semiconductor Dr.
P.O. Box 58090
Santa Clara, CA 95052-8090

INDUSTRY CATEGORY High Technology

♦　♦　♦　♦　♦　♦　♦

New York Life

| **OUR MISSION**

New York Life and its affiliates are in the business of providing financial security through insurance and other products. We are committed to being the soundest, strongest, and easiest company to do business with. Every decision we make, every action we take has one overriding purpose: To be here when our customers need us. That's why we call ourselves The Company You Keep.®

| **OUR BELIEFS**

We are a Company founded on strong beliefs, beliefs that manifest themselves in the way we do business, through our employees and agents, and in the products we sell and the services we provide.

We believe in FINANCIAL STRENGTH. We believe in maintaining and enhancing our sound financial position so we can continue to do what we have always done: be there for our customers.

We believe in INTEGRITY. We believe adherence to the highest standards of integrity is the principal measure of the success of our products, our dealings with our customers, and our contributions to society. Our integrity keeps us dedicated to providing our clients with value and financial security in the products we offer and quality and responsiveness in the services we provide.

And most of all, we believe in HUMANITY. We believe in treating our customers, agents, and employees with compassion, consideration, and respect. Our business is unique in that we possess the ability to help people provide for their futures and make their lives less worrisome, and our enduring belief in humanity keeps us from losing sight of this fact.

From the time New York Life was founded over 150 years ago to the present day, we've stayed true to these beliefs. They are the driving force behind what we were, what we are, and what we strive to become. Through every change that has taken place and will take place in our Company or in society at large, these beliefs keep us focused on the fact that we are in a business that can make a difference in people's lives.

CORPORATE DESCRIPTION

New York Life Insurance Company, a *Fortune* 100 company, is one of the largest insurance and financial services companies in the United States and the world. Founded in 1845 and headquartered in New York City, New York Life and its affiliates offer traditional life insurance and annuities. On the investment side, New York Life and its affiliates provide institutional asset management and trust services and, through a subsidiary, NYLIFE Distributors Inc., provide an array of securities products and services such as institutional and retail mutual funds, including 401(k) products.

ADDRESS   51 Madison Ave.
New York, NY 10010

INDUSTRY CATEGORY   Insurance

◆ ◆ ◆ ◆ ◆ ◆ ◆

Niagara Mohawk Power Corp.

STATEMENT | **Vision**

We will become the most responsive and efficient energy services company in the Northeast to achieve maximum value for customers, shareholders and employees.

| **Mission**

Niagara Mohawk is an energy services company committed to maximizing value to its customers, shareholders and employees.

The Company seeks to satisfy customers' energy needs with high quality, competitively priced electric and gas energy products and services; increase shareholder value through above average growth in earnings; and provide an atmosphere for employees which promotes empowerment and rewards or excellence.

Niagara Mohawk promotes safe and efficient practices in the supply, delivery and use of energy. The Company is committed to a cleaner, healthier environment through an active, positive approach to its environmental responsibilities. The Company supports improvement in the social and economic well-being of the communities it serves and seeks cooperative and constructive relationships with all of its regulators.

Niagara Mohawk's business emphasis focuses on results, aggressive and responsible leadership, responsiveness to customer needs and continuous improvement in operations.

CORPORATE DESCRIPTION

Niagara Mohawk Power Corp. is an investor-owned utility providing energy to the largest customer service area in New York.

ADDRESS   300 Erie Blvd. W.
Syracuse, NY 13202

INDUSTRY CATEGORY   Utility

◆ ◆ ◆ ◆ ◆ ◆ ◆

Nike

STATEMENT │ **Corporate Mission**

To maximize profits to shareholders through products and services that enrich people's lives.

CORPORATE DESCRIPTION

Nike operates predominantly in one industry segment, that being the design, production, and marketing of athletic and casual footwear, apparel, and accessories.

ADDRESS   One Bowerman Dr.
Beaverton, OR 97005-6453

INDUSTRY CATEGORY   Consumer Goods and Services

◆ ◆ ◆ ◆ ◆ ◆ ◆

Norfolk Southern Corporation

| ### Our Vision

Be the safest, most customer-focused and successful transportation company in the world.

Our Mission

Norfolk Southern's mission is to enhance the value of our stockholders' investment over time by providing quality freight transportation services and undertaking any other related businesses in which our resources, particularly our people, give the company an advantage.

Our Creed

We are responsible to our Stockholders, Customers, Employees, and the Communities we serve.

For all our constituencies,

we will make safety our highest priority.

For our Customers,

we will provide quality service, always trying to reduce our costs in order to offer competitive prices.

For our Stockholders,

we will strive to earn a return on their equity investment which will increase the value of their ownership. By generating a reasonable return on invested capital, we will provide the security of a financially strong company to our customers, employees, stockholders, and communities.

For our Employees,

our greatest asset, we will provide fair and dignified treatment with equal opportunity at every level. We will seek talented Management with the highest standards of honesty and fairness.

For the Communities we serve,

we will be good corporate citizens, seeking to enhance their quality of life through service, jobs, investment, and the energies and good will of our Employees.

CORPORATE DESCRIPTION

Norfolk Southern Corporation is a Virginia-based holding company that owns all the common stock and controls a major freight railroad, Norfolk Southern Railway Company, and a motor carrier, North American Van Lines, Inc. The railroad system's lines extend over more than 14,500 miles of road in 20 states, primarily in the Southeast and Midwest, and the Province of Ontario, Canada. North American provides household moving, truckload general freight and specialized handling freight services in the United States and Canada, and offers certain motor carrier services worldwide.

ADDRESS   Three Commercial Pl.
Norfolk, VA 23510-2191

INDUSTRY CATEGORY   Transportation

◆　◆　◆　◆　◆　◆　◆

Northeast Utilities

STATEMENT | **Corporate Mission Statement**

Northeast Utilities is dedicated to providing safe, dependable, and reasonably priced energy and related services as an ethical, environmentally responsible, and financially sound private enterprise committed to the efficient use of resources, responsive to the needs of customers and their communities, sensitive to the well-being of employees, and yielding a fair return to shareholders.

CORPORATE DESCRIPTION

Northeast Utilities is the parent company of the NU system (collectively referred to as NU). NU is among the 20 largest electric utilities in the country and the largest in New England, serving about 1.7 million customers in Connecticut, New Hampshire, and western Massachusetts.

ADDRESS   P.O. Box 270
Hartford, CT 06141-0270

INDUSTRY CATEGORY   Utility

◆　◆　◆　◆　◆　◆　◆

Northern States Power Company

STATEMENT | **NSP**

Our commitment to our customers is to be:

Your Energy Partner of Choice

By exhibiting this commitment, NSP will be the leader in growth and profitability in the expanding markets where the Company competes.

As employees of NSP, we will increase the value provided to our customers by surrounding them with options from the NSP portfolio of energy products and services. We will continuously improve the ways we benefit our shareholders, customers, the communities we serve and each other.

CORPORATE DESCRIPTION

Northern States Power (NSP), with headquarters in Minneapolis, serves customers in Minnesota, Wisconsin, North Dakota, South Dakota, and Michigan's Upper Peninsula.

ADDRESS   414 Nicollet Mall
Minneapolis, MN 55401

INDUSTRY CATEGORY   Utility

◆　◆　◆　◆　◆　◆　◆

Northwestern Mutual Life

STATEMENT | **The Northwestern Mutual Way**

The ambition of The Northwestern has been less to be large than to be safe; its aim is to rank first in benefits to policyowners rather than first in size. Valuing quality above quantity, it has preferred to secure its business under certain salutary restrictions and limitations rather than to write a much larger business at the possible sacrifice of those valuable points which have made The Northwestern pre-eminently the policyowner's Company.

Executive Committee, 1888

CORPORATE DESCRIPTION

Northwestern Mutual offers life insurance, disability income, and annuities for the protection of human life value.

ADDRESS   720 E. Wisconsin Ave.
Milwaukee, WI 53202

INDUSTRY CATEGORY   Insurance

◆   ◆   ◆   ◆   ◆   ◆   ◆

Office Depot

STATEMENT | **Our Mission**

Office Depot's mission is to be the most successful office products company in the world. Our success is driven by an uncompromising commitment to:
   ◆ **Superior Customer Satisfaction**
A company-wide attitude that recognizes that customer satisfaction is everything.

◆ **An Associate-Oriented Environment**

An acknowledgment that our associates are our most valuable resource. We are committed to fostering an environment where recognition, innovation, communication and the entrepreneurial spirit are encouraged and rewarded.

 ◆ **Industry Leading Value, Selection and Services**

A pledge to offer only the highest-quality merchandise available at everyday low prices, providing customers with an outstanding balance of value, selection and services.

 ◆ **Ethical Business Conduct**

A responsibility to conduct our business with uncompromising honesty and integrity.

 ◆ **Shareholder Value**

A duty to provide our shareholders with superior Return-On-Investment.

CORPORATE DESCRIPTION

Office Depot is the world's largest seller of office products operating more than 700 stores throughout the United States, Canada, and France.

ADDRESS   2200 Old Germantown Rd.
Delray Beach, FL 33445

INDUSTRY CATEGORY   Business Products

◆ ◆ ◆ ◆ ◆ ◆ ◆

OfficeMax, Inc.

STATEMENT | **The OfficeMax Mission**

Serve our customers, build significant value for our shareholders and provide growth opportunities for our associates.

CORPORATE DESCRIPTION

OfficeMax, Inc. operates a chain of high-volume, deep-discount office products superstores.

ADDRESS   3605 Warrensville Center Rd.
Shaker Heights, OH 44122

INDUSTRY CATEGORY   Business Products

◆ ◆ ◆ ◆ ◆ ◆ ◆

Oklahoma Natural Gas Company

STATEMENT | **Mission Statement**

Providing reliable natural gas services to customers in Oklahoma.

| **Vision Statement**

We will be a recognized model of excellence, challenging traditional boundaries, seizing opportunities, setting the standard to become a renowned provider of energy and innovative products and services.

| **Core Values of Oklahoma Natural Gas Company**

Ethics

Our actions are founded on trust, honesty, and integrity through open communications and adherence to the highest standards of business ethics.

Quality

Our commitment to quality is driven by continuous improvement and our quest for excellence.

Loyalty

We acknowledge the dignity and worth of each employee and the necessity for a workplace environment that provides opportunities and rewards for teamwork, innovation, and loyalty.

Value

We are committed to maximizing value for all investors, customers, employees, and the public, recognizing their concern for optimum development and utilization of our resources.

Service

We will provide responsive flexible service while enthusiastically embracing our commitment to improving quality of life and preserving the environment.

CORPORATE DESCRIPTION

Oklahoma Natural Gas Company provides natural gas to customers in Oklahoma. It is a division of ONEOK Inc., a diversified energy company headquartered in Tulsa, Oklahoma. It is primarily a natural gas company with three divisions and 15 subsidiaries.

Oklahoma Natural Gas Company division and ONG Transmission Company division provide natural gas utility services to three-quarters of Oklahoma. These divisions purchase, gather, compress, transport, distribute, sell and store natural gas. They also lease pipeline capacity and provide the link for interstate gas transportation. Oklahoma Natural has been in existence since 1908.

ADDRESS   100 W. Fifth St.
Tulsa, OK 74103-0871

INDUSTRY CATEGORY   Utility

◆　◆　◆　◆　◆　◆　◆

Old Kent Financial Corporation

STATEMENT | **Old Kent Financial Corporation**

Philosophy of the Corporation

Our corporate mission and culture statement reflect our long-standing commitment to shareholders, customers, employees and the communities we serve. Key tenets of the Corporation's business philosophy are—to maximize the value of shareholders' investment, to meet the needs of customers with quality products and services, to provide a meaningful and challenging work environment for our employees, and to serve communities as a good citizen.

Corporate Mission

Increase shareholder value as a high performing independent regional bank holding company serving select communities with quality products and services.

Corporate Culture

The management of Old Kent has the ultimate responsibility for achieving profit levels which assure the quality of the balance sheet and the continuation of the Corporation, for the benefit of our shareholders, communities we serve and our employees.

Old Kent's purpose is to understand and fulfill the needs of our customer groups resulting in long-term, multiple-service client relationships. This customer-driven purpose requires that we earn and retain the respect, confidence and loyalty of our customers by serving them so that they will benefit from their association with us.

CORPORATE DESCRIPTION

Old Kent Financial Corporation is a bank holding company headquartered in Grand Rapids, Michigan, with total assets of $10 billion. Old Kent is in the business of commercial banking and related services through its 16 banking subsidiaries and five non-banking subsidiaries. Old Kent's principal markets for financial services are communities within Michigan and Illinois, where its 228 banking offices are located.

ADDRESS   One Vandenberg Center
Grand Rapids, MI 49503

INDUSTRY CATEGORY   Banking

◆　◆　◆　◆　◆　◆　◆

Oneida Ltd.

STATEMENT | **Oneida Ltd. Mission Statement**

"To profitably and ethically satisfy our customers' needs in a manner that enhances the welfare of our stockholders, our employees and the communities in which we reside."

CORPORATE DESCRIPTION

A manufacturer and marketer of two diversified product groups— tableware for the consumer and foodservice markets, and industrial wire for original equipment manufacturers.

ADDRESS   Kenwood Station
Oneida, NY 13421

INDUSTRY CATEGORY   Manufacturing

◆　◆　◆　◆　◆　◆　◆

Owens & Minor

STATEMENT | **Our Mission ...**

To provide our customers and suppliers with the most responsive, efficient and cost-effective distribution system for the delivery of healthcare products and services in the markets we serve; to earn a return on our invested capital consistent with being an industry leader; and to manage our business with the highest ethical standards in a socially responsible manner with particular emphasis on the welfare of our teammates and the communities we serve.

CORPORATE DESCRIPTION

Owens & Minor is the nation's second largest medical/surgical supply distributor. The company strives to reduce costs in the healthcare delivery system by adding efficiency to the supply chain through improved linkage between healthcare providers and manufacturers of medical/surgical supplies. Stockless, just-in-time, materials management, information flow, electronic data interchange (EDI) and logistics programs are part of Owens & Minor's array of customer services, in conjunction with the delivery of its 100,000+ items product offering.

ADDRESS   4800 Cox Rd.
P.O. Box 27626
Richmond, VA 23261-7626

INDUSTRY CATEGORY   Medical Products and Services

◆   ◆   ◆   ◆   ◆   ◆   ◆

PacifiCorp

The mission statement explains our reason for being in business, our key constituents, and the overall way in which we choose to conduct our business:

PacifiCorp's mission is to help our customers prosper in our economic system by satisfying their electric energy wants and needs with electricity, energy efficiency and other related value-added products and services. PacifiCorp can only do this by maintaining competitive prices and quality services for its customers, creating a favorable work environment for its employees, being a responsible steward of the natural environment, and in the end growing value for its shareholders.

CORPORATE DESCRIPTION

As the third largest electric utility west of the Rocky Mountains, PacifiCorp serves 1.3 million customers through Pacific Power and Utah Power. PacifiCorp also holds a major telecommunications utility. Pacific Telecom, an 87 percent-owned subsidiary, is one of the nation's largest nonBell telephone companies.

ADDRESS   700 N.E. Multnomah St.
Portland, OR 97231-4116

INDUSTRY CATEGORY   Utility

◆ ◆ ◆ ◆ ◆ ◆ ◆

Penney (J.C. Penney Company, Inc.)

STATEMENT | **The Penney Idea**

- To serve the public, as nearly as we can, to its complete satisfaction.
- To expect for the service we render a fair remuneration and not all the profit the traffic will bear.
- To do all in our power to pack the customer's dollar full of value, quality and satisfaction.
- To continue to train ourselves and our associates so that the service we give will be more and more intelligently performed.
- To improve constantly the human factor in our business.
- To reward men and women in our organization through participation in what the business produces.
- To test our every policy, method and act in this wise: "Does it square with what is right and just?"

Adopted 1913

CORPORATE DESCRIPTION

J.C. Penney is 5th among the 50 largest retailers, according to *Fortune* magazine. J.C. Penney is a national department store, the largest department store retailer in the United States.

ADDRESS   P.O. Box 10001
Dallas, TX 75301-8105

INDUSTRY CATEGORY   Retail

◆   ◆   ◆   ◆   ◆   ◆   ◆

Pennsylvania Power & Light Company

STATEMENT

[Author's note: This entry for Pennsylvania Power & Light Company is unusually lengthy because it includes

1. The updated, current versions of the company's Vision, Values, and Principles
2. The earlier versions of the company's Vision, Values, Mission, and Philosophy (developed in the 1980s) that the current versions replace.

Please see the case history on PP&L in Part I, which includes an interview with James Marsh, director of corporate communications at PP&L. Mr. Marsh explains how and why the versions differ, as well as the process involved in creating a new set of statements. The case history includes the valuable "definition of terms" (from the earlier versions), which explains the meaning of a Vision, Values, Mission, and Business Philosophy statement. The case history also reflects the company's significant commitment to expressing and communicating such statements that clarify the company's direction and focus.

The two sets of statements are reprinted with the expressed permission of PP&L.]

(Current Version)

Our Vision

PP&L—People Leading, Growing and Winning in the Changing Electric Energy Markets

Our vision is a statement of where we are going. To get there, we will have to transform our company by building on our solid reputation and acquiring new skills. Supporting this new vision are the three cornerstones of competitive performance, creating change and a commitment to excellence.

First, we are performance-driven. Our financial strength is a result of our commitment to continuous improvement and a commitment by all of us to perform to our real potential. We are accountable for personal and organizational success.

Second, we embrace change. Everyone must be willing to fundamentally challenge our existing ways of doing business. Everyone is encouraged to contribute new and better ideas for improved performance in every area of our business. We will be pioneers in the new electricity marketplace—out front leading the market through innovation. **Finally, we strive for excellence in all areas.** This is a common personal goal shared by all of us. Our commitment to excellence unifies and strengthens us. It differentiates us from other organizations.

With more companies competing for our customers, we will have to reaffirm our commitment to our guiding values and commit to the CPIP principles that will help us achieve our vision. **Our success in a competitive environment hinges on our commitment to the values that will help us achieve our vision.**

Our Values

While our vision provides direction and our principles identify the behaviors that will help us succeed in the future, we are committed to certain guiding values that continue to govern the way we do business.

Integrity—We are honest, open and fair. Respect for individuals is not to be compromised.

Safety—We create a culture that promotes the safety and well-being of employees and the public.

Diversity—We seek a diverse work force at all levels of the organization, as well as a variety of experience and ideas. Differing points of view and opinions will be sought and valued.

Environmental Commitment—We operate our facilities and serve our customers in a manner that protects the environment for present and future generations.

Our Principles

The following eight key principles of the CPIP program are integral to the successful implementation of our vision:

1. Serving our customers.
2. Striving to meet customer, employee and shareowner expectations by being a cost-competitive producer.

3. Measuring and assessing performance constantly.
4. Ensuring that all employees understand and support strategic and operational plans.
5. Leaders role modeling the behavior they expect from others.
6. Creating a climate of trust.
7. Empowering people to think and act.
8. Creating a high level of teamwork throughout the organization.

◆ ◆ ◆

(Older Version)

Our Vision

PP&L will be the energy supplier of choice.

Our Values

PP&L stands for integrity, customer satisfaction, financial strength, excellence, employee fulfillment, equal opportunity, teamwork, safety, environmental commitment and public service commitment.

Integrity

As stated in our "Standards of Integrity," we are an organization that is here to serve people efficiently in ways that are decent and honorable. Integrity is essential to pursue our vision and to ensure that all other values are meaningful.

Integrity means:

◆ living up to our responsibilities, meeting our obligations, fulfilling our commitments;
◆ maintaining our credibility by open, accurate and timely communications with customers, employees, regulators, investors, and all others affected by our business;
◆ instilling confidence in all who deal with the company that PP&L people can be depended upon to act with highest moral and ethical standards. Unethical behavior to accomplish a desired end result is not acceptable.

Customer Satisfaction

Satisfied customers are the lifeblood of our business. Customers are not only those who purchase our service, but also our fellow employees who rely on each other for business-related services. All are entitled to have their needs and expectations realized. Customer satisfaction means:

- exceeding customer expectations;
- treating them with respect in an open and forthright manner;
- adding value to our customer services;
- putting ourselves in their place, asking how we can provide better service, and then improving our performance to provide that service;
- seeking continual feedback on how well we are meeting customer expectations.

Financial Strength

PP&L can successfully accomplish its mission only if it has the financial resources to do so. Financial strength results from:

- applying sound judgment to all expenditures to assure that full value is obtained for every dollar spent;
- setting financial objectives that increase shareowner value and implementing thoughtful business plans to achieve these objectives;
- providing superior service—on time, every time.

Excellence

We set high standards in all aspects of our business, measure our performance against those standards and focus on continuous improvement. Commitment to excellence means:

- satisfying ourselves that excellent performance is more than mere adherence to rules, regulations and requirements;
- assessing ourselves, identifying opportunities to improve our performance;
- admitting our mistakes and learning from them to do better the next time;

- going the "extra mile" to improve performance;
- setting challenging goals and embracing the concept of rising expectations. Rising expectations recognizes that today's challenging goals will evolve into tomorrow's standards of performance.

Employee Fulfillment

A work force that is productive, well-trained, properly equipped and motivated is an essential element to success. Employee fulfillment means:
- providing a work environment that encourages all employees to fully utilize their skills to effectively meet our mission;
- valuing each employee's contributions to achieving objectives;
- being aware of, and responsive to, the needs and values of employees;
- committing ourselves to sound safety, health, compensation and communications practices.

Equal Opportunity and Affirmative Action

An integral part of our commitment to people is to take positive actions to assist each PP&L person to become the best that he or she can be. To accomplish this, we must open our doors to every qualified person and remove all barriers to their development.

Equal Opportunity/Affirmative Action means:
- taking a positive stand against discrimination of any sort;
- ensuring that no person is excluded from full participation in our company and its activities due to race, color, religion, sex, age, national origin or handicap;
- seeking qualified, motivated, enthusiastic candidates for job openings; welcoming them as part of the PP&L team, and taking active steps to improve their capabilities.

Teamwork

Change is an inevitable part of our business life. Identifying, understanding and shaping change to the benefit of our company requires creative thinking and innovation from each employee. As part of our problem solving and decision-making process, we encourage a climate which is open and supportive of suggesting and trying new approaches or ideas. Teamwork means:

- employee participation, engaging employees at all levels in molding the future of the company;
- reaching out, soliciting input from those who may be affected by what we do and how we do it;
- encouraging teamwork among employees and cooperation among work groups to achieve our common goals and objectives more effectively.

Safety

Maintaining a work environment that promotes the safety and well being of employees and the public is a top priority at PP&L. No job is so important, or so urgent, that safety precautions can be bypassed. Safety means:

- providing tools, equipment and training to enable PP&L people to carry out their responsibilities safely and productively;
- maintaining a safety awareness among PP&L people for themselves, their co-workers and the public;
- searching for new initiatives to improve safety performance.

Environmental Commitment

PP&L will serve its customers in a manner that protects the environment for present and future generations. Environmental Commitment means:

- being alert to the environmental voices of customers, employees and the general public;
- demonstrating leadership in sound environmental management;
- promoting open and honest communication about environmental impacts of, and on, our operations;
- using our expertise to assist in resolving public environmental issues.

PP&L is an integral part of the economic, political, and social structure of Central Eastern Pennsylvania. Our success depends upon the vitality of our service area. PP&L people participate in community activities that contribute to enhancing the quality of life in the area we serve. Community Involvement means:

- being a responsible and responsive corporate citizen;
- caring about the cultural and civic values of the communities we serve, and operating our business in harmony with those values;
- sharing our knowledge and experience to enhance economic prosperity and quality of life.

PP&L's Vision and Values will have maximum benefit when communicated, understood and practiced throughout the organization. Our Vision and Values should become an ongoing topic for discussion among all employees; they are the foundation for development of vision and values for work groups throughout the company. Our Vision and Values will require periodic review and modification to reflect changing conditions or circumstances.

Our Mission

To meet our customers' ongoing needs for economical and reliable electric service in ways that merit the trust and confidence of our publics.

Our Business Philosophy

PP&L will strive to accomplish its mission in conformance with our Standards of Integrity and within the framework of the following philosophies and policies:

- We will be an institution that is humane, responsible and contributive to the betterment of society, with special emphasis on helping to develop both economic prosperity and a better quality-of-life in our service area. We will not compromise safety, public health or environmental quality in carrying out our mission.

- We will maintain an open and full disclosure policy with customers, employees, investors, and others affected by our business.
- We will seek public input in the development and implementation of plans to meet our commitment to provide economical and reliable electric service. We will inform the public about our progress and about probable effects of our plans and actions.
- We will search for new ideas and perspectives so as to anticipate and effectively respond to change.
- We will support the development and application of sound governmental policies that we believe to be in the best interests of our publics.
- We will create and maintain a work environment that attracts and retains capable people, encourages self-development and enables them to take pride and satisfaction in their work.
- We will support improved coordination among interconnected utilities in the planning and operation of generation and bulk power transmission facilities.
- We will strive to earn a fair return on the capital provided by investors, maintain a sound credit standing and have the financial strength required to raise needed capital at reasonable costs.
- We recognize our responsibility to be good stewards of the resources entrusted to us. We will utilize these resources efficiently and effectively to carry out our mission. We will promote the wise use of electricity and provide excellent customer service.
- We will constantly look for methods to improve the operating efficiency of the electric supply system, search out cost-effective programs to improve continuity of service and develop ways to minimize adverse impacts of unforeseen circumstances.

- We will pursue a climate of excellence and intend to be a well-run, responsive, cost-effective company. We will measure our performance by regularly comparing it to the best that others achieve under similar conditions.

CORPORATE DESCRIPTION

Pennsylvania Power & Light Co. headquartered in Allentown, PA, provides electric service to approximately 1.2 million homes and businesses throughout a 10,000-square-mile area in 29 counties of Central Eastern Pennsylvania.

ADDRESS   2 N. 9th St.
Allentown, PA 18103

INDUSTRY CATEGORY   Utility

◆   ◆   ◆   ◆   ◆   ◆   ◆

PepsiCo, Inc.

STATEMENT │ (Objective and Strategy)

Our overriding objective is to maximize shareholder value. Our strategy is to concentrate our resources on growing our businesses, both through internal growth and carefully selected acquisitions within these businesses. The corporation's success reflects our continuing commitment to growth and a focus on those businesses where we can drive our own growth and create opportunities.

│ (Values)

Results—PepsiCo people are recognized and rewarded for achieving results. To create shareholder value, we must perform brilliantly on millions of consumer transactions each day.

Integrity—At PepsiCo, integrity means more than corporate honesty. It takes openness and trust to run a huge flexible corporation. Warmth and good humor help, too.

People—In the end, it's always the special efforts of people that make great things happen. We value our employees, customers, business partners, franchises, suppliers and shareholders. We know without them there would be no PepsiCo.

CORPORATE DESCRIPTION

PepsiCo operates on a worldwide basis within three industry segments: beverages, snack foods, and restaurants. The beverage segment markets Pepsi, Diet Pepsi, Mountain Dew and other brands worldwide and 7UP outside the U.S. The snack food segment manufactures and markets snack chips worldwide, with Frito-Lay representing the domestic business. The restaurant segment includes operations of the worldwide Pizza Hut, Taco Bell, and KFC (Kentucky Fried Chicken) chains.

ADDRESS   700 Anderson Hill Rd.
Purchase, NY 10577-1444

INDUSTRY CATEGORY   Food/Beverage

◆　◆　◆　◆　◆　◆　◆

Perini Corporation

STATEMENT | **Statement of Beliefs**

As a recognized leader in the construction industry, we believe we must:

- ◆ Strive to meet or exceed our customers' expectations and to be the best in our businesses;
- ◆ Foster a business environment in which Perini employees, subcontractors and suppliers work together with customers to provide a quality product;
- ◆ Earn an equitable financial return for our shareholders;

- Be responsible citizens, concerned at all times for the safety of our employees and the public, and responsive to the needs of the communities in which we live and work;
- Develop and maintain a highly motivated, diverse, competent, well-trained management team and workforce who strive for continuous improvement in their jobs and who are proud to work for Perini;
- Provide competitive compensation with advancement based on merit and reward for innovation and performance in a workplace in which nondiscrimination and equal opportunity are the norm;
- Earn the respect, confidence and good will of our clients, subcontractors, suppliers, workforce and shareholders;
- Build upon our 100-year tradition of integrity and excellence.

CORPORATE DESCRIPTION

Perini Corporation, headquartered in Framingham, Massachusetts, is engaged in two principal businesses: Construction and Real Estate Development.

Perini provides general contracting, both building and heavy, and construction management services to private clients and public agencies throughout the United States and in selected overseas locations.

Real estate development operations are conducted by Perini Land & Development Company, a wholly owned subsidiary with offices in Arizona, California, Florida, Georgia and Massachusetts.

ADDRESS   73 Mt. Wayne Ave.
Box 9160
Framingham, MA 01701-9160

INDUSTRY CATEGORY   Construction

◆ ◆ ◆ ◆ ◆ ◆ ◆

Pfizer

Purpose

We at Pfizer dedicate ourselves to helping humanity and delivering exceptional financial performance by discovering, developing and providing innovative health care products that lead to healthier and more productive lives.

Mission

Over the next five years, we will achieve and sustain our place as the world's premier research-based health care company. Our continuing success as a business will benefit patients and our customers, our shareholders, our families, and the communities in which we operate around the world.

In each of its global health care businesses, Pfizer will secure a leading position through excellence in the following areas:

- Research and Development
- Marketing Innovative Products
- Financial Performance

Research and Development

We will develop an unmatched number of new products that are recognized worldwide as significantly enhancing health and quality of life.

We will sustain unparalleled vitality in all our product pipelines.

We will attract and retain world-class researchers and product developers who will utilize ever-expanding scientific knowledge to discover life-saving and life-enhancing medicines and health care products.

Marketing Innovative Products

We will be the most effective organization in commercializing innovative health care products, in launching new products, in attaining rapid market penetration, and in sustaining the commercial success of our products over their entire life cycles.

We will understand the realities and needs of our diverse customers. Patients worldwide will recognize Pfizer for providing safe and effective health care products. Doctors, health care institutions, and governments will recognize Pfizer's superior product quality and supporting expertise and the value our products and people add to health care.

We will employ our worldwide resources to advantage, while appropriately tailoring our efforts to suit local market requirements.

In recognition of our development and marketing capabilities, we will be the preferred partner for product innovators throughout the industry.

Financial Performance

Each business will attain sales and operating income growth that is significantly higher than its industry competitors.

As a company we will:

Measure and reward high performance and recruit superior talent.

Actively strive to shape our business environment, leveraging our understanding of consumers and the health care industry and our experience in public policy initiatives worldwide.

Fiercely defend our intellectual property and work to expand the protection of innovation throughout the world.

Maintain a stringent business review process to assure accountability and ensure that each business lives up to our leadership aspirations.

Ensure that each of our businesses has the resources and skills—in managing research and development, in dealing with regulatory authorities, in manufacturing, and in marketing—that are essential to leadership.

Promote collaboration among our businesses to achieve research, development, manufacturing, and marketing synergies.

Values

To fulfill our purpose and achieve our mission, we abide by the enduring values that are the foundation of our business:

Integrity
Innovation
Respect for People
Customer Focus
Teamwork
Leadership
Performance
Community

Integrity

We demand of ourselves and others the highest ethical standards, and our products and processes will be of the highest quality. Our conduct as a company, and as individuals within it, will always reflect the highest standards of integrity. We will demonstrate open, honest, and ethical behavior in all dealings with customers, clients, colleagues, suppliers, partners, the public, and governments. The Pfizer name is a source of pride to us and should inspire trust in all with whom we come in contact.

We must do more than simply do things right—we must also do the right thing.

Innovation

Innovation is the key to improving health and sustaining Pfizer growth and profitability. The quest for innovative solutions should invigorate all of our core businesses and pervade the Pfizer community worldwide.

In our drive to innovate, we support well-conceived risk-taking and understand that it will not always lead to success. We embrace creativity and consistently pursue new opportunities. We look for ways to make our research and development capabilities, our products and services more useful to our customers, and our business practices, processes, and systems more efficient and effective. We listen to and collaborate with our customers to identify and make widely available potential new products.

Respect for People

We recognize that people are the cornerstone of Pfizer's success. We come from many different countries and cultures, and we speak many languages. We value our diversity as a source of strength. We are proud of Pfizer's history of treating employees with respect and dignity and are committed to building upon this tradition.

We listen to the ideas of our colleagues and respond appropriately. We seek a business environment that fosters personal and professional growth and achievement. We recognize that communication must be frequent and candid and that we must support others with the tools, training, and authority they need to succeed in achieving their responsibilities, goals, and objectives.

Customer Focus

We are deeply committed to meeting the needs of our customers and constantly focus on customer satisfaction. We take genuine interest in the welfare of our customers, whether internal or external. We recognize that we can prosper only if we anticipate and meet customer needs, respond quickly to changing conditions, and fulfill customer expectations better than our competitors. We seek long-term relationships based on our comprehensive understanding of all our customers' needs and on the value we provide through superior products and services.

Teamwork

We know that to be a successful company we must work together, frequently transcending organizational and geographic boundaries to meet the changing needs of our customers.

We want all of our colleagues to contribute to the best of their ability, individually and in teams. Teamwork improves the quality of decisions and increases the likelihood that good decisions will be acted upon. Teamwork sustains a spirit of excitement, fulfillment, pride, and passion for our business, enabling us to succeed in all of our endeavors and continually learn as individuals and as a corporation.

Leadership

Leaders advance teamwork by imparting a clarity of purpose, a shared sense of goals, and a joint commitment to excellence. Leaders empower those around them by sharing knowledge and authority and by recognizing and rewarding outstanding individual effort. We are dedicated to providing opportunities for leadership at all levels in our organization.

Leaders are those who step forward to achieve difficult goals, envisioning what needs to happen and motivating others. They utilize the particular talents of every individual and resolve conflict by helping others to focus on common goals.

Leaders build relationships with others throughout the company to share ideas, provide support, and help assure that the best practices prevail throughout Pfizer.

Performance

We strive for continuous improvement in our performance. When we commit to doing something, we will do it in the best, most complete, most efficient, and most timely way possible. Then we will try to think of ways to do it better the next time. We will measure our performance carefully, ensuring that integrity and respect for people are never compromised. We will compete aggressively, establishing challenging but achievable targets and rewarding performance against those targets. We wish to attract the highest caliber employees, providing them with opportunities to develop to their full potential and to share in the success that comes from winning in the marketplace.

Community

We play an active role in making every country and community in which we operate a better place to live and work. We know that the ongoing vitality of our host nations and localities has a direct impact on the long-term health of our business. As a company and as individuals, we give of ourselves to serve the needs of communities and people in need throughout the world.

Pfizer is a research-based pharmaceutical company with global operations.

ADDRESS   235 E. 42nd St.
New York, NY 10017

INDUSTRY CATEGORY   Pharmaceutical/Biotechnology

◆ ◆ ◆ ◆ ◆ ◆ ◆

The Pillsbury Company

STATEMENT | **Mission Statement**

WE ASPIRE TO BE THE BEST FOOD COMPANY
In the eyes of our employees, shareholders, consumers, trade customers, communities and suppliers.

We will achieve this through a dedication to and relentless pursuit of our governing objective:

TO BUILD SHAREHOLDER VALUE
Pillsbury will be a principal contributor to Diageo's doubling of shareholder returns every 4 years:

BY VALUING OUR PEOPLE
Unleashing the passion and creativity of all our employees around the world

BY WINNING IN THE MARKETPLACE
Turning superior understanding of consumers, trade customers and the competition into growth of volume, share and brand equity

BY BUILDING LEADING INTERNATIONAL BRANDS

| **OUR VALUES**

Freedom To **Succeed**
Be The **Best**
Passionate About Consumers
Proud Of What We Do

We Make **Lips Smile** Everywhere
By Making Everyday **Food Special**

CORPORATE DESCRIPTION

Founded in 1869 as a Minneapolis-based flour miller, Pillsbury has evolved into a highly regarded food company. The company still markets flour for home, retail and institutional use, and provides a wide range of value-added food products: refrigerated baked goods, desserts and baking mixes, breakfast and snacks, vegetables, Mexican food, soup, frozen desserts, and bakeries and foodservice.

ADDRESS

200 S. 6th St.
Minneapolis, MN 55402

INDUSTRY CATEGORY   Food/Beverage

◆ ◆ ◆ ◆ ◆ ◆ ◆

Pioneer Hi-Bred International, Inc.

STATEMENT | Mission Statement

♦ Our mission is to provide products and services which increase the efficiency and profitability of the world's farmers.
♦ Our core business is the broad application of the science of genetics.
♦ We will ensure the growth of our core business and develop new opportunities which enhance the core business.

CORPORATE DESCRIPTION

Pioneer Hi-Bred's business is the broad application of the science of genetics. Pioneer was founded in 1926 to apply newly discovered genetic techniques to hybridize corn. Today, the Company develops, produces, and markets hybrids of corn, sorghum, and sunflower, and varieties of soybean, alfalfa, wheat, canola, and vegetables.

◆   ◆   ◆   ◆   ◆   ◆   ◆

Ply Gem Industries, Inc.

STATEMENT

Our goal is to become the supplier of choice to the home improvement industry. By supplying top quality products, delivering excellent customer service and working in partnership with our customers to satisfy their needs, we aim to be the best. As we see it, that's the best way we can properly serve the long-term interests of all our constituents: customers, suppliers, employees and stockholders.

CORPORATE DESCRIPTION

Ply Gem is a national manufacturer and distributor of specialty products for the home improvement industry. The company was founded in 1943 and is headquartered in New York City. Ply Gem's 11 independent operating companies employ over 4,000 people in more than 50 locations throughout the United States and Canada.

ADDRESS   777 Third Ave.
New York, NY 10017

INDUSTRY CATEGORY   Construction

◆   ◆   ◆   ◆   ◆   ◆   ◆

Potlatch Corporation

Potlatch People Make It Better

By consistently living our values, we provide superior results for shareholders, customers, ourselves, and future generations.

People: We share a common purpose and values, and treat each other with respect and dignity. We are accountable for a safe, healthy, and productive work environment. Individual contribution, team achievements, and diversity are valued. Enthusiasm and fun are encouraged.

Open Communication: Communication flows in a timely and open fashion in all directions. Information is power when it is shared, not withheld. We listen respectively to each other's ideas and concerns with the intent to understand and respond. Leaders are accessible. We debate openly, honestly, and constructively.

Trust: We earn trust by keeping our commitments and promises and by treating people fairly, ethically, and honestly. We expect the same of others.

Life-Long Learning: We are life-long learners with an unwavering commitment to expanding our knowledge, experience, and training to attain life-long employability. We use and share what we know and learn.

Adaptiveness: We anticipate and creatively adapt to changes in the business climate, customer needs, technology, and social expectations. We solicit and utilize new ideas, creativity, and innovation to achieve long-term success. We are leaders not followers.

Treatment of Others: We treat all shareholders, customers, suppliers, contractors, local communities, and other stakeholders as valued partners.

Competence: We accept responsibility and accountability to excel in all that we do. We take pride in our work, but believe that it can always be improved. We are well matched to our jobs and internal culture.

Honesty and Integrity: We will never compromise our honesty and integrity, even if it is unpleasant or causes financial hardship. We always do what we say, and our actions are consistent with our core values and beliefs.

Value: We provide superior returns to our shareholders by providing value to customers. We cooperate internally to aggressively compete externally.

Involvement: We participate in decisions that affect us, and strive for true partnership. We encourage interdependence through power-sharing, teamwork, and collaboration with all customers, both internal and external.

Strategy: Our strategy is to be a low-cost producer of quality forest products.

Impartiality: We treat everyone fairly and consistently. We select, reward, promote, and recognize based on performance and ability rather than favoritism.

Opportunity: We constantly search for opportunities to create a more prosperous future for our stakeholders and ourselves. We reward risk-taking as well as results. We are proactive not reactive.

Natural Resources: We are responsible stewards of all resources, including forest, soil, water, air, and wildlife. Our future depends on natural resources, and we recognize that they are important to our communities, the general public, and future generations. We set the standards by which others are judged in our use of the best practices to sustain all resources.

CORPORATE DESCRIPTION

Founded in 1903, Potlatch is one of North America's largest integrated forest products companies, with more than 18 manufacturing sites and timberlands in Idaho, Minnesota, and Arkansas. Currently, the company's product lines are divided into three segments:

- ◆ Wood Products Group
- ◆ Minnesota Pulp and Paper Division
- ◆ Pulp and Paper Group

ADDRESS   601 West Riverside Ave.
Spokane, WA 99201

INDUSTRY CATEGORY   Forest Products, Wood Processing, Paper

◆　◆　◆　◆　◆　◆　◆

Principal Financial Group

| **Mission**

What we do

To help individuals, groups and businesses meet their financial goal by providing high quality insurance and financial services.

| **Vision**

Where we want to be

To become the financial services company of choice for individuals, groups, businesses and their employees, and communities around the world.

| **Core Values**

These four values are the soul of our company ... our culture. They define how we conduct ourselves, shape our business approach and form our unique perspective on the world. These basic values, and the points that follow each one, comprise what is necessary for our success.

Customer Service

♦

Quality

♦

Strength

♦

Integrity

Customer Service

- **Service**—Our reason for existence is to provide excellent service to customers. We believe excellent service is defined by the customer.
- **Mutuality**—We have no stockholders; we operate on behalf of our customers. Mutuality provides a strong focus on customers and enables us to concentrate on the long-term view.
- **Financial Stability**—Maintaining and improving our financial soundness is a fundamental part of serving customers well. Financial stability gives The Principal® flexibility. In short, it prepares us for good times and bad.

- **Marketing**—We will know our customer markets well, understand and meet a variety of their financial needs.
- **Cost**—Our commitment to customers includes offering the lowest possible cost for high quality service. We emphasize both expense control and growth in numbers of customers to reduce the cost per customer.

Quality

- **Management**—We work toward continuous improvement in our operations, which over time, has a large positive impact.
- **Products and Services**—We find out what customers need and then build quality products and services to meet their needs. We continually seek to improve and enhance existing products and services to meet customers' changing needs.
- **Corporate Identity**—Our identity and image distinguishes us from the competitors. We strive to increase recognition of The Principal Financial Group and improve our quality reputation as a financially sound, customer-oriented company.

Strength

- **Human Resources**—We are only as strong as our people. The Principal is committed to giving employees the training, tools, opportunities and rewards, along with a stimulating work environment, to do their jobs well. We seek diversity to draw excellence from all available sources.
- **Growth and Profit**—We strive to balance orderly growth with adequate profits. Growth enables us to provide economies of scale; in other words we can provide more for less. Profit allows us to keep our promises to customers, continue growth and provide new services.
- **Asset Management**—We seek above average, long-range rates of return from our investments. In managing our assets (what we own), we consider our own liabilities (what we owe) and the level of risk our customers desire.
- **Diversification**—As the economy changes and as customer needs change, our various businesses may grow and decline over time. We diversify into a number of businesses so that the

decline of any one business doesn't have an overwhelming impact on the entire company and our customers.

♦ **Decentralization**—The Principal will continue to offer products and services through separate business units. Our business units are empowered to conduct their ongoing businesses and make decisions regarding their operations, customer service and products and service offerings. This autonomy brings success to the whole company because the business units can be flexible and efficient in responding to customers' needs. However, communication and coordination through a central company management group is crucial. This central management group will be the focus of decisions regarding the businesses we are in and the allocation of resources. The group will also review all business plans.

♦ **Globalization**—We are committed to becoming a global financial services organization.

Integrity

♦ **Ethics**—We operate in an ethical and legal manner. We are dedicated to being honest and straightforward in our dealings with customers, the public and each other.

♦ **Social Responsibility**—The Principal is a responsible member of the communities in which it operates. We do our best to support society, the global community, the economy, the insurance and financial services industries and the nations, states and local communities where our employees and customers work and live.

CORPORATE DESCRIPTION

The Principal Financial Group is a diversified family of financial companies offering a full range of insurance and financial products and services for businesses, groups and individuals.

ADDRESS   711 High St.
Des Moines, IA 50392

INDUSTRY CATEGORY   Insurance

♦ ♦ ♦ ♦ ♦ ♦ ♦

Protective Life Corporation

Protective Life Corporation provides financial security through life and health insurance and investment products. Our vision is to enhance the quality of life of our customers, our stockholders, and our people.

We hold to three preeminent values—quality, serving people, and growth—which by tradition and choice transcend all others. They are the foundation of our aspirations, our plans, our best energies, and our life together in this Company.

Quality

The heart of quality is integrity. Quality is the cornerstone on which all our activity rests—quality products, services, people, and investments. We strive for superior quality and continuous quality improvement in everything we do.

Serving People

Serving people is vital. We find our ultimate reward in the service and support of three groups:

Customers: Our customers come first. We prosper only to the extent that we create long-term relationships with satisfied customers. We do so in discerning their needs and responding to them; in providing high value, distinctive products; in prudent investment of policyholder funds; in systems, information, and counsel which help our customers solve problems; and in prompt, accurate, innovative, and courteous service which is the best in the business.

Stockholders: Our stockholders provide the equity essential for our success. We are stewards of their investment and must return a profit to them. Profit is essential for implementing our commitment to quality, serving people, and growth. It is a critical measurement of our performance. Our objective is to rank at the top of the industry in long-range earnings growth and return on equity.

Protective People: The accomplishment of our mission depends on all Protective people working together. We want our people to enjoy their work and take pride in Protective Life, its mission and values. We are committed to opportunity and training for all to help us fulfill our potential; open, candid communication; the input, initiative, and empowerment of all our people; the encouragement of one another; and creating a place where a zeal to serve our customers, stockholders, and each other permeates the Company.

Growth

We are dedicated to long-term growth in sales, revenues, and profit, not only for our stockholders but also for personal growth and development of Protective people. We achieve growth through resourceful marketing, superior service, and acquisitions. Growth is critical for improving quality and serving people. It is essential to maintaining a position of strength in our marketplace and attracting and retaining high caliber people.

CORPORATE DESCRIPTION

Protective Life Corporation provides financial services through the production, distribution, and administration of insurance and investment products. It has five marketing divisions: Agency, Group, Guaranteed Investment Contracts, Financial Institutions, and Investment Products.

Founded in 1907, the Company's principal operating subsidiary is Protective Life Insurance Company (Protective Life).

ADDRESS   P.O. Box 2606
Birmingham, AL 35202

INDUSTRY CATEGORY   Insurance

◆　◆　◆　◆　◆　◆　◆

Public Service Enterprise Group Incorporated

STATEMENT | **Mission Statement**

Enterprise is dedicated to providing, through its principal subsidiary, PSE & G, the competitively priced electric and gas services that customers desire. Enterprise will also enter new markets when its experience and knowledge offer special advantages and when market needs and opportunities can be pursued on a sound and profitable basis. These activities are designed to enhance the social and economic well-being of customers, employees, shareholders and the communities which Enterprise serves.

| **Enterprise Vision**

Working together to set the standard of excellence in delivering energy services to customers.

CORPORATE DESCRIPTION

Public Service Enterprise Group Incorporated is a diversified public utility holding company. Public Service Electric and Gas Company (PSE & G), the principal subsidiary of Enterprise, is an operating public utility company providing electric and gas service to residents of New Jersey. It is the state's largest utility and one of America's largest combined electric and gas companies.

ADDRESS   80 Park Plaza – T6B
Newark, NJ 07102-4194

INDUSTRY CATEGORY   Utility

◆　◆　◆　◆　◆　◆　◆

Raytheon Aircraft Company

STATEMENT | **The Beechcraft Vision**

To be the world standard for quality and performance in general aviation, related products, and services.

| **The Beechcraft Mission**

To build and sell the best aircraft and aerospace products in their class through continuous quality improvement, effective use of resources, and the full involvement and contribution of Beech employees, in order to increase market-share, customer satisfaction and profitability.

CORPORATE DESCRIPTION

Raytheon Aircraft Company is one of the world's leading manufacturers of business aircraft and dual use aircraft for the military. With headquarters and major facilities in Wichita, Kansas, and major manufacturing operations in Andover and Salinas, Kansas, Little Rock, Arkansas, and the United Kingdom, the company offers the broadest and strongest product lines in business aviation.

The Raytheon Aircraft Company was formed following the combination of Beechcraft Aircraft Corporation, founded in 1932 and one of the world's oldest, most prestigious aviation companies, and Raytheon Corporate Jets, manufacturer of the Hawker line of business aircraft. Together, the two entities have produced more than 51,000 airplanes.

ADDRESS   P.O. Box 85
9707 E. Central
Wichita, KS 67206

INDUSTRY CATEGORY   Aerospace

◆ ◆ ◆ ◆ ◆ ◆ ◆

Research Industries Corporation

STATEMENT | **Corporate Mission Statement**

To provide cardiovascular & other specialty surgeons with innovative, low-priced disposable products that are cost-effective & improve therapeutic outcomes—thereby providing challenging employment opportunities while enhancing long-term shareholder value.

CORPORATE DESCRIPTION

The Company develops, manufactures and sells disposable medical products and specialty pharmaceuticals to hospitals, distributors and other medical related facilities.

ADDRESS   6864 S. 300 West
Midvale, UT 84047

INDUSTRY CATEGORY   Pharmaceutical/Biotechnology

◆   ◆   ◆   ◆   ◆   ◆   ◆

Reynolds Metals Company

STATEMENT | **Our Vision**

We, the men and women of Reynolds Metals Company, are dedicated to being the premier supplier and recycler of aluminum and other products in the global markets we serve.

| **Our Mission**

Working together, our mission is to provide our customers with uncompromising quality, innovation and continuous improvement, which will result in the profitable growth and financial strength of our company.

Exceed customer expectations
Employee empowerment
Continuous improvement
Stockholder satisfaction
Supplier involvement
Social responsibility

We are committed to the success of our customers, employees, stockholders, suppliers, and the communities in which we operate.

CORPORATE DESCRIPTION

Founded in 1919, Reynolds Metals Company is the second largest aluminum company in the United States and the third largest in the world.

ADDRESS   6601 W. Broad St.
Richmond, VA 23230

INDUSTRY CATEGORY   Manufacturing

◆ ◆ ◆ ◆ ◆ ◆ ◆

Rhône-Poulenc Rorer Inc.

STATEMENT | **The Rhône-Poulenc Rorer Mission**

Our Mission is to become the BEST pharmaceutical company in the world by dedicating our resources, our talents and our energies to help improve human health and the quality of life of people throughout the world.

Being the Best Means:

◆ Being the BEST at satisfying the needs of everyone we serve: patients, healthcare professionals, employees, communities, governments and shareholders;

- Being BETTER AND FASTER than our competitors at discovering and bringing to market important new medicines in selected therapeutic areas;
- Operating with the HIGHEST professional and ethical standards in all our activities, building on the Rhône-Poulenc and Rorer heritage of integrity;
- Being seen as the BEST place to work, attracting and retaining talented people at all levels by creating an environment that encourages them to develop their potential to the full;
- Generating consistently BETTER results than our competitors, through innovation and a total commitment to quality in everything we do.

The Rhône-Poulenc Rorer Principles

Satisfying the needs of our customers
We will strive for the highest quality and continuous improvement in our products and services for all our customers, external and internal, maintaining the highest standards of integrity in all our relationships.

Global communication and collaboration
We will be a global company, fostering open communications, receptivity to new ideas and (worldwide) collaboration on strategies that support the growth and sales of the company.

Being entrepreneurial and acting quickly
We will be entrepreneurial, working with a great sense of urgency, encouraging teamwork and quick decision-making, rewarding innovation and results at every level of the organization.

Treating each other fairly and valuing diversity
We will treat each other fairly, with trust and respect, valuing cultural and individual differences so that our company is strengthened by our diversity.

Caring for our communities and the environment
We will be good neighbors, working to improve the safety of the environment and the vitality of our communities and our workplace.

When we operate according to these principles, Rhône-Poulenc Rorer will grow and prosper as a company and so will we as individuals.

CORPORATE DESCRIPTION

Rhône-Poulenc Rorer Inc. is a global pharmaceutical company dedicated to the discovery, development, manufacturing, and marketing of human pharmaceuticals.

ADDRESS   500 Arcola Rd.
P.O. Box 1200
Collegeville, PA 19426-0107

INDUSTRY CATEGORY   Pharmaceutical/Biotechnology

◆   ◆   ◆   ◆   ◆   ◆   ◆

Rich Products Corporation

STATEMENT | **The Rich Family Vision**

We will excel as an innovative family-owned company who treats our customers like family. We will be their first choice as a long-term business partner because we are reliable, responsive to their needs, easy-to-do business with and committed to providing great-tasting, quality products and customized solutions to help them grow their business.

| **The Rich Mission**

The Rich Mission strives to set new standards of excellence in customer satisfaction and to achieve new levels of competitive success in every category of business in which we operate. We will achieve this by working together as a team to:
Impress Our Customers
Provide exceptional service to our external and internal customers the first time and every time.
Improve, Improve, Improve!
Continuously improve the quality and value of the goods we produce and services we provide.

Empower People

Unleash the talents of all our Associates by creating an environment that is safe, that recognizes and rewards their achievements, and encourages their participation and growth.

Work Smarter

Drive out all waste of time, effort and material—all the barriers and extra steps that keep us from doing our jobs right.

Do The Right Things!

Maintain the highest standards of integrity and ethical conduct and behave as good citizens in our communities.

Think Outside The Box

Challenge the status quo and look for opportunities to make breakthrough innovations in Products, Processes & Services.

CORPORATE DESCRIPTION

Rich Products Corporation is the nation's largest family-owned frozen food manufacturer supplying the bakery, food service and retail food industry with non-dairy, bakery, and specialty food items.

ADDRESS   One W. Ferry St.
P.O. Box 245
Buffalo, NY 14240

INDUSTRY CATEGORY   Food/Beverage

◆　◆　◆　◆　◆　◆　◆

Rockwell International Corporation

We believe maximizing the satisfaction of our customers is our most important concern as a means of warranting their continued loyalty.

We believe in providing superior value to customers through high-quality, technologically-advanced, fairly-priced products and customer service, designed to meet customer needs better than all alternatives.

We believe Rockwell people are our most important assets, making the critical difference in how well Rockwell performs and, through their work and effort, separating Rockwell from all competitors.

We believe we have an obligation for the well-being of the communities in which we live and work.

We believe excellence is the standard for all we do, achieved by encouraging and nourishing:

- Respect for the individual
- Honest, open communication
- Individual development and satisfaction
- A sense of ownership and responsibility for Rockwell's success
- Participation, cooperation and teamwork
- Creativity, innovation and initiative
- Prudent risk-taking
- Recognition and rewards for achievement

We believe success is realized by:

- Achieving leadership in the markets we serve
- Focusing our resources and energy on global markets where our technology, knowledge, capabilities and understanding of customers combine to provide the opportunity for leadership
- Maintaining the highest standards of ethics and integrity in every action we take, in everything we do

We believe the ultimate measure of our success is the ability to provide a superior value to our shareowners, balancing near-term and

long-term objectives to achieve both competitive return on investment and consistent increased market value.

CORPORATE DESCRIPTION

Rockwell is a global electronic controls and communications company with leadership positions in industrial automation, avionics and
communications, and electronic commerce.

ADDRESS P.O. Box 5090
Costa Mesa, CA 92628

INDUSTRY CATEGORY Electronics

◆ ◆ ◆ ◆ ◆ ◆ ◆

Rollins Inc.

STATEMENT | **Mission of Excellence**

Our Mission is to be the Nation's Best Service Company. We will
accomplish this goal by delivering the finest quality services and value
to our customers, while being environmentally responsible. This will
provide opportunities and security for employees, as well as maximize
long-term financial performance for stockholders.

CORPORATE DESCRIPTION

Rollins, Inc. owns and operates Orkin Exterminating Company, Inc.
and Rollins Protective Services. Orkin is the world's largest termite
and pest control company, and also provides plantscaping and lawn
care services. Rollins Protective Services is a leader in electronic security systems.

ADDRESS 2170 Piedmont Rd., N.E.
Atlanta, GA 30324

INDUSTRY CATEGORY Diversified

◆ ◆ ◆ ◆ ◆ ◆ ◆

Rubbermaid Incorporated

Rubbermaid's philosophy is based upon these fundamental beliefs:

We believe that partnerships with our customers, suppliers, communities, governments, shareholders, and Rubbermaid associates are the most effective and efficient means of continuously improving the value we create for our consumers.

We believe that value is a carefully balanced and consumer-defined combination of quality, price, timeliness, service, and innovation. We believe these value attributes are based on a solid foundation of innovation which is the main driver of Rubbermaid's Continuous Value Improvement Process.

We believe that internal partnerships, meaningful teamwork, and ongoing learning will instill in every Rubbermaid associate the skills, the understanding, and the desire to achieve continuous improvement in every link of our value chain.

We believe in partnerships which strive for:

♦ A relationship of mutual respect, recognition, and reward for performance
♦ A commitment to a highest standards of integrity and ethical conduct
♦ A dedication to safety and protection of the environment, and
♦ A fair return on investment

We believe that through this partnership and teamwork philosophy, Rubbermaid will be greater than the sum of its parts.

We believe that the best way to create shareholder wealth consistently and sustainably is to best satisfy the needs of consumers. We will excel when we make them happy. We will make them happy by delighting them with our value.

(Signed)

Wolfgang R. Schmitt
Co-Chairman of the Board
and Chief Executive Officer

Charles A. Carroll
President and Chief Operating Officer

(June 1994)

Management Principles

We believe our primary responsibility is to the consumers and customers who buy Rubbermaid's products and services. We will consistently delight them with our quality, innovation, and prompt and accurate service. We will use teamwork, benchmarking, and advanced technologies to compress time and improve our business processes. Every associate must contribute to continuously improving the value being created by the business. We will eliminate boundaries between our business partners as the best means of improving our total value chain.

We believe our partners are entitled to share in the economic benefits derived from Rubbermaid's development, production, sourcing, and marketing of products worldwide.

For our consumers, we will strive to:
- Be creatively responsive to their changing needs
- Consistently improve our value for them
- Stand behind our products and services, and
- Help protect and improve the environment.

For our customers we will strive to:
- Work as partners with integrity and principled negotiation
- Invest aggressively in research, new products, capacity, and advanced technologies
- Offer on-trend products of exceptional design, fashion, quality, and utility
- Work together to reduce or eliminate non-value activities to improve productivity

- Provide mass customization and creative, aggressive marketing programs, and
- Understand and respond innovatively to their changing requirements

For our suppliers we will strive to:
- Foster mutually beneficial long-term strategic partnerships
- Consider all their attributes, not just price
- Utilize their capabilities to improve the total value chain
- Be objective and ethical in all our business dealings

For our associates, we will strive to:
- Have management lead by example
- Provide an environment which is positive, reality-based, and reinforces initiative
- Encourage experimentation, attentive listening, and risk taking
- Nurture diversity and variety of thought
- Offer a continuous learning environment
- Empower associates to the fullest extent with accountability
- Offer equal opportunity for career growth and advancement
- Provide rewards and opportunities which recognize associate contributions
- Develop a global view of customers, consumers, vendors, and opportunities

For our communities and governments, we will strive to:
- Support the economy and general welfare
- Conduct business in an ethical and responsible manner
- Encourage associates to participate actively in community affairs
- Communicate the many benefits of the free enterprise system, and
- Be a good corporate citizen

For our shareholders, we will strive to:
- Prove an attractive and consistent return on investment
- Continuously improve our people, products, processes, plans, and programs

- Optimize and utilize the full resources of Rubbermaid
- Provide superior management with depth and continuity
- Provide leadership which is proactive and demands excellence
- Balance our incremental and leap growth strategies
- Communicate financial performance effectively on a timely basis

For all our stakeholders, we will strive to:
- Ensure that every Rubbermaid associate acts with high integrity and observes our shared ethical standards

Vision and Mission

Rubbermaid's vision is to grow as a leading global business by creating the best value solutions as defined by our customers and consumers.

Our mission is to be the leading marketer under our global umbrella brands of products and services which are responsive to consumer needs and trends and make life more productive and enjoyable. We will achieve this mission by creating the best value for the consumer, commercial, and industrial markets.

We will think, plan, and manage strategically to execute a balanced combination of the following Incremental and Leap Avenues of Growth.

Incremental Avenues of Growth

- *Continuous Value Improvement*—Make today's products a better value
- *Market Penetration*—Creatively sell more current products and enter emerging distribution channels
- *Product Enhancement*—Upgrade and revitalize our current product designs and features
- *Product Line Extension*—Expand our current product lines
- *Licensing*—Leverage our strengths and those of strategic partners
- *New Products*—Add new product lines to strength current market positions

- *New Markets*—Enter new core businesses where our strengths can create leadership value positions
- *New Technology*—Aggressively apply new materials and processes to create innovative new products
- *Global Expansion*—Think and compete internationally
- *Service*—Make our products easy to buy, easy to handle, and easy to sell
- *Acquisition*—Acquire selected complementary businesses
- *Joint Venture and Alliance*—Capitalize upon synergistic expertise

Increment and Leap Avenues of Growth

- *Rubbermaid Resources*—Share all of Rubbermaid's unmatchable resources to leverage the technology and knowledge existing within the Company for growth and global competitiveness.

Objectives

Associate Objectives Are To:

- Stress open and frequent communications
- Invest consistently in growing our capabilities
- Train associates to achieve Continuous Value Improvement and Creative Innovation goals
- Create a global competitive capability
- Recognize, reinforce and reward teamwork, results and excellence

Growth Objectives Are To:

- Double sales every five years
- Maintain 33% of yearly sales from new products introduced in the previous five-year period
- Enter a new market every 12 to 18 months
- Attain more than 30 percent of sales outside the United States by the year 2000
- Create leading destination brands worldwide

Profit Objectives Are To:

- Double earnings per share every five years
- Achieve a 13.5% return on assets employed
- Improve our value position by $335 million by 1998
- Utilize profits for people and productivity improvement, growth, and dividends

Leadership Objectives Are To:

- Achieve and maintain the leading value position
- Create compelling competitive advantages in each marketing mix element
- Be proactive on environmental and safety issues
- Embrace the process of change and make it an integral part of the corporate culture
- Be recognized for excellence by customers, suppliers, the media, governments, communities, financial constituencies, and our associates.

Technological Objectives Are To:

- Utilize the basic and applied research and technology capabilities of supplier partners
- Enhance our applied research capabilities
- Encourage experimentation and learning by all associates
- Use common global management information systems as a competitive advantage.

Competency Objectives Are To:

- Recognize and strengthen the core competencies of:
  —Corporate associates
  —Division associates
  —Centralized capabilities
  —Business teams
  —Project, process, partner, and self-directed teams

Shareholder Objectives Are To:

- Consistently create wealth on a sustainable long-term basis
- Deliver a superior 20% return on equity
- Communicate the Company's performance clearly and in a timely fashion

© 1994 Rubbermaid Incorporated

CORPORATE DESCRIPTION

Rubbermaid produces plastic products for consumer, institutional, office products, agricultural, and industrial markets.

ADDRESS   1147 Akron Rd.
P.O. Box 6000
Wooster, OH 44691-6000

INDUSTRY CATEGORY   Consumer Goods and Services

◆   ◆   ◆   ◆   ◆   ◆   ◆

Ryder System, Inc.

STATEMENT | **Ryder's Vision Statement**

Ryder will serve its customers with the best value in logistics and transportation solutions around the world or around the corner.

CORPORATE DESCRIPTION

Ryder System is an international company which provides highway transportation services throughout the United States and in Canada, Puerto Rico, the United Kingdom, Germany and Poland.

ADDRESS   3600 N.W. 82 Ave.
Miami, FL 33166

INDUSTRY CATEGORY   Transportation

◆   ◆   ◆   ◆   ◆   ◆   ◆

Rykoff-Sexton, Inc.

STATEMENT | **Mission Statement**

- Be the leader in our industry by providing the finest people, products and services.
- Assist our customers to be successful by building long-term business relationships through our people, proven quality products, demonstrated integrity and superior service.
- Have a business environment, based on sincerity of purpose, for all of our people that provides opportunity for growth and advancement as a reward for excellence and individual accomplishments.
- Achieve for our shareholders a premium return on investment through optimal utilization of capital and human resources.
- Continue our tradition: All who come here to trade fairly, whether to buy or to sell, are always welcome.

CORPORATE DESCRIPTION

Established in 1911, Rykoff-Sexton, Inc. is a leading manufacturer and distributor of high quality foods and related non-food products and services for the food service industry throughout the United States.

The Company's products and services are sold wherever food is prepared and consumed away from home. Customers include restaurants, industrial cafeterias, health care facilities, schools and colleges, hotels, airlines, membership warehouse stores and other segments of the travel and leisure markets.

ADDRESS   761 Terminal St.
Los Angeles, CA 90021

INDUSTRY CATEGORY   Food/Beverage

◆ ◆ ◆ ◆ ◆ ◆ ◆

Safety-Kleen Corporation

STATEMENT | **Corporate Mission**

"To maximize the value of the Company's unique marketing, distribution, and recycling capabilities by becoming the world's leading specialty reclaimer of hazardous and quasi-hazardous automotive and industrial fluids, with primary emphasis on serving the needs of the small quantity generator of these fluids."

CORPORATE DESCRIPTION

Safety-Kleen is the world's largest recycler of automotive and industrial hazardous and non-hazardous fluids. The Company provides safe and environmentally responsible services that are targeted primarily at small quantity generators of such fluids. The Company collects, processes and recovers contaminated fluids for reuse, or use in another manner that is in harmony with the environment.

[*Author's note:* Safety-Kleen provided the following statement.]

"The mission statement was issued in 1987 when the company was almost exclusively a parts cleaner service company. The company's mission statement became the strategic focal point for subsequent action. Five years later, in 1992, Safety-Kleen achieved its stated mission. Our company has continued to build on this position in succeeding years."

ADDRESS   1000 Randall Rd.
                Elgin, IL 60123

INDUSTRY CATEGORY   Industrial, Specialized

◆   ◆   ◆   ◆   ◆   ◆   ◆

Sanwa Bank

**Sanwa Bank California
Vision Statement**

"The Best Quality Bank in the U.S."

The main objective of Sanwa Bank California is to become among the best-quality banks in the U.S.:

♦ To demonstrate superior financial and management practices
♦ To embody the highest standards of quality
♦ To be a firm our peers want to emulate
♦ To have employees proud to be a "SanwaBanker"
♦ To have the public express "I want a Sanwa . . . [relationship]"

While these goals won't be achieved easily or quickly, they reflect the breadth of the strides we intend and the depth of our commitment. We won't be an "also ran" in what we do and therefore cannot do everything. We can be the best at providing relationship-oriented financial services primarily among small- to medium-sized commercial and retail customers in selected markets.

We will be measured against top-quality peers on common standards of profitability, efficiency and loan quality. We will achieve distinction through the QUALITY of our organization and the services provided, the UNIQUENESS of our approach to meeting financial needs and the TEAMWORK that guides our diverse staff of winning people.

QUALITY

We will portray an image of high quality while building strength in markets where we are now represented by:

♦ Improving sustainable returns to our shareholders
♦ Being customer-needs focused and customer driven
♦ Concentrating on markets where we have competence
♦ Leveraging our international affiliations to become known in the Western U.S. as the premier Pacific Rim bank
♦ Either strengthening or exiting areas of weakness

The heart of our quality will be our winning people and the professional manner in which they represent the bank.

To support this, we will:

♦ Invest in the development of our people to assure they are top quality
♦ Encourage, expect and reward excellence of conduct, performance and business production
♦ Encourage creativity
♦ Not accept individual performance which reflects poorly on the bank or inhibits bank performance

Investment in technology will be made to enable us to excel at managing information vital to our business success and quality customer service.

UNIQUENESS

We will not be limited by perceptions of what is traditional in banking. We will:

♦ Chart innovative paths to success that differentiate us
♦ Strive to be unique in the ways we do business

We will build strength in both our retail and commercial banking capabilities.

We envision:

♦ Being a first-tier regional bank that stays close to and responsive to its customers
♦ Being relationship-oriented in our style and quality of service, combined with the strength of one of the largest banks in the world
♦ Actively supporting the communities we serve
♦ Positioning ourselves as the No. 1 alternative to mega-banks

TEAMWORK

We benefit from a diversity of talents and viewpoints that will be united to build a winning team.

Open communication, sharing of ideas and mutual support will be hallmarks of our management style.

While our Parent provides us with the pride of worldwide strength, the Sanwa Team is self-sufficient and our success will be self-determined.

CORPORATE DESCRIPTION

Sanwa Bank California is the largest overseas subsidiary of The Sanwa Bank, Limited. With $7.3 billion in assets, Sanwa Bank is the sixth largest and one of the best capitalized banks in the state. Sanwa offers both quality service and strength for businesses and consumers in over 100 communities from Sacramento to San Diego.

ADDRESS   601 S. Figuero St.
Los Angeles, CA 90017

INDUSTRY CATEGORY   Banking

◆　◆　◆　◆　◆　◆　◆

SAS Institute Inc.

STATEMENT | **Our Mission and Philosophy**

SAS Institute develops and maintains the SAS Systems for Information Delivery, the world's leading integrated system of hardware-independent software, as well as other software products. Our primary goal is to help the organizations we serve—in business, industry, education, and governments—become the beneficiaries of advanced technology by providing software and services to help them meet their organizational goals. To this end, we are dedicated to:

◆ providing the most capable and reliable software in the industry

◆ devoting a significant portion of our human and financial resources to research and development

◆ establishing an uncommon commitment to customer service and support through a continuous dialogue with our worldwide community of users

◆ attracting and retaining the most talented people in the industry by providing the highest quality work environment where productivity, creativity, and personal and professional growth can flourish.

CORPORATE DESCRIPTION

Incorporated in 1976, SAS Institute is one of the world's largest independent software companies. The Institute is devoted to the development, support and maintenance of its software and related services. The Institute's flagship product—the SAS® System—is an integrated suite of software for enterprise-wide information delivery.

ADDRESS   SAS Campus Dr.
Cary, NC 27513

INDUSTRY CATEGORY   High Technology

◆   ◆   ◆   ◆   ◆   ◆   ◆

Saturn Corporation

STATEMENT | **The Saturn Mission Statement**

To market vehicles developed and manufactured in the United States that are world leaders in quality, cost and customer enthusiasm through the integration of people, technology and business systems, and to exchange knowledge, technology and experience through General Motors.

| **Our Philosophy**

We, the Saturn Team, in concert with the UAW and General Motors, believe that meeting the needs of Customers, Saturn Team Members, Suppliers, Retailers and Neighbors is fundamental to fulfilling our mission.

| **Shared Values**

We at Saturn are committed to being one of the world's most successful car companies by adhering to the following values: commitment to customer enthusiasm, commitment to excel, teamwork, trust and respect for the individual, and continuous improvement.

CORPORATE DESCRIPTION

Saturn Corporation is a wholly owned subsidiary of General Motors Corporation and manufactures automobiles under the Saturn name.

ADDRESS   100 Saturn Pkwy.
Spring Hill, TN 37174

INDUSTRY CATEGORY   Motor Vehicles and Related

◆ ◆ ◆ ◆ ◆ ◆ ◆

Savannah Foods & Industries, Inc.

STATEMENT | **Savannah Foods' Vision Statement**

Savannah Foods' vision is to strive for excellence in products, service, and profitability through honesty, integrity, respect for the individual and concern for those we serve.

CORPORATE DESCRIPTION

Savannah Foods & Industries, Inc., one of the nation's largest refined cane and beet sugar producers, markets products primarily in the eastern half of the United States under the labels Dixie Crystals®, Evercane®, Colonial®, and Pioneer®, as well as private and control labels.

Savannah Foods operates cane sugar refineries in Georgia, Florida, and Louisiana, four sugar beet processing plants in Michigan, a sugar beet processing plant in Ohio, and a raw sugar mill in Louisiana.

ADDRESS   2 E. Bryan St.
P.O. Box 339
Savannah, GA 31402-0339

INDUSTRY CATEGORY   Food/Beverage

◆ ◆ ◆ ◆ ◆ ◆ ◆

Schwab (The Charles Schwab Corporation)

STATEMENT | **The Mission Statement For Our Company**

Our mission as a company is to serve the needs of investors. We have all kinds of customers: individuals, professional money managers, companies and their employees. We know our customers have many different needs in meeting their own financial goals. We will focus our resources on the financial services that best meet our customers' needs, whether they are transactional, informational, custodial services, or something new. We will strive to deliver to our customers:

- High quality, reliable, ethical products and services at a fair price,
- Superior service from the best team of trained, motivated and ethical employees, supported by the best technology,
- A strong company, financially viable under any circumstance.

CORPORATE DESCRIPTION

The Charles Schwab Corporation provides financial services for more than 2 million investors with $66 billion in assets.

ADDRESS   101 Montgomery St.
San Francisco, CA 94104

INDUSTRY CATEGORY   Financial Investment Services

♦ ♦ ♦ ♦ ♦ ♦ ♦

Scripps (The E.W. Scripps Company)

STATEMENT | **Mission**

The Company aims at excellence in the products and services it produces and responsible service to the communities in which it operates. Its purpose is to engage in successful, growing enterprises in the fields of information and entertainment. The Company intends to expand, to develop and acquire new products and services and to pursue new market opportunities. Its focus shall be long-term growth for the benefit of its stockholders and employees.

CORPORATE DESCRIPTION

The E.W. Scripps Company is a diversified media company that operates 19 daily newspapers with aggressive circulation of 1.3 million daily and 1.4 million Sunday, 9 television stations, and cable television systems in 10 states with 718,000 basic subscribers. Through its emerging entertainment division, the Company operates 2 television production companies, a 24-hour cable channel (The Home & Garden Television Network), and United Media, a worldwide syndicator and licensor of newspaper features and comics.

ADDRESS   P.O. Box 5380
Cincinnati, OH 45201

INDUSTRY CATEGORY   Media

◆   ◆   ◆   ◆   ◆   ◆   ◆

Sensormatic

Our mission is to strengthen our position as the world leader in the design, production, marketing, sales, and servicing of electronic loss prevention systems for the retail industry. It is also our mission to become a leading worldwide provider of electronic loss prevention and asset control systems for the commercial and industrial marketplace and a significant supplier of electronic loss prevention systems to government agencies. Our mission will be achieved by providing superior customer service and unique, high quality products which will enhance customer productivity and profitability. Our products will be designed and manufactured at the lowest cost, consistent with our customers' needs and requirements.

We will accomplish this mission while attaining superior profitability which will fund our continued rapid growth.

We are committed to maintain the Sensormatic culture of dedicated, spirited and ethical performance while fulfilling our responsibilities to:

- Serve our <u>customers</u> well, driven by the need to stay close to, anticipate, listen and respond to their changing requirements while providing products and services of superior quality.
- Serve our <u>shareholders</u> by preserving and building the value of the shareholders' investment.
- Serve our <u>employees</u> by creating an environment where they can contribute, learn, grow and advance based on merit.
- Serve the business, social and cultural needs of the <u>communities</u> in which we operate.

CORPORATE DESCRIPTION

Sensormatic is a fully integrated market-driven company which develops, manufactures, sells, and services electronic security systems on a worldwide basis to the retail, commercial and industrial markets.

◆   ◆   ◆   ◆   ◆   ◆   ◆

Shaklee U.S., Inc.

STATEMENT | **Mission**

To be a highly visible, scientifically supported health and wellness company that enables all people to own their lives, make a positive difference in the world and earn the respect of customers and communities

| **Vision**

Shaklee Corporation is a values based, innovative, global marketing company driven by passionate leadership throughout the enterprise that provides the opportunity for individuals to take control and improve the quality of their lives

CORPORATE DESCRIPTION

Founded in 1956 and headquartered in San Francisco, Shaklee Corporation is a diversified consumer products company with multilevel marketing, research and technology development and contract manufacturing under the Shaklee name. The Shaklee Companies include Shaklee North America, Shaklee International and Shaklee Technica. Yamanouchi Shaklee Pharma is a division of Shaklee Corporation focused on developing new, novel drug delivery technologies. Bear Creek Corporation is a subsidiary with direct mail, wholesale, and retail store operations.

ADDRESS   Shaklee Terraces
44 Market St.
San Francisco, CA 94111

INDUSTRY CATEGORY   Consumer Goods and Services

◆   ◆   ◆   ◆   ◆   ◆   ◆

Shell Chemical Company

STATEMENT | **Shell Chemical Company's Mission Statement**

Shell Chemical Company's mission is to be a leading chemical company by:

- Growing with our customers as their preferred supplier.
- Utilizing and building the skills and creativity of our people.
- Building on our strengths in markets, technology and feedstocks.

CORPORATE DESCRIPTION

Shell Chemical Company is a fully integrated manufacturer and supplier of basic industrial chemicals and performance products.

ADDRESS   One Shell Plaza
P.O. Box 2463
Houston, TX 77252

INDUSTRY CATEGORY   Oil and Gas

◆ ◆ ◆ ◆ ◆ ◆ ◆

SkyWest Airlines, Inc.

STATEMENT | **The New SkyWest Airlines Vision**

To provide airline service that exceeds our customers' expectations.

| **Dedicated to Excellence**

Each of us is dedicated to excellence in the air transportation system.
We are dedicated to:

- Safety first
- On-time every time
- Fairness and consistency in everything we do
- Working together as a team
- Personal and corporate integrity
- Maintaining profitability

CORPORATE DESCRIPTION

SkyWest Airlines, a large regional airline operating as a Delta Connection carrier, offers scheduled passenger and cargo air service to 42 cities in nine western states and completes over 500 flights daily.

In 1987, SkyWest became a Delta Connection carrier and continues its affiliation with Delta Air Lines at hubs in Los Angeles and Salt Lake City. On October 1, 1997, SkyWest began its affiliation with United Airlines and serves United hubs at Seattle/Tacoma, Portland, San Francisco, and Los Angeles. SkyWest is the nation's eighth largest regional airline.

ADDRESS   444 S. River Rd.
St. George, UT 84770

INDUSTRY CATEGORY   Transportation

◆   ◆   ◆   ◆   ◆   ◆   ◆

Sonoco Products Company

STATEMENT | **Mission Statement**

We will be a customer-focused, global packaging leader, recognized for superior quality and high-performance results. Integrity and a commitment to excellence will be the hallmarks of our culture.

CORPORATE DESCRIPTION

Sonoco is a major packaging manufacturer serving a wide variety of consumer and industrial markets with containers and carriers made from paper, plastic, metal and wood. Sonoco has a high degree of vertical integration, producing most of its adhesives, paperboard and paper converting machinery.

ADDRESS   P.O. Box 160
N. Second St.
Hartsville, SC 29550-0160

INDUSTRY CATEGORY   Manufacturing

◆   ◆   ◆   ◆   ◆   ◆   ◆

Southern California Edison Company

STATEMENT | **Vision and Values**

Our Vision

We will be a great company that provides business and regional leadership.
Business Leadership: We will set the national standard of performance among utilities. We will provide our customers cost-competitive, reliable electricity; energy-saving services; and creative solutions to their energy needs.

Regional Leadership: We will anticipate and address the challenges of economic competitiveness and environment quality facing our customers and communities. As a public utility, we are committed to helping Southern California prosper as an excellent place to live and do business.

Our Values

Challenge:
We will challenge ourselves to continuously improve our performance and constantly renew our understanding of our changing business.
Candor:
We will conduct ourselves with honesty, openness and integrity in all our relationships.
Commitment:
We will achieve:

- Value for our customers
- Leadership for our community and environment
- Excellence as a team
- Shared purpose with regulators, and
- Value for our shareholders

CORPORATE DESCRIPTION

Southern California Edison Company is the nation's second-largest electric utility, providing service to customers in Central and Southern California.

ADDRESS   P.O. Box 800
8631 Rush St.
Rosemead, CA 91770

INDUSTRY CATEGORY   Utility

♦ ♦ ♦ ♦ ♦ ♦ ♦

Southern Company

Vision Statement
Southern Beyond 2000

The Challenges We Face

The future of our company is being shaped by increasing competition and change across our industry ...

- The global marketplace is placing competitive pressures on our customers and forcing us to further reduce our costs.
- Technology is compounding these competitive pressures by driving down the cost of new generation to less than half of what it used to be.
- Power marketers are pushing hard for more competition. Multiple players—including Southern Company—are flooding this market in anticipation of new markets opening up.
- Wholesale rates are being driven down by wholesale transmission access and numerous new suppliers.
- Federal regulators are advocating a sweeping restructuring of our industry. Members of Congress are calling for market competition. And over 80 percent of all states are considering retail competition.
- Retail access may or may not be inevitable, but we must plan as if it is. Clearly, competition at the retail level will accelerate. Just the threat of retail access has unleashed forces that will have a far-reaching impact on our markets, competitive position, and structure.
- All customer groups are demanding more choices, greater control over their energy use and costs, and new energy services and products.
- Even without competition, the growth potential of our core business is limited by economic factors and slower growth in energy use.

... Despite the challenges, we have more influence on the future success of our company than any other force. So we are embarking on a course to ensure our success today and into the 21st century, a course that will stamp us as ...

America's Best Diversified Utility

What does that mean?

It means that our target is not limited to just the Southeast—that we truly intend to be "America's Best." It also means we will be involved in areas beyond our traditional business. We will not attempt things we are not qualified to do. But we will diversify geographically—even beyond the United States, as we have already shown. And we can enter certain other utility businesses in which we have expertise.

Clearly, we will remain a utility. Specifically, we will be in four major businesses:

♦ The core business—our electric operating companies.
♦ The international electric power business.
♦ The domestic power generation and power marketing businesses.
♦ Major new business lines we choose to enter—future utility business units.

What are our strategies?

The core business will continue to be our dominant business for the foreseeable future, although it will be threatened by additional competitors. We will defend this market by continuing to drive down costs and drive up customer satisfaction. We will maintain and increase our market share through price leadership.

While defending our core business, we will seek growth through our non-core business. Internationally, we will continue to seek attractive projects with superior financial results.

Domestically, we will offset the challenges to our core business by aggressively seeking new markets that evolve with changing regulation.

We will explore major new utility business opportunities. Expansion of our core business and expansion into other utility services will provide a growth opportunity for us.

Goals for Success

Our Bold Aggressive Goal (BAG)

+ To be America's Best Diversified Utility

Measuring the BAG will be simple; the financial markets do it every day. We will be successful if an investment in Southern Company is better than an investment in any other electric utility. In other words, any time in the future, $1,000 of Southern Company stock should have cost less than $1,000 of stock of any other electric utility—no matter when it was purchased.

Our Big Intermediate Goals (BIGs)

We intend to be in the best quartile of all meaningful measures—with a view toward the top—but in order to reach our ultimate objective, we must achieve major goals along the way. These will be our mileposts on the pathway to becoming America's Best:

+ Achieve a kilowatt-hour cost that is at or below the competitive market price.
+ Reduce overhead costs by 20 percent by 1998.
+ Grow revenue in the core business while maintaining competitive pricing.
+ Generate positive cash flow—above capital expenditures and dividend requirements.
+ Be the No. 1 power marketer in the Southeast by 1998. Be among the top 10 power marketers nationally by 1997 and among the top 5 nationally by 2003.
+ Generate 30 percent of the company's net income from non-core businesses by 2003, earning a higher ROE than in the core business.
+ Grow earnings per share an average of 5 percent to 6 percent annually.
+ Rank in the best quartile of top companies as a "great place to work."

Southern Style

Our people are our company. We will be recognized by the actions of our people. Our successful people exhibit these behaviors and model these values, which are The Southern Style of doing things.

Ethical Behavior
- ♦ We tell the truth.
- ♦ We keep our promises.
- ♦ We deal fairly with everyone.

Consumer First
Our business is customer satisfaction. We will think like customers …

Shareholder Value
… and act like owners. We work to increase the value of our investment.

Great Place to Work
We are a first-name company. We enjoy our work and celebrate our successes. We seek opportunities to learn. We do not compromise safety and health.

Teamwork
We communicate openly and value honesty. We listen. We respect all opinions and expect differing viewpoints as we work together toward common goals. We emphasize cooperation—not turf.

Superior Performance
We continue to set high goals for ourselves. We take personal responsibility for success. We act with speed, decisiveness, and individual initiative to solve problems. We use change as a competitive advantage.

Citizenship
We are committed to the environment and to the communities we serve.

CORPORATE DESCRIPTION

The Southern Company is the parent firm of one of the nation's largest investor-owned electric utility groups. The company includes five utilities—Alabama Power, Georgia Power, Gulf Power, Mississippi Power, and Savannah Electric—as well as Southern Company Services, Southern Electric International, and Southern Nuclear.

The Southern Company supplies energy to customers in most of Alabama and Georgia, the panhandle of Florida, and Southeastern Mississippi.

ADDRESS   64 Perimeter Center East
Atlanta, GA 30346-6401

INDUSTRY CATEGORY   Utility

◆ ◆ ◆ ◆ ◆ ◆ ◆

SouthTrust Corporation

STATEMENT | **SouthTrust Corporation Mission Statement**

As a high-performing Southeastern regional bank holding company, our mission is to offer banking and specialized financial services to customers found in select geographic markets and market segments. To attain a superior return for our shareholders through quality earnings growth, we will distinguish ourselves by our excellence in—

◆ Customer Service
◆ Employee and Team Performance
◆ Risk Management
◆ Local Leadership
◆ Business Ethics and
◆ Community Involvement

CORPORATE DESCRIPTION

SouthTrust Corporation, a multibank holding company with headquarters in Birmingham, Alabama, currently owns 40 banks and several bank-related affiliates in Alabama, Florida, Georgia, North Carolina, South Carolina, and Tennessee. The banks serve their customers from 400 offices located throughout the six-state area.

ADDRESS   P.O. Box 2554
Birmingham, AL 35290

INDUSTRY CATEGORY   Banking

◆ ◆ ◆ ◆ ◆ ◆ ◆

Southwest Airlines Co.

STATEMENT | **The Mission of Southwest Airlines**

The mission of Southwest Airlines is dedication to the highest quality of Customer Service delivered with a sense of warmth, friendliness, individual pride, and company Spirit.

To Our Employees

We are committed to provide our employees a stable work environment with equal opportunity for learning and personal growth. Creativity and innovation are encouraged for improving the effectiveness of Southwest Airlines. Above all, employees will be provided the same concern, respect, and caring attitude within the organization that they are expected to share externally with every Southwest Customer.

(January 1998)

CORPORATE DESCRIPTION

Southwest Airlines Co. is the nation's low fair, high Customer Satisfaction airline. It primarily serves shorthaul city pairs, providing single class air transportation, which targets the business commuter as well as leisure travelers. The Company, incorporated in Texas, commenced Customer Service on June 18, 1971 with three Boeing 737 aircraft serving three Texas cities—Dallas, Houston, and San Antonio. At year end 1993, Southwest, together with newly acquired Morris Air, operated 178 Boeing 737 aircraft and provided service to 52 airports in 51 cities principally in the midwestern, southwestern, and western regions of the United States.

ADDRESS   P.O. Box 36611
Dallas, TX 75235-1611

INDUSTRY CATEGORY   Transportation

◆ ◆ ◆ ◆ ◆ ◆ ◆

SpaceLabs Medical, Inc.

In business, success is best attained when there is commonality of purpose. SpaceLabs Medical is committed to accomplishing our mission guided by a framework of shared principles.

Mission Statement

SpaceLabs Medical's mission is to be the leading worldwide provider of quality, cost-effective systems that gather, analyze, and present clinical information beneficial to the delivery of healthcare.

Corporate Values

Respect for individuals and development of their potential
Excellence in product quality and customer service
The importance of innovation
The spirit of persistence and entrepreneurism
The power of teamwork
The importance of ethical behavior
Sound financial performance
The urgency of today and the promise of the future

Operating Philosophy

Understand and support SpaceLabs Medical's mission, priorities, and Corporate Values
Set clear objectives, plan well, prioritize, measure progress, reassess as needed
Practice systematic and continuous improvement to be the best at what we do
Align personal career objectives with the long-term needs of the corporation
Accept responsibility, admit mistakes, learn, and improve as a result
Manage financial resources in the best interest of the corporation
Reduce politics, bureaucracy, and gamesmanship
Emphasize fundamentals—keep it simple
Have fun

CORPORATE DESCRIPTION

SpaceLabs Medical is a leading worldwide supplier of patient monitoring equipment and clinical information systems.

ADDRESS   15220 N.E. 40th St.
P.O. Box 97017
Redmond, WA 98073-9713

INDUSTRY CATEGORY   Medical Products and Services

◆ ◆ ◆ ◆ ◆ ◆ ◆

Sprint

STATEMENT | **Vision and Values**

| **VISION**

To be a world-class telecommunications company—the standard by which others are measured

| **GOALS**

Exceptional customer satisfaction
Inspired, innovative and empowered employees
Superior financial results

| **VALUES**

Customer first
Integrity in all we do
Excellence through quality
Respect for each other
Growth through change
Community commitment
Productive work environment
Representative work force
Shareholder value

CORPORATE DESCRIPTION

Sprint serves consumers, businesses and telecom carriers with a wide array of voice, video and data services across local, long distance, wireless, international, Internet and paging markets.

ADDRESS   2330 Shawnee Mission Pkwy.
Westwood, KS 66205

INDUSTRY CATEGORY   Communications and Telecommunications

◆ ◆ ◆ ◆ ◆ ◆ ◆

St. Paul Bancorp, Inc.

STATEMENT | **Our Mission**

At St. Paul Bancorp, Inc. our mission is to provide quality, innovative, and competitive consumer financial products and services to our customers and the community we serve. We believe that our success is rooted in sound business practices coupled with respect and responsiveness to our customers, stockholders, employees and communities.

In support of this, we are committed to:

—Understand and respond to the financial needs of our customers and provide them with a variety of financial products to help realize their life's visions and dreams;

—Provide our stockholders with maximum value achieved through a steady focus on profitability and financial strength principally through the investment of our customers' deposits in quality real estate mortgages;

—Provide an equal opportunity for all employees to contribute to the bank in an environment which links pay and advancement to performance and accomplishments;

—Maintain an active partnership with our neighborhoods, characterized by a sensitivity to their housing, credit and savings needs, and the understanding that contributing to the community's well-being is vital to our future.

CORPORATE DESCRIPTION

St. Paul Bancorp, Inc. is the holding company for St. Paul Federal Bank For Savings, the largest independent Illinois-based thrift. Founded in 1889, St. Paul Federal offers a complete range of checking, savings, mortgage and consumer loan products and services through 52 offices in metropolitan Chicago.

ADDRESS   6700 W. North Ave.
Chicago, IL 60635

INDUSTRY CATEGORY   Banking

◆   ◆   ◆   ◆   ◆   ◆   ◆

Sta-Rite Industries

STATEMENT | **Sta-Rite Mission Statement**

Sta-Rite will be a leading innovative provider of water moving and improving equipment in the world. We will act aggressively to profitably grow our business, satisfy our customers and responsively meet the needs of our employees and the communities in which we do business.

(Water Systems Group Vision)

| **Our Vision**

Profitably grow in the defined markets by increasing market share, introducing new products, and acquiring complementary product lines. It is our goal to be a global leader in our defined markets. We will be market-driven focusing on the following areas:
PRODUCT PERFORMANCE
CUSTOMER SUPPORT
TECHNICAL SUPPORT/SERVICE
We will gain competitive advantage by building on existing strengths and developing new competencies. We will be the best-cost manufacturer.

CORPORATE DESCRIPTION

Sta-Rite, headquartered in Delavan, Wisconsin, is a leading world-wide manufacturer of pumps and water processing equipment serving agricultural, residential and industrial markets. Its products are sold in 110 countries.

ADDRESS   293 Wright St.
Delavan, WI 53115

INDUSTRY CATEGORY   Manufacturing

◆   ◆   ◆   ◆   ◆   ◆   ◆

The Standard Register Company

STATEMENT | **the Mission**

A Commitment to Excellence

Standard Register's Forms Division serves the information and transactional needs of business with superior quality printed and associated products and services at a fair price.

We are a people-oriented, customer-focused organization:

—Committed to providing exceptional service to our customers.

—Committed to sustaining growth over the long term.

—Committed to showing appreciation to our dedicated employees.

—Committed to encouraging a free flow of information and an open style of management with emphasis on the team concept.

—Committed to contributing to the communities in which we operate.

—Committed to supporting and expanding on environmentally acceptable programs.

—Committed to providing an acceptable return for our corporate shareholders.

Standard Register's vision is to be a customer-driven organization whose primary direction is to serve the information and transactional needs of business, focused on key market segments.

It is our purpose to increase revenues and profits by providing high quality, value-desired products and services through innovation and technological development.

Key to the achievement of the Company's growth plans and strategies is the Standard Register employee, who through his or her daily commitment to quality work and customer services, makes our vision a reality.

CORPORATE DESCRIPTION

Standard Register serves the information and transaction needs of its customers as a leading provider of business forms, pressure sensitive labels, business equipment and systems, direct marketing materials and materials management software.

ADDRESS   600 Albany St.
Dayton, OH 45408

INDUSTRY CATEGORY   Business Products

◆　◆　◆　◆　◆　◆　◆

Staples

STATEMENT | **Core Values: C.A.R.E. (Customers, Associates, Real Communications and Execution)**

Customers

Value every customer

- Strive to exceed our customers' expectations (internal and external)
- Provide a courteous and efficient shopping experience
- Sell the Staples way: engage, qualify, close
- Remember, without customers, we have nothing
- Empower associates to satisfy their customers by moving decision-making close to the customer, whenever it makes sense to do so

Associates

Support as valuable resource

- Attract and retain the very best associates
- Develop our associates' skills so they can grow with the company
- Celebrate the individual and team successes
- Treat associates with respect, offering them attractive rewards and flexibility, to keep them in our family for a long time
- Conduct all affairs with integrity and openness
- Create a diverse, motivating, rewarding, and safe environment

Real Communications

Share information with people when they need it

- Keep associates informed of their job responsibilities, how well they are doing, how well the company is doing, where the company is headed, and how they can help
- Explain the reasoning behind decisions
- Meet regularly with associates in the work group
- Engage in honest, concise communications

Execution

Achieve our business goals

- Generate dynamic growth in sales and earnings, while producing a great return on capital
- Fulfill our commitments and deliver the numbers
- Find innovative ways to serve our customers, taking intelligent risks as we do so
- Be cost-effective in everything we do
- Embrace change and new ideas, and share in the passion of doing great things
- Foster teamwork
- Have a bias toward action, recognizing speed is critical for competitiveness; this may lead to occasional mistakes, which we own up to and learn from
- Hold ourselves accountable for quality results
- Invest in technology to allow our associates to better satisfy their customers

CORPORATE DESCRIPTION

Staples is a $6 billion retailer of office supplies, furniture and technology to consumers and business from home based businesses to *Fortune* 50 companies in the United States, Canada, the United Kingdom and Germany. Headquartered outside Boston, Staples invented the office superstore concept and today is the largest operator of office superstores in the world. The Company has over 37,000 employees serving customers through more than 900 office superstores, mail order catalogs, e-commerce and contract business.

ADDRESS   1 Research Dr.
Westborough, MA 01581

INDUSTRY CATEGORY   Business Products

♦   ♦   ♦   ♦   ♦   ♦   ♦

State Auto Insurance Companies

STATEMENT | **Mission Statement**

Your Company's mission is to excel by providing a strong and stable insurance market and overwhelming service to its customers, both policyholders and agents.

We believe that regardless of the insurance industry cycles, responsible pricing and underwriting will bring about profit, consistent growth and opportunities for shareholders, agents, employees and policyholders.

CORPORATE DESCRIPTION

State Auto Financial Corporation is a holding company located in Columbus, Ohio. The company and its subsidiaries are affiliated with State Automobile Mutual Insurance Company, which owns 68% of the Company's common shares.

State Auto Property and Casualty (P&C) Insurance Company produces more than 99% of the revenues of State Auto Financial. Stateco, Inc., a premium finance subsidiary, produces nominal revenues, and State Auto National Insurance Company, a specialty insurer, is a new company that began insurance operations in 1992. State Auto Life Insurance Company has no effect on State Auto Financial's earnings.

ADDRESS   518 E. Broad St.
Columbus, OH 43216

INDUSTRY CATEGORY   Insurance

◆   ◆   ◆   ◆   ◆   ◆   ◆

Stride Rite Corporation

The Stride Rite we will create builds on the foundation we have inherited, affirms the best of our Company's traditions and makes our policies and practices consistent with our principles.

Our goal is to sustain responsible financial success by achieving superior profitability. To accomplish this, we will build a Company where associates are proud and committed, and where all have an opportunity to contribute, learn, grow and advance based on merit. Associates will be respected, treated fairly, heard, involved and challenged. Above all, we want satisfaction from accomplishments, balanced personal and professional lives, to support the community, and to have fun in our endeavors.

We will make these goals a reality by being committed to new behaviors such as:

♦ Diversity: Valuing a diverse workforce and diversity in experience and perspectives. Diversity will be valued and honesty rewarded.

♦ Recognition: Recognizing individual and team contributions to our success. Recognition will be given to all who contribute—those who create and innovate as well as those who support the day-to-day business requirements.

♦ Ethical Management Practices: Behaving in a manner consistent with the Company's high standards for business ethics, enforced throughout the Corporation.

♦ Communication: Clarity regarding Company, divisional and individual goals. Associates will know what is expected and will receive ongoing communication that is timely, open, direct and honest.

- **Empowerment:** Increasing the authority and responsibility of those closest to our products and customers. By empowering associates and building trust, we will encourage and unleash the full capabilities of our people.
- **Risk Taking:** Encouraging and properly recognizing calculated risk-taking, regardless of the results. Openness to change will stimulate and support creative ideas and solutions.
- **Customer Service:** Striving for excellence with internal and external customers.
- **Career Opportunities:** Providing opportunities for career growth, where advancement within the Company becomes the normal practice, not the exception.
- **Strategic Decision Making:** Anticipating and supporting change by making decisions based on long-term strategies.
- **Continual Improvement:** Constantly striving for excellence and high standards by challenging old methods and offering creative solutions.
- **Having Fun:** While we work very hard to achieve our goals, we must not lose sight of a very important element in our lives—having fun!

By committing to these new behaviors and showing support and trust toward all members of The Stride Rite Team, we will achieve our overall goal of commercial success.

CORPORATE DESCRIPTION

The Stride Rite Corporation is the leading marketer of high quality children's footwear in the United States and is a major marketer of athletic and casual footwear for children and adults.

The Company markets children's footwear under the trademarks STRIDE RITE®️ and KEDS®️, Pro-Keds®️, SPERRY TOP-SIDER®️, GRASSHOPPERS®️, Street Hot®️, Tommy Hilfiger®️ and Nine West Kids®️.

The Company is predominantly a wholesaler of footwear, selling its products nationwide to independent retail shoe stores, department stores, sporting good stores and marinas. The Company also markets its products directly to consumers by selling children's footwear through its Stride Rite Bootery stores, Great Feet concept stores and leased operations within leading department stores.

ADDRESS   191 Spring St.
P.O. Box 9191
Lexington, MA 02420

INDUSTRY CATEGORY   Consumer Goods and Services

◆　◆　◆　◆　◆　◆　◆

The Stroh Brewery Company

STATEMENT | **Vision**

Our vision of The Stroh Brewery Company is one of a growing and prospering company with a dynamic and motivated organization providing our shareholders with a reasonable return on their investment.

| **Mission**

To achieve this vision, our mission is to produce, distribute, and market a variety of high-quality beers in a manner that meets or exceeds the expectations of our customers.

CORPORATE DESCRIPTION

The Stroh Brewery is a producer of high-quality alcoholic and non-alcoholic beverage products sold globally.

ADDRESS   100 River Pl.
Detroit, MI 48207-4291

INDUSTRY CATEGORY   Food/Beverage

◆　◆　◆　◆　◆　◆　◆

Sun Company

| **Our purpose:**

To be a source of excellence for our customers; to provide a challenging professional experience for our employees; to be a rewarding investment for our shareholders; to be a respected citizen of community and country.

| **Our values:**

Sun Company is committed to:

Profitable Growth—Seeking sustainable, profitable growth through relentless pursuit of our vision, simplicity of style, speed of action, innovation and leadership in all of our chosen business activities.

Positive Change—Embracing and capitalizing on change, recognizing that every employee must be empowered to stimulate continuous improvement in all aspects of our business.

Enthusiastic Customers—Enhancing our reputation as a company that customers can rely on to deliver products so excellent in their quality, and service so outstanding in its responsiveness, that Sun will be recognized for leadership in the marketplace.

Involved Employees—Striving for a workplace where opportunity, openness, enthusiasm, diversity, teamwork, accountability and a sense of purpose combine to provide a rewarding professional experience that promotes fairness, dignity and respect for all employees.

Confident Shareholders—Managing all parts of our business in a manner that builds value into the investment of all shareholders, confirming their confidence in participating in the ownership of this company.

Responsible Citizenship—Conducting our business with the highest standards of ethics, adherence to the law, and "doing what's right"—thereby continuing Sun's legacy of encouraging a healthy and safe workplace, responsible government, a highly competitive free enterprise system, environmental excellence and community enrichment.

CORPORATE DESCRIPTION

Sun operates six domestic refineries and markets gasoline under the Sunoco brand in 18 states from Maine to Indiana and the District of Columbia. Sun also markets under the Atlantic brand in Pennsylvania and New York State. It is converting Atlantic gasoline outlets to Sunoco. Sun sells lubricants and petrochemicals worldwide, operates domestic pipelines and terminals, and produces crude oil and natural gas internationally. Sun is 55 percent owner of Suncor, a fully integrated Canadian oil company.

ADDRESS   Ten Penn Center
1801 Market St., 27th Floor
Philadelphia, PA 19103-1699

INDUSTRY CATEGORY   Oil and Gas

◆ ◆ ◆ ◆ ◆ ◆ ◆

Sundstrand Corporation

STATEMENT | **Sundstrand Corporation Commitments**

Mission

- To satisfy the needs of selected worldwide aerospace and industrial markets by developing and manufacturing high quality, proprietary, technology-based components and subsystems and by achieving customer satisfaction.
- To serve market segments where we can either be a market leader or have a strategy to become one while achieving returns that reward shareholders and employees and permit the business to grow and prosper.

Goals

- To provide superior rewards to investors by achieving returns on equity among the top quartile of Fortune 500 manufacturing companies.

- To anticipate and fully satisfy customer needs by providing superior products utilizing appropriate advanced technology and customer service.
- To recognize that every member of the Sundstrand team is a valued individual and important contributor.
- To be a responsible Corporate citizen by being an active participant and a positive contributor both in the local community and at the national level.
- To team with strong business partners with similar philosophies and objectives.

Beliefs

- Continuously improving the way we do our jobs, managing our businesses and serving our customers.
- Having a genuine concern for cost while fulfilling all commitments and providing total value to our customers.
- Maintaining the highest level of integrity and trust in all our relationships, reflecting respect and fairness in all our actions.
- Adhering strictly to our Code of Business Conduct and Ethics.
- Managing our businesses aggressively yet prudently.
- Encouraging the personal and professional growth of each member of the Sundstrand team.
- Developing a sense of ownership and belonging in each team member through effective two-way communications.
- Fostering innovation in all business and technical activity by recognizing and rewarding superior contribution.
- Developing and maintaining relationships rather than just executing transactions.
- Providing superior quality in all things. This is our most important belief.

CORPORATE DESCRIPTION

Sundstrand Corporation is a market leader in the design, manufacture, and sale of a variety of proprietary technology-based components and subsystems requiring significant research, development engineering, and processing expertise. The business segments of the Corporation are: Industrial and Aerospace.

ADDRESS 4949 Harrison Ave.
P.O. Box 7003
Rockford, IL 61125-7003

INDUSTRY CATEGORY Aerospace

♦   ♦   ♦   ♦   ♦   ♦   ♦

SYSCO Corporation

STATEMENT

[*Author's note:* SYSCO stresses that the following is not their mission statement, but is instead their philosophy of doing business.]

The SYSCO Philosophy

The scale and scope of its operations are such that SYSCO can:
- Provide high levels of customer service;
- Buy in quantity on favorable terms;
- Retain professional marketing and merchandising personnel who possess a wide knowledge of the many different supply markets;
- Accumulate broad experience which enables the company to work with manufacturers, processors and customers to reduce operating costs;
- Assure quality and consistency of products in thousands of locations;
- Maintain minimum levels of inventory while supplying customers' needs;

- Consolidate expenses for promotions and advertising;
- Test new merchandising and marketing methods on a pilot basis;
- Provide sales aids and training tools to enable marketing associates to represent the SYSCO product line effectively; and therefore
- Undergird the success of SYSCO's customers.

Meanwhile, SYSCO's corporate structure ensures that the entrepreneurial spirit and drive is as strong in the parent company as in each of its subsidiary companies.

That spirit—a combination of personal interest, drive, creativity and determination to benefit customers—is the guiding philosophy of SYSCO Corporation, the key to its past success and to continued growth.

CORPORATE DESCRIPTION

SYSCO is the largest foodservice marketing and distribution organization in North America. Generating annual sales of excess of $15 billion, the company provides products and services to approximately 300,000 restaurants, healthcare and educational institutions, lodging establishments and other foodservice operations. The SYSCO distribution network extends throughout the entire continental United States, as well as portions of Alaska and Canada.

ADDRESS   1390 Enclave Pkwy.
Houston, TX 77077-2099

INDUSTRY CATEGORY   Food/Beverage

◆　◆　◆　◆　◆　◆　◆

Tandy Corporation (RadioShack)

| **Tandy Corporation and RadioShack Mission Statement**

"To Demystify Technology for the Mass Market"

Our people are different because we get excited about helping people understand technology. We care about our customers, whether they're in our store for a $3.00 or $300.00 purchase. Every day, we give peace of mind to thousands of people who need help from someone. We're there to solve their problems and to connect them to the wonders of modern technology. We are about people helping people. When America needs answers, we're there at every turn.

CORPORATE DESCRIPTION

Tandy Corporation is a retailer of consumer electronics and computers. The Company is best known for its 6,900+ RadioShack® stores and dealers across the U.S.

ADDRESS   100 Throckmorton St.
Fort Worth, TX 76102

INDUSTRY CATEGORY   Retail

♦ ♦ ♦ ♦ ♦ ♦ ♦

TCF Financial Corporation

- TCF believes in community banking. TCF serves primarily middle- and lower-income individuals and small to medium-sized businesses in its market areas. We believe that community banking is the most consistently profitable type of banking.

- TCF believes that community banking operates best with separate bank charters in each state with local management and boards of directors.

- TCF emphasizes those businesses that meet our return on average assets and return on average equity goals. POWER ASSETS^{SM} (consumer loans, commercial loans and leases) and POWER LIABILITIES^{SM} (checking, savings, and money market deposit accounts) produce the majority of TCF's net interest margin and fee income.

- TCF operates like a partnership, organized by function with profit center goals and objectives emphasizing return on average assets and return on average equity. We know which products are profitable and contribute to these goals. Managers are incented to increase return on average assets and return on average equity.

- TCF encourages stock ownership by our officers, directors and employees. We have a mutuality of interest with our shareholders, and our goal is to earn above-average returns for our shareholders by maximizing return on average assets and return on average equity.

- TCF believes interest rate risk should be minimized. Interest rate speculations do not generate consistent profits and are high risk.

- TCF is primarily a secured lender and emphasizes credit quality over asset growth. The costs of poor credit far outweigh the benefits of unwise asset growth.

- TCF places a high priority on the development of technology to enhance productivity, customer service, and new products. Properly applied technology reduces costs and enhances service. We centralize paper processing and decentralize the banking process.
- TCF is committed to providing extra services to broad markets through longer hours, convenient access, innovative products, and good customer relations.
- TCF encourages open employee communications. TCF promotes from within whenever possible and places the highest priority on honesty, integrity, and ethical behavior.
- TCF believes in community participation, both financially and through volunteerism. We feel a responsibility to help those less fortunate.
- TCF does not discriminate against anyone in employment or the extension of credit. As a result of TCF's community banking philosophy, we market to all the customers in our communities.

CORPORATE DESCRIPTION

TCF Financial Corporation is a stock savings bank holding company. TCF Bank operates primarily in Minnesota, Illinois, Wisconsin and Michigan. TCF affiliates include mortgage banking, title insurance, annuity, mutual fund, and consumer finance companies.

ADDRESS   801 Marquette Ave.
Minneapolis, MN 55402

INDUSTRY CATEGORY   Banking

◆ ◆ ◆ ◆ ◆ ◆ ◆

Texas Instruments

STATEMENT | **TI Vision Statement**

World leadership in digital solutions for the networked society.

| **TI Values**

Integrity
Innovation
Commitment

| **TI Principles**

We respect and value people.
We are honest.
We learn and create.
We act boldly.
We take responsibility.
We commit to win.

CORPORATE DESCRIPTION

Texas Instruments Incorporated is a global semiconductor company and the world's leading designer and supplier of Digital Signal Processing Solutions, the engines driving the digitization of electronics. The company's businesses also include materials and controls, educational productivity solutions, and digital imaging.

ADDRESS 8505 Forest Ln.
Dallas, TX 75243

INDUSTRY CATEGORY High Technology

◆ ◆ ◆ ◆ ◆ ◆ ◆

Time Warner

STATEMENT | **Mission Statement**

We strive to be the most respected and successful media company—the leader in each of our businesses—renowned for quality, excitement and performance. The soul of our success lies in bringing together exceptionally talented people, including the world's finest journalists and artists, and empowering all of us to think and act creatively.

CORPORATE DESCRIPTION

Time Warner is the world's leading media company, whose principal business objective is to create and distribute branded information and entertainment copyrights throughout the world. Time Warner classifies its business interests into four fundamental areas: Entertainment, Cable Networks (cable television programming), Publishing, and Cable (cable television systems).

ADDRESS   75 Rockerfeller Plaza
New York, NY 10019

INDUSTRY CATEGORY   Media

◆   ◆   ◆   ◆   ◆   ◆   ◆

Times Mirror Company

Our mission is to be the information partner of choice in each market we serve—helping people gain the knowledge they need to work, live and govern themselves.

Values

In accomplishing this mission, we are guided by an abiding set of values:

Adhering to the highest standards of ethics and integrity.

Exceeding our customers' expectations for editorial excellence, product quality, and service.

Fostering a creative working environment with development, openness, challenge, accountability, diversity, teamwork and respect for every colleague.

Actively contributing to the social, cultural and environmental well-being of the communities we serve.

Operating Goals

We strive to make Times Mirror an attractive investment by:

Providing superior total shareholder returns and dividend growth.

Adopting the best operating practices as judged by world standards of excellence.

Managing risk through business diversity and financial flexibility.

Making our wide array of information resources available in all desirable forms, including traditional and electronics.

CORPORATE DESCRIPTION

Times Mirror is a diversified media and information company. Its holdings include newspapers and magazines; information and educational products and services for professional markets; and cable television in 13 states.

The company publishes the *Los Angeles Times, Newsday* and *New York Newsday,* the *Baltimore Sun* newspaper, *The Hartford Courant, The Morning Call, The (Stamford) Advocate* and *Greenwich Time.*

Book publishing includes Matthew Bender law books, Mosby-Year Book medical books, journals and college texts; Wm. C. Brown Communications, Inc., science, mathematics and social science textbooks and products; Richard D. Irwin business and economics textbooks; and CRC Press scientific and technical books. Jeppesen Sanderson produces aeronautical charts and pilot training materials. Learning International Zenger-Miller, Inc. and Kaset International are in the professional training field The company also publishes Abrams art and illustrated works.

Times Mirror Magazines publishes nine special-interest magazines, two trade magazines and has a custom publishing division.

ADDRESS   Time Mirror Square
Los Angeles, CA 90053

INDUSTRY CATEGORY   Media

◆ ◆ ◆ ◆ ◆ ◆ ◆

Tootsie Roll Industries, Inc.

STATEMENT | **Corporate Principles**

We believe that the differences among companies are caused by the differences among their people, and therefore we strive to attract and retain the best people available for the job.

We believe that an open, family atmosphere at work combined with professional management fosters cooperation and enables each individual to maximize his or her contribution to the company and realize the corresponding rewards.

We do not jeopardize long-term growth for immediate, short-term results.

We view our well known brands as prized assets to be aggressively advertised and promoted to each new generation of consumers in the United States and selected foreign markets.

We run a trim operation and continually strive to eliminate waste, minimize cost and seek performance improvements.

We invest in the latest and most productive equipment to deliver the best quality product to our customers at the lowest cost.

We seek to vertically integrate operations to the greatest practical extent.

We maintain a conservative financial posture in the employment and management of our assets.

CORPORATE DESCRIPTION

Tootsie Roll Industries, Inc. has been engaged in the manufacture and sale of candy since 1896. The Company's products are primarily sold under the familiar brand names Tootsie Roll, Tootsie Roll Pops, Child's Play, Charms, Blow Pop, Blue Razz, Cella's, Mason Dots, Mason Crows, Junior Mints, Charleston Chew, Sugar Daddy and Sugar Baby.

ADDRESS   7401 S. Cicero Ave.
Chicago, IL 60629

INDUSTRY CATEGORY   Food/Beverage

◆　◆　◆　◆　◆　◆　◆

Total System Services, Inc.

STATEMENT | **TSYS® Mission Statement**

To Exceed the Expectation of Our Customers through the Delivery of Superior Service and Continuous Quality Improvement that Rewards Our Employees and Enhances the Value of Our Shareholders' Investment.

CORPORATE DESCRIPTION

Total System Services Inc.^{SM} (TSYS®) is a bankcard and private label card processing company based in Columbus, Georgia, which provides card-issuing institutions with a comprehensive on-line system of data processing services marketed as THE TOTAL SYSTEM^{SM}. It is an 80.8 percent-owned subsidiary of Synovus Financial Corp.®, a $5.6 billion multi-financial services company composed of TSYS, 31 banking affiliates in three states, and a full-service brokerage firm.

TSYS® is a federally registered service mark of Total System Services, Inc., and THE TOTAL SYSTEM^{SM} and Total System Services, Inc.^{SM}, are service marks of Total System Services, Inc. Synovus Financial Corp.® is a federally registered service mark of Synovus Financial Corp.

ADDRESS   1000 Fifth Ave.
P.O. Box 120
Columbus, GA 31902

INDUSTRY CATEGORY   Business Services

◆　◆　◆　◆　◆　◆　◆

TravelSmith

STATEMENT | **TravelSmith Mission Statement**

| **Our Business**

TravelSmith seeks to be the premier direct marketer, in the U.S. and abroad, of functional products for travelers. We offer products for travel that are lightweight, practical, packable and supremely reliable. We will be the leading authority on the needs of serious travelers and deliver a level of service that consistently exceeds their expectations.

Values

We believe travel enhances and deepens our understanding of other cultures and people and underscores our shared responsibility for the world's economic, environmental and social issues. TravelSmith is committed to creatively supporting efforts to overcome these challenges.

People

TravelSmith's people are its greatest asset. The Company will support each individual's efforts to reach his/her full potential as each contributes to the achievement of the above business goals. TravelSmith will create a productive and rewarding environment for its people in which each individual has the opportunity to build and share in the Company's success.

Value Creation

TravelSmith seeks profitable, sustainable and controlled growth as the basis for delivering superior returns and creating value for its customers.

CORPORATE DESCRIPTION

TravelSmith makes clothing for active travelers sold direct through its catalog and website.

ADDRESS   60 Leveroni Court
Novato, CA 94949

INDUSTRY CATEGORY   Consumer Goods and Services

◆　◆　◆　◆　◆　◆　◆

Tribune Company

| **Mission**

We build businesses that inform, educate and entertain our customers in the ways, places, and at the times they want. Doing so creates value for our customers, our employees and our shareholders.

| **Strategies**

We have distinct growth plans for each of our businesses, but there are certain common elements underlying how we create value in all of our businesses:

- Create premier branded content
- Build communities using multiple media in our local markets
- Apply technology imaginatively
- Encourage creativity in a diverse workplace
- Use financial resources aggressively to create shareholder value

| **Values**

We have been guided by strong values since the company's founding in 1847:

- Integrity
- Customer Satisfaction
- Innovation
- Employee Involvement
- Financial Strength
- Citizenship
- Diversity
- Teamwork

CORPORATE DESCRIPTION

Tribune is a leading information and entertainment company with businesses in 13 of the nation's largest metropolitan markets. Through the Company's print and broadcast media, it can reach more than half of U.S. households daily. Tribune publishes six daily newspapers, as well as books and information in print and digital formats. Tribune also provides editorial and advertising services to client newspapers and electronic media. Tribune's broadcasting and entertainment business operates eight independent television stations and six radio stations, produces and syndicates television and radio programming, and owns a major-league baseball team. In addition to its media business, the Company has an ownership interest in one of Canada's largest newsprint manufacturers.

ADDRESS   435 N. Michigan Ave.
Chicago, IL 60611

INDUSTRY CATEGORY   Media

♦　♦　♦　♦　♦　♦　♦

TRW Inc.

STATEMENT | **TRW Mission & Values**

Mission

TRW is a global company focused on providing superior products and services to customers in the space and defense, automotive, and information systems markets. Our mission is to achieve leadership position in these markets by serving the needs of our customers in innovative ways—by being the best in everything we do. We will create value for our shareholders by balancing short-term performance and long-term financial strength.

Customers

Customer satisfaction is essential. We will deliver superior value to our customers through quality, reliability and technology. We grow and prosper by serving the needs of our customers better than our competitors, while effectively controlling costs.

People

The men and women of TRW make our success possible. We encourage involvement and reward the contributions of each employee. We value open and honest communications. We create a workplace where every employee can share a sense of ownership for TRW's success. We provide equal opportunity in our employment and promotion practices.

Quality

Quality is important in everything we do. Quality is everyone's responsibility and is achieved through continuous improvement. We routinely seek ways to do things better.

Integrity

We pursue our business interests worldwide in a socially responsible manner. We conduct our business in accordance with the highest standards of legal and ethical conduct. We encourage every TRW employee to participate in and support community activities.

CORPORATE DESCRIPTION

TRW Inc. manufactures automotive systems, including occupant restraints, steering systems and engine components; spacecraft, electronics and defense systems; and commercial information systems.

ADDRESS   1900 Richmond Rd.
　　　　　　　Cleveland, OH 44124

INDUSTRY CATEGORY   Diversified

◆　◆　◆　◆　◆　◆　◆

Tultex Corporation

| **Tultex ... Our Values**

Trust ... Integrity ... Respect

| **Tultex ... Our Vision**

Our Mission is to provide superior returns to our Stakeholders (our Shareholders, Employees, Customers and the Communities where our people work and live).

Our Vision for these Stakeholders, toward which we will continually strive, is as follows:

SHAREHOLDERS

Shareholders would see their investment appreciate by at least 15 percent per year (a 15 percent Return on Equity).

EMPLOYEES

Employees would receive compensation that is above industry average in return for working together as an effective team. It is through teamwork that we will achieve the industry's lowest cost with the best quality and best customer service. All Tultex people would have the opportunity to participate directly in the profits, ownership and decisions of the business.

We will create, through the contribution of each of us, a quality of worklife that is recognized by the caring, openness and understanding of each other. We will create an environment that fosters the building of trust, integrity and respect among all of our employees. Work should be challenging, satisfying and rewarding. We will create a company attitude that encourages, recognizes and rewards excellence and team performance.

CUSTOMERS

Customers will receive high quality and high value products from Tultex—with service and support better than anyone else in the business. We will establish among each other a sincere feeling of pride ... in our products, our quality, our service and pride in each other and this pride will be obvious to our customers. Through building partnerships, all of us will constantly focus on delighting our customers.

COMMUNITIES

Communities of Tultex people will be made significantly better by the presence of our company as a major employer.

CORPORATE DESCRIPTION

Tultex Corporation is a vertically integrated marketer and manufacturer of quality activewear and licensed sports apparel. The company is headquartered in Martinsville, Virginia.

Tultex offers a wide range of activewear apparel products under the Tultex®, Discus Athletic®, Brittania®, and Logo7® and Logo Athletic® brand names, as well as numerous private label brands for various customers. Tultex products can be found with the Levi Strauss, Nike, Gitano and Pro Spirit label.

ADDRESS   P.O. Box 5191
Martinsville, VA 24115

INDUSTRY CATEGORY   Consumer Goods and Services

◆ ◆ ◆ ◆ ◆ ◆ ◆

The Turner Corporation

STATEMENT | **Mission Statement**

Turner will be the recognized leader in providing building construction services, both nationally and in every location in which Turner operates. We will achieve this by consistently exceeding our commitments to and the expectations of clients, design professionals, subcontractors and vendors, and the community at large. These services will be delivered by team-oriented, responsive, innovative, reliable, ethical and skilled staff who participate in a world-class training and development program and benefit from a career employment opportunity.

CORPORATE DESCRIPTION

The Turner Corporation, through Turner Construction Company and other construction subsidiaries, is the nation's leading builder. Turner provides a complete range of construction and program management services in all segments of the non-residential building market. With more than sixty percent of Turner's business coming from repeat clients, we are a recognized leader in providing quality service in diverse markets. Turner, operating through more than 34 offices, has construction projects underway throughout the United States and abroad. During 1993, The Turner Corporation completed $2.8 billion of construction.

ADDRESS   375 Hudson St.
New York, NY 10014

INDUSTRY CATEGORY   Construction

◆   ◆   ◆   ◆   ◆   ◆   ◆

Union Carbide

STATEMENT | **Corporate Mission**

♦ To grow the value of the Corporation by successfully pursuing strategies that capitalize on our business strengths in chemicals and polymers;

♦ To successfully execute wealth creation strategies that consistently deliver value to all stakeholders over the course of the business cycle.

| **Corporate Vision**

♦ Union Carbide is a leading global chemical company, focused on being the low cost and preferred supplier of chemicals and polymers in the industry segments in which we participate. We have the best olefins chain petrochemicals businesses, augmented by a related portfolio of high quality, focused performance product businesses.

♦ Our leadership is measured by our technology and cost positions, customer satisfaction, product performance, people excellence, earnings performance, and investor returns.

Corporate Value

♦ Safety and Environmental Excellence
♦ Customer Focus
♦ Technology Leadership
♦ People Excellence
♦ Simplicity and Focus

CORPORATE DESCRIPTION

Union Carbide is a basic chemicals company with many of the industry's most advanced process technologies and some of the most efficient large-scale chemical production facilities found anywhere in the world.

ADDRESS   39 Old Ridgebury Rd.
                Danbury, CT 06817-0001

INDUSTRY CATEGORY   Chemicals

♦   ♦   ♦   ♦   ♦   ♦   ♦

Union Electric

STATEMENT | **Statement of Policy**

We are a business enterprise—dependent for success on the high quality and fair price of our service; on the skill, courtesy, and loyalty of our employees; on the confidence of our investors; and on the ability of our management to forecast and provide for the energy requirements of our area.

In the conduct of our business, we will render service of the highest quality to our customers—promptly, courteously, and efficiently—at the lowest price consistent with paying fair wages and affording job satisfaction and security to our employees; providing modern facilities for our customers' expanding needs for energy service; and paying a fair return to our investors who have provided the funds to make such service possible.

As a private enterprise entrusted with an essential public service, we recognize our civic responsibility in the communities we serve. We shall strive to advance the growth and welfare of these communities and shall participate in civic activities which fulfill that goal ... for we believe this is both good citizenship and good business.

CORPORATE DESCRIPTION

Union Electric is a utility company, primarily engaged in providing energy to 1.2 million customers in the strategic center of America—a 24,500-square-mile area in Missouri and Illinois.

ADDRESS   P.O. Box 149
                 St. Louis, MO 63166

INDUSTRY CATEGORY   Utility

◆　◆　◆　◆　◆　◆　◆

Unisys Corporation

| **Our Corporate Mission**

We build long-term relationships with clients helping them creatively use information and apply technology to improve service to their customers, enhance their competitive position in the marketplace, and increase their profitability.

CORPORATE DESCRIPTION

Unisys is one of the largest providers of information services, technology, and software in the world. The Company does business in some 100 countries. About 80 percent of its revenue is derived from commercial information systems and services, with the remainder coming from electronic systems and services for the defense market. Slightly more than one-half of their revenue is from business in the United States.

Unisys specializes in providing business-critical solutions, based on open information networks, for organizations that operate in transaction-intensive environments. These organizations include financial services companies, airlines, telephone companies, government agencies, and other commercial enterprises. The Company's solutions are used by 41 of the world's 50 largest banks, 140 airlines worldwide, 35 of the world's largest telecommunications companies, and more than 1,600 governmental agencies worldwide.

ADDRESS   P.O. Box 500
Blue Bell, PA 19424-0001

INDUSTRY CATEGORY   Business Services

◆　◆　◆　◆　◆　◆　◆

United Dominion Industries

STATEMENT | **Mission**

Provide superior manufactured products, engineering and construction services through engineering-driving, market-leader businesses which serve construction and industrial markets worldwide.

CORPORATE DESCRIPTION

A community of companies, United Dominion Industries is a worldwide manufacturing, engineering and construction enterprise built on more than a century of serving a wide range of construction markets and providing superior, value-added products for industrial and commercial markets.

ADDRESS   2300 One First Union Center
301 S. College St.
Charlotte, NC 28202-6039

INDUSTRY CATEGORY   Diversified

◆   ◆   ◆   ◆   ◆   ◆   ◆

United Parcel Service

STATEMENT | **Corporate Mission and Strategy**

UPS Corporate Mission Statement

Customers

Serve the ongoing package distribution needs of our customers worldwide and provide other services that enhance customer relationships and complement our position as the foremost provider of package distribution services, offering high quality and excellent value in every service.

People
Be a well-regarded employer that is mindful of the well-being of our people, allowing them to develop their individual capabilities in an impartial, challenging, rewarding, and cooperative environment and offering them the opportunity for career advancement.

Shareowners
Maintain a financially strong, manager-owned company earning a reasonable profit, providing long-term competitive returns to our shareholders.

Communities
Build on the legacy of our company's reputation as a responsible corporate citizen whose well-being is in the public interest and whose people are respected for their performance and integrity.

UPS Corporate Strategy Statement

UPS will achieve worldwide leadership in package distribution by developing and delivering solutions that best meet our customers' distribution needs at competitive rates. To do so, we will build upon our extensive and efficient distribution network, the legacy and dedication of our people to operational and service excellence, and our commitment to anticipate and respond rapidly to changing market conditions and requirements.

CORPORATE DESCRIPTION

United Parcel Service is in the business of delivering parcels and documents worldwide.

ADDRESS   55 Glenlake Pkwy. N.E.
Atlanta, GA 30328

INDUSTRY CATEGORY   Package Delivery Service

◆ ◆ ◆ ◆ ◆ ◆ ◆

United States Fidelity and Guaranty Corporation

STATEMENT | **Vision Statement**

We aspire to build a company with a strong character of integrity and ethical conduct dedicated to providing very competitive, innovative, high quality insurance products and services to our customers.

We will secure a leadership position in our served markets and earn a superior return for our shareowners by adhering to four fundamental precepts of strategy:

- Create a performance driven culture and work environment conducive to the development and growth of our employees which enables them to exercise competitively superior skills.
- Compete only in attractive markets and businesses where we have the financial capability and market opportunity to attain a leadership position and earn acceptable return.
- Build market-driven, highly-focused businesses that provide value-added, differentiated products and services to our customers.
- Organize in a manner than best leverages people, capital, and technology.

CORPORATE DESCRIPTION

USF&G Corporation, with assets of 14.3 billion (at year-end 1993), is composed of property/casualty and life insurance subsidiaries. The principal subsidiary is United States Fidelity and Guaranty Company (USF&G Insurance), one of the nation's largest property/casualty insurers, founded in 1896. Life insurance products are written through Fidelity and Guaranty Life Insurance Company, founded in 1959. USF&G provides a wide variety of quality commercial, personal, fidelity-surety, and reinsurance products targeted to meet the diverse insurance needs of its customers.

ADDRESS   P.O. Box 1138
Baltimore, MD 21203-1138

INDUSTRY CATEGORY   Insurance

◆ ◆ ◆ ◆ ◆ ◆ ◆

The United States Shoe Corporation

STATEMENT | **The U.S. Shoe Corporation Strategy**

BUILD DOMINANT BRANDS by aggressively developing and growing winning consumer brands in well-defined retail niches.

PROVIDE LEGENDARY CUSTOMER SERVICE by achieving significantly higher customer satisfaction than competitors. Respond to customer needs by bringing preferred products to market faster than competitors.

EMPOWER ASSOCIATES by establishing a highly organized, decentralized organization that aggressively shares expertise.

ACT WITH UNCOMPROMISING INTEGRITY in all our business endeavors.

CORPORATE DESCRIPTION

The United States Shoe Corporation is a specialty retailing company operating 2,468 retail stores, outlets and leased departments in three segments: women's apparel, optical and footwear. U.S. Shoe also manufactures, imports and wholesales prominent footwear brands, primarily for women.

ADDRESS   One Eastwood Dr.
Cincinnati, OH 45227-1197

INDUSTRY CATEGORY   Retail

◆ ◆ ◆ ◆ ◆ ◆ ◆

United Vision Group

STATEMENT | **Mission Statement**

As a company and as individuals we will do our best to become a model company. We will achieve this by offering products of the highest quality at the right price with a standard of service that is rooted in our desire to serve others.

CORPORATE DESCRIPTION

United Vision Group is the parent company of the corporations that retail, manufacture, and import furniture, jewelry and fresh cut flowers. United Vision Group had 1994 sales of $33 million and 310 employees.

ADDRESS 34 State St.
Ossining, NY 10562

INDUSTRY CATEGORY Diversified

◆　◆　◆　◆　◆　◆　◆

Universal Foods Corporation

STATEMENT | **Our Vision**

Universal Foods will add value to customers' products worldwide by developing and delivering technically superior ingredients and ingredient systems for foods and other applications. Through dedication to our customers and employees, and commitment to continuous improvement and innovation, we will achieve superior quality, service and operating performance.

To drive above average earnings growth, we must:
Shift to <u>HIGHER</u> <u>GROWTH</u> Opportunities
Develop new products internally.
Make acquisitions.
Adjust product mix in existing businesses.

Provide <u>BEST</u> <u>VALUE</u> as Perceived by the Customer

Deliver operations excellence.

Add value through responsiveness to customers.

Lead in product innovation.

Capitalize on core competencies.

Establish <u>MARKET</u> <u>LEVERAGE</u>

Build similar positions outside of the U.S. to achieve #1 or #2 position in U.S. non-volatile niche markets.

Operate <u>GLOBALLY</u>

Seek opportunities worldwide.

Leverage technology and product enterprise.

<u>IMPROVE</u> Operating Margins

Target capital expenditures to boost efficiency.

Provide above-industry average spending on research and development.

Achieve low-cost operating structure.

<u>INVOLVE</u> <u>OUR</u> <u>PEOPLE</u>

Train people in skills that will allow them to make a difference in our business.

Foster teamwork and continuous improvement, The Universal Way.

Create a work environment that fosters innovation.

Our Creed

Universal Foods Corporation is committed to conducting a business enterprise which is of real and continuing value to society. This requires bringing together, in an optimal manner, shareholders, employees, suppliers, and civic resources so that customers are well served, profits are fairly earned in the competitive marketplace, investors are rewarded, employees grow in their careers, and the needs of communities are recognized by appropriate commitment of corporate time and wealth.

CORPORATE DESCRIPTION

Universal Foods is an international manufacturer and marketer of key ingredients, primarily for food processors. Key ingredients include flavors and colors, yeast products and dehydrated vegetables. The Company's divisions maintain significant market shares in their respective businesses through attention to product quality, technological innovation and customer service.

ADDRESS   433 E. Michigan St.
Milwaukee, WI 53202

INDUSTRY CATEGORY   Food/Beverage

◆   ◆   ◆   ◆   ◆   ◆   ◆

Unocal Corporation

STATEMENT | **Our Mission**

Unocal produces and sells a broad array of essential energy resources, petroleum products, chemical fertilizers, and specialty minerals that help improve the quality of life for people around the world. Our primary mission is to maximize—ethically and responsibly—the total long-term returns to the owners of the company, our stockholders.

| **Our Vision**

To be recognized leaders in creating value by identifying, developing, and producing crude oil, natural gas, and geothermal energy resources.

To manufacture, transport and market high-quality petroleum and chemical products safely and efficiently.

To combine the strengths of a large company with the speed and agility of a small business.

To achieve excellence in all staff functions, providing cost-effective, value-added services to company operations.

To be innovators, who find creative and cost-effective ways to produce new energy resources, develop needed technologies, and protect the environment.

Our Values

Achieve continuous improvement in all of our business activities through teamwork, accountability, and sharing of ideas. Meet our customers' requirements by providing quality products and services.

Act quickly to solve problems and seize opportunities.

Spend wisely and safeguard every company asset as if it were our own.

Create a work environment in which employees can develop their full potential.

Take appropriate business risks, encourage creativity and reward results.

Treat everyone fairly and with respect.

Communicate openly and honestly.

Meet the highest ethical standards in all of our business activities.

Maintain a safe and healthful workplace.

Protect the environment.

Obey the law and comply with all regulations.

Improve the quality of life in all the communities where we do business.

CORPORATE DESCRIPTION

Unocal Corporation is the parent of Union Oil Company of California, a fully integrated, high-technology energy resources company whose worldwide operations comprise all aspects of energy production. Virtually all operations are conducted by Union Oil Company of California, which does business as Unocal.

ADDRESS   1201 W. 5th St.
Los Angeles, CA 90051

INDUSTRY CATEGORY   Oil and Gas

◆　◆　◆　◆　◆　◆　◆

UNUM Corporation

| **Our Mission is:**

To relieve clients of insurable financial risk.

We protect clients from financial hardship that results from retirement, death, sickness and from disability or other casualty events.

| **Vision**

We will achieve leadership in our business. Leadership does not necessarily mean a dominant market share. Rather, we will achieve leadership in areas which are meaningful and important to our business and the market, e.g., profitability, quality, reputation.

We will focus our business on specialty, risk-relieving products for which we can establish and sustain profitable positions. Development of these products will be driven by the needs of customers, in both domestic and international markets.

We will be a products-offered company:

- Developing products which meet customer needs and leveraging our expertise and strengths. Our product development efforts will focus on providing the right solution.
- Seeking market segments which are appropriate for our products.
- Delivering our products in a high-quality and efficient manner utilizing existing and new channels.

Our products will be perceived by customers as representing superior value in quality and price, and will consist of a total offering including risk, service, delivery and reliability.

We will be known for:

- Superior knowledge, expertise and risk management
- Quality service
- Being responsive to the needs of customers and intermediaries
- Being reliable, dependable and trustworthy
- Providing the right solutions to current and emerging needs
- Implementing good ideas well

We will be a well-managed company:

♦ Consistently growing profits, an efficient cost structure, leadership returns and financially sound
♦ Anticipating, shaping and effectively responding to relevant external forces and events
♦ Making decisions in the best long-term interests of our stakeholders
♦ Planning well; making clear and sound business decisions

Values

We take pride in ourselves and the organization's leadership position:

♦ Acting with integrity and high ethical standards
♦ Achieving leadership in performance, the community and the industry
♦ Setting and meeting individual goals consistent with business goals, and owning our individual performance
♦ Being motivated and excited about the organization
♦ Believing in what we are doing
♦ Emphasizing the positives, celebrating our successes and strengths, and constantly striving to improve our performance
♦ Delivering results

We value and respect people:

♦ Dealing with each other as individuals, and treating each other as we would like to be treated
♦ Developing people to their fullest potential
♦ Working together in a common endeavor: recognizing each other as important elements to the success to the whole
♦ Having a common understanding of each other's role and how we fit with the corporate objectives
♦ Collaborating with each other and having a sense of team
♦ Recognizing and accepting differences among people, but sharing the same values

We value customers:

- ♦ Building long-term relationships with our customers and intermediaries
- ♦ Maintaining a strong orientation to service and the customer
- ♦ Delivering what we promise

We value communication:

- ♦ Communicating clearly, consistently and openly with everyone we deal with
- ♦ Building an environment which encourages open communication, participation, honesty and candor
- ♦ Listening

CORPORATE DESCRIPTION

UNUM is a publicly held specialty insurance holding company that provides income protection through a range of disability, life, health, long term care and retirement income products and services.

ADDRESS   2211 Congress St.
Portland, ME 04122

INDUSTRY CATEGORY   Insurance

♦　♦　♦　♦　♦　♦　♦

U.S. Bancorp

STATEMENT | **The U.S. Bancorp Vision**

| **Mission**

We build high-performing banking franchises where we can create and sustain market leadership.

Goal

We will be one of the top-performing banks, measured in terms of market share and long-term profitability. We will achieve this goal through:

Customer service commitment

Cost control

Credit quality

Capital strength

Core business concentration

Cross-selling aggressively and effectively

Community commitment

Communicating clearly and honestly

Values

As a company, we value:

Integrity

We are honest, ethical and fair. We tell the truth and expect to hear the truth from others.

Leadership

As a company and as individuals, we take positions and lead by example in all things important to us.

Performance

We know there is no substitute for outstanding performance. We continually seek ways to reward excellence.

Quality

We understand that our customers define quality and we strive to consistently meet their expectations.

Diversity

We value individual differences and work to leverage their inherent creative potential.

We will work together to achieve our common goals. Openness and flexibility are important.

CORPORATE DESCRIPTION

Minneapolis-based U.S. Bancorp, with $76 billion in assets, is the 13th largest bank holding company in the nation and operates approximately 1,000 banking offices in 17 Midwestern and Western states. The company provides comprehensive banking, trust, investment and payment systems products and services to consumers, businesses and institutions. The Company is the largest provider of Visa corporate and purchasing cards in the world, and is one of the largest providers of corporate trust services in the nation.

ADDRESS   601 2nd Ave. S.
Minneapolis, MN 55402

INDUSTRY CATEGORY   Banking

◆ ◆ ◆ ◆ ◆ ◆ ◆

UTILX Corporation

STATEMENT

Our mission is what we focus and work on to achieve accomplishment now and forever.

Mission Statement

Our mission is to assist companies of the world in the installation and maintenance of a segment of their underground infrastructure. We will do this by providing UTILX services and products in a way that helps our customers achieve their goals and solve their problems. We will achieve success by making our customers successful.

In the process of providing the highest quality product and services to our customers, we will be admired and possibly held in awe by our competitors. This will occur because our technology will be the best in the world and because the people of UTILX, through their pride, commitment, teamwork and their ability to focus on doing what it takes to make our customers successful, will be absolutely unbeatable by our competition.

Through exceptional customer service and world class safety, quality and technology, our mission includes being the best in the entire world in what we do.

CORPORATE DESCRIPTION

UTILX® Corporation provides services and products used in the replacement and renovation of underground utilities and related construction. The Company's FlowMole® and CableCure® divisions give UTILX a strategic advantage in solving the utility needs of the nation and the world. The FlowMole technology provides economic alternatives for the installation needs of electric, telephone, gas, water and sewer utilities while meeting the increasing demand for environmental remediation. CableCure dielectric enhancement technology restores water-damaged power and telephone cables at substantial savings compared to the cost of cable replacement. Domestically, UTILX provides its technology as a service, while internationally it supplies equipment, parts and training.

ADDRESS   22404 66th Ave. S.
Kent, WA 98064

INDUSTRY CATEGORY   Industrial, Specialized

◆　◆　◆　◆　◆　◆　◆

Valassis Communications, Inc.

STATEMENT | **Pledge to Shareholders**

As employees and fellow "owners" of Valassis Communications, we are committed to achieving maximum profits, short- and long-term growth, and an excellent return on your investment. We realize that next to our customers, our shareholders are the key to our success. Therefore, we promise to manage your investment like you would— by working hard and smart. We will constantly look for ways to improve our products and services, set and accomplish the highest objectives for ourselves and for our company, increase efficiencies through training and innovation, and conduct our business ethically and responsibly.

CORPORATE DESCRIPTION

Valassis Communications, Inc. is one of the world's largest publishers of printed sales promotion materials.

ADDRESS   19975 Victor Pkwy.
Westwood Office Park
Livonia, MI 48152

INDUSTRY CATEGORY   Media

◆　◆　◆　◆　◆　◆　◆

Varlen Corporation

STATEMENT | **The Varlen Mission**

Varlen's primary objective is to increase the long-term value of its shareowners' investment. This will be achieved by building upon our employees' creativity and their commitment to serving customers better and more efficiently than our competitors do in the markets where Varlen chooses to compete.

Varlen will invest resources in selected industrial markets where it has, or can obtain, a leadership position; we will redeploy resources from markets where we cannot. We will continue to enhance our global presence. Varlen's engineered products for the niche markets in which it participates are characterized by differentiable process technology employed in their manufacture and/or superior performance attributes. Our dedication to continuous improvement will be unrelenting.

CORPORATE DESCRIPTION

The Company designs, manufactures, and markets a diverse range of products in its transportation products and laboratory and other products business segments. These products are marketed to the railroad, heavy duty truck and trailer and automotive industries, as well as to the life science research, petroleum, and consumer products industries.

ADDRESS   55 Shuman Blvd.
P.O. Box 3089
Naperville, IL 60566-7089

INDUSTRY CATEGORY   Manufacturing

◆ ◆ ◆ ◆ ◆ ◆ ◆

VF Corporation

| **VF Corporation Code of Business Conduct**
Statement of Mission and Purpose

VF is a diversified apparel company whose mission it is to provide above average shareholder returns by being the industry leader in marketing and servicing basic fashion apparel needs while maintaining conservative financial strategies.

The purpose of the Company is to manufacture and market products which offer superior real value to the customer and consumer compared to competition. In doing so, it is a cornerstone of our business philosophy to achieve a leadership position in every facet of our business and to judge our actions by the highest standards of excellence. We will restrict growth only by the stability and quality of profits and our ability to develop and market products offering superior value.

The Company intends to achieve profit levels sufficient to provide an attractive return to its shareholders and to provide adequate resources necessary to achieve corporate objectives.

The Company desires to provide stable employment in positions which will allow employees to develop personally and professionally. It is the Company's aim that our employees will derive satisfaction from achieving corporate objectives through superior performance in an organization environment characterized by competence, integrity, teamwork and fairness.

The conduct of business with employees, customers, consumers, suppliers, and all others shall be based on an honest, fair and equitable basis. It has been and will continue to be the Company's policy to obey the laws of each country and to honor our obligations to society by being an economic, intellectual, and social asset to each community and nation in which the Company operates.

The Board of Directors and Management of the Company have adopted the Code of Business Conduct as set forth below.* This Code is intended to establish minimum general standards of conduct encompassing the most common and sensitive areas in which the business operates. Other specific corporate policies and guidelines will expand on broad statements made in this policy and will cover other subjects relative to the management of the business.

All managers will be responsible for the distribution of this Code to their employees. Every employee is responsible for complying with these principles, guidelines and policies. Any violation may be grounds for dismissal.

*[*Author's note:* The Code of Business Conduct has not been included here.]

CORPORATE DESCRIPTION

VF Corporation is one of the largest apparel manufacturers in the world and an international leader in the jeanswear, intimate apparel, knitwear and specialty apparel markets.

ADDRESS   628 Green Valley Rd.
Greensboro, NC 21488

INDUSTRY CATEGORY   Consumer Goods and Services

♦ ♦ ♦ ♦ ♦ ♦ ♦

The Vons Companies, Inc.

STATEMENT | **The Vons Companies, Inc.**
Mission Statement & Visions

[Mission Statement]

Vons is a premier retailer of foods and related categories including products and services associated with drug stores. We respond to needs and preferences of a wide spectrum of customer segments with a dense and growing state-of-the-art store network employing several names and store types. All are merchandised, staffed and operated with highest integrity providing quality shopping experiences designed to create and keep customers. We are good corporate citizens of the communities in which we operate. We provide a rewarding work environment which attracts, develops and retains quality people. In this manner, we grow our business in volume, share and profits to maximize shareholder value.

[#1 Vision]

The Vons Companies is primarily an operator of supermarkets, super stores, and combination stores, all of which focus on food, drug store products and services, plus select related categories. Special emphasis is placed on perishable product categories and departments. Our stores are merchandised, staffed and operated with an understanding of customer needs and preferences. This understanding enables us to operate our stores with sustainable competitive advantage.

[#2 Vision]

The Vons Companies is committed to being a growth company. We view opportunities for growth in the further development of our existing businesses, new store additions to our network and strategic acquisitions. We strive to be the share leader in our markets in order that we can most fully utilize our assets and our infrastructure.

[#3 Vision]

The Vons Companies is a customer driven company. We continuously identify value-added factors that create customer satisfaction. In response to our diverse customer base, we operate several separate state-of-the-art store chains each with different store types. Each is managed by a separate retail business unit organization that is served by a central umbrella of support services. This structure contains our non-customer operating costs and enables us to respond quickly to customers changing preferences so as to deliver a Quality Shopping Experience.

[#4 Vision]

Vons believes in involving its employees in managing the business. The Company respects all of its employees and provides them with good working conditions and "open door" policies. The Company fosters a "give a darn" attitude on the part of all employees to generate products and services of outstanding quality.

[#5 Vision]

The Vons Companies is a part of an industry that exists as the purchasing agent of its customers. Faithful to this purpose, we work with our suppliers in a constructive and participative manner to assure the lowest possible cost of product. Simultaneously, we diligently control expenses so as to provide customers with outstanding value from the goods and services we sell.

[#6 Vision]

The Vons Companies will operate from a position of financial strength by maintaining a solid yet flexible capital structure. We emphasize utilization of existing resources to maximize profitability.

[#7 Vision]

Vons has achieved technological leadership which it strives to maintain. We see technology as a vehicle by which to increase customer loyalty, enhance employee satisfaction and improve profitability.

[#8 Vision]

The Vons Companies is committed to being a good corporate citizen. We operate our business with the highest integrity.

[#9 Vision]

The Vons Companies is committed to maximizing shareholder value through consistent earnings per share growth. The Company operates its business for the long term.

CORPORATE DESCRIPTION

The Vons Companies, Inc. is the ninth largest supermarket chain in the nation and the market share leader in Southern California.

ADDRESS   618 Michillinda Ave.
Arcadia, CA 91007-6300

INDUSTRY CATEGORY   Food/Beverage

◆　◆　◆　◆　◆　◆　◆

Vulcan Materials Company

Mission

VULCAN MATERIALS COMPANY is an international producer of industrial materials and commodities that are essential to the standard of living of advanced and developing societies.

OUR mission is to provide quality products and services that consistently meet our customers' expectations; to be responsible stewards with respect to the safety and environmental impact of our operations and products; and to earn superior returns for our shareholders.

WE recognize that success in all of our activities is related directly to the talents, dedication and performance of our employees throughout the company.

Guiding Principles

INTEGRITY: We will work constantly to earn the respect and trust of all parties we interact with by acting fairly and honorably. We will observe high ethical standards and obey all laws and regulations.

EXCELLENCE: We are committed to excellence in all of our activities. We value innovation. We intend to maintain a position of leadership in each of our industries.

PEOPLE: We will maintain a high respect for people—for their dignity, their talents and their interests.

Commitments

Following are our most important commitments. They embody goals that we strive to attain and values that guide our conduct.

WE will strive to be the low cost producer in each of our industries and to be the standard-setter with regard to quality, service and technical support.

WE will respect the dignity of each of our employees and deal with them fairly. We will strive to maintain an environment that encourages them to develop their talents, exercise creativity and achieve superior performance. We will keep our compensation programs at fair and competitive levels. Employment and advancement will be based on qualifications, performance and organizational needs. We will maintain a firm commitment to employee health and safety.

WE will provide technical and educational assistance so that customers may use our products in an efficient, safe and environmentally proper manner. We will maintain a steadfast commitment to minimize any adverse impacts our activities have on the environment in which we operate. We will comply with all environmental laws and regulations.

WE will compete vigorously in each of our industries while maintaining a strict regard for compliance in all respects with the antitrust laws.

WE will be a good corporate citizen in each community in which we operate. We will support and take an active part in public and charitable projects.

WE will maintain a strong commitment to divisional autonomy consistent with high accountability and performance. Corporate and group staffs will be kept lean and highly competent so that their contributions will add value to divisional results without restricting the initiative and accountability of division managers. Corporate, group and divisional relationships will be marked by goodwill, teamwork and open communications.

WE are determined to achieve superior rates of return on the capital our shareholders have entrusted to us. We intend to rank in the top quartile of U.S. industrial companies as measured by profitability and growth in earnings. We will aggressively pursue profitable growth opportunities through extension of existing product lines, addition of new products, development of greenfield sites and business acquisitions.

CORPORATE DESCRIPTION

Vulcan is a producer of industrial materials and commodities with significant positions in two industries. It is the nation's foremost producer of construction aggregates and a leading chemicals manufacturer, producing a diversified line of chlorinated solvents and other industrial chemicals.

ADDRESS   P.O. Box 530187
Birmingham, AL 35253-0187

INDUSTRY CATEGORY   Industrial, Specialized

◆ ◆ ◆ ◆ ◆ ◆ ◆

The Wackenhut Corporation

STATEMENT | **Corporate Vision:**

By the year 2000, The Wackenhut Corporation will be recognized throughout the world as a uniquely diversified, superior performing and profitable protective and support services company.

Operating and Financial Goals.

The Wackenhut Corporation will

- Conduct all Corporate relationships according to the highest moral and ethical standards.
- Increase earnings per share and shareholder value on a continuing basis.
- Attract and retain a skilled work force, using only the highest standards in the recruitment and selection of personnel.
- Increase the productivity and professionalism of personnel at all levels within the organization, by emphasizing sound initial and ongoing training.
- Respect the dignity, rights and contributions of its employees.
- Maintain Return on Equity (ROE) at consistently high levels.
- Develop and retain a prestigious client base, including companies listed on the Fortune 500 and important agencies within federal, state and local governments.

- Seek long term relationships with our clients, based upon quality of service, not lowest price.
- Establish and maintain a mechanism for identifying and satisfying real customer needs through a total Corporate quality improvement program.
- Continue to improve the quality of Corporate services, to internal as well as external customers.
- Develop and achieve meaningful market share goals for each Business Unit.
- Continue to diversify into areas that will maximize profits and cash flow, and/or improve market penetration.
- Develop a balanced plan of short, medium and long-term interests while achieving sustained, profitable growth.

CORPORATE DESCRIPTION

The Wackenhut Corporation is a diversified provider of security-related services to government, industrial, and business organizations worldwide. It is one of the world's largest security organizations, with offices in over 125 U.S. cities, and in over 50 other countries on six continents. Its uniformed security officers can be found protecting the assets of Fortune 500 companies, major industrial and government complexes, the business and professional communities, retail outlets and residential neighborhoods. Its capabilities also include: investigations, fire and emergency services, facility management, training and educational services, prison/jail foodservice, and privatization of public services.

ADDRESS   4200 Wackenhut Dr.
Palm Beach Gardens, FL 33410

INDUSTRY CATEGORY   Business Services

◆ ◆ ◆ ◆ ◆ ◆ ◆

Warner-Lambert Company

OUR VISION at Warner-Lambert is to be the best by offering the most innovative, highest quality products to advance the health and well-being of people around the world. Toward this vision we will provide an environment where people can innovate and excel. To achieve this vision, we make these commitments to those whose lives we touch.

Our Creed

To Our Customers

WE COMMIT OURSELVES to anticipating customer needs and responding first with superior products and services. We are committed to continued investment in the discovery of safe and valuable products to enhance people's lives.

To Our Colleagues

WE COMMIT OURSELVES to attracting and retaining excellent people, and providing them with an open and participative work environment, marked by equal opportunity for personal growth. Performance will be evaluated candidly, on the basis of fair and objective standards. Creativity, speed of action, and openness to change will be prized and rewarded. Colleagues will be treated with dignity and respect. They will have the shared responsibility for continuously improving the performance of the company and the quality of work.

To Our Shareholders

WE COMMIT OURSELVES to providing fair and attractive economic returns to our shareholders. We are prepared to take prudent risks to achieve sustainable long-term corporate growth.

To Our Business Partners

WE COMMIT OURSELVES to dealing with our suppliers and other business partners fairly and equitably, recognizing our mutual interests.

WE COMMIT OURSELVES to being responsible corporate citizens, actively initiating and supporting efforts concerning the health of society and stewardship of the environment. We will work to improve the vitality of the worldwide communities in which we operate.

ABOVE ALL, our dealings with these constituencies will be conducted with the utmost integrity, adhering to the highest standards of ethical and just conduct.

CORPORATE DESCRIPTION

Warner-Lambert is a leading worldwide company engaged in the research and development, manufacturing, and marketing of quality health care and consumer products. The company's prescription pharmaceutical business is focused on such major areas of medical need as cardiovascular disease, central nervous system disorders, women's health care, and infectious disease. Warner-Lambert also ranks as the world's leading supplier of empty hard-gelatin capsules for pharmaceutical use. The company's broad range of consumer products includes over-the-counter health care products, shaving and other personal care products, confectionery products, and home aquarium products. These products contribute to the health and well-being of people in more than 130 countries.

ADDRESS   201 Tabor Rd.
Morris Plains, NJ 07950

INDUSTRY CATEGORY   Health Care

◆ ◆ ◆ ◆ ◆ ◆ ◆

Washington Gas

STATEMENT | **Our Mission**

TO PROVIDE THE BEST ENERGY VALUE—A SUPERIOR PRODUCT AND QUALITY SERVICE AT A COMPETITIVE PRICE.

THE CUSTOMER IS THE KEY. **Customers have choices.** We compete with others to add and retain customers. To be the customer's choice, we must continuously and rapidly improve service and productivity. **We listen to our customers.** That is the only way we can identify and meet their changing needs and expectations. **We share community concerns.** We care about the quality of life in our communities and are committed to protecting the environment. We emphasize safety, encourage conservation, and promote efficient energy services at fair prices.

EMPLOYEES ARE THE COMPANY. **Washington Gas is a team.** We must draw strength from diversity and work in partnership with each other and with our customers, communities, investors and suppliers. **We listen to each other.** By doing so, we can build an environment of openness and mutual respect where we can be our best and grow in our jobs. **We set high standards.** We must observe the highest ethical and professional standards in all that we do.

INVESTORS ARE ESSENTIAL. **The company must succeed financially.** We must earn competitive returns for our investors, since they provide the financial underpinning to meet customer, employee, and community needs.

CORPORATE DESCRIPTION

Washington Gas and its distribution subsidiaries provide natural gas service to more than 700,000 customers in the growing Washington, D.C. metropolitan and surrounding areas.

Sales to residential and small commercial customers account for 86% of the company's revenues.

ADDRESS   1100 H St. N.W.
Washington, D.C. 20080

INDUSTRY CATEGORY   Utility

◆ ◆ ◆ ◆ ◆ ◆ ◆

Washington Mutual Inc.

ETHICS

All actions are guided by absolute honesty, integrity and fairness.

RESPECT

People are valued and appreciated for their contributions.

TEAMWORK

Cooperation, trust and shared objectives are vital to success.

INNOVATION

New ideas are encouraged and sound strategies implemented with enthusiasm.

EXCELLENCE

High standards for service and performance are expected and rewarded.

| OUR MISSION

To be one of the nation's premier financial services companies by:
- ♦ providing exceptional service to customers
- ♦ making our communities better places to live and work
- ♦ recognizing outstanding efforts of employees
- ♦ delivering a superior long-term return to shareholders

CORPORATE DESCRIPTION

Washington Mutual Inc., founded in 1889, is a financial services company serving consumers and small- to mid-sized businesses. The company operates principally in California, Washington, Oregon, Florida and Utah but has operations in a total of 36 states.

ADDRESS   1201 3rd Ave.
Seattle, WA 98101

INDUSTRY CATEGORY   Banking

♦ ♦ ♦ ♦ ♦ ♦ ♦

Weirton Steel Corporation

Weirton Steel Corporation will lead the industry in satisfying customers with high quality products and services. We are committed to accomplishing this through highly trained and informed employee-owners who participate fully in the continuous process of improving performance, achieving the highest possible level of personal development.

Vision for Success

WE ARE BOUND TOGETHER IN THESE COMMON BELIEFS AND VALUES

We must ...

FOR THE CUSTOMERS

- Have a total quality commitment to consistently meet the product, delivery and service expectations of all customers.
- Give customers increased value through processes that eliminate waste, minimize costs and enhance production efficiency.

FOR THE EMPLOYEE

- Reward teamwork, trust, honesty, openness and candor.
- Ensure a safe workplace.
- Recognize that people are the corporation and provide them with training and information that allows for continuous improvement.
- As employee-owners, obligate ourselves to provide a high level of performance and be accountable for our own actions.
- Respect the dignity, rights and contributions of others.

FOR THE COMPANY

- Continuously invest in new technology and equipment to ensure competitiveness and enhance stockholder value.
- Manage our financial and human resources for long-term profitability.

FOR THE COMMUNITY
- ♦ Commit to environmental responsibility.
- ♦ Fulfill our responsibility to enhance the quality of community life.

CORPORATE DESCRIPTION

Weirton Steel Corporation, a major integrated steel producer, was formed in 1982 for the purpose of acquiring the Weirton Steel Division of National Steel Corporation. The Company produces flat rolled carbon steels in sheet and strip form.

ADDRESS   400 Three Springs Dr.
Weirton, WV 26062-4989

INDUSTRY CATEGORY   Manufacturing

♦ ♦ ♦ ♦ ♦ ♦ ♦

Wellman, Inc.

STATEMENT | **Wellman, Inc.**
The Fibers Division
Mission Statement

The mission of the Wellman Fibers Division is to enhance the value of the company by achieving excellence in the production and marketing of high quality products. We will provide earnings, develop people, and produce value-added products, including those from recycled materials, to support the long term growth of the corporation.

CORPORATE DESCRIPTION

Wellman, Inc., the nation's largest plastics recycler, manufactures and markets high-quality Fortrel® polyester textile fibers, recycled polyester and nylon staple fibers, PET and nylon resins, PET sheet and thermoformed packaging and various related products.

◆ ◆ ◆ ◆ ◆ ◆ ◆

Wendy's International, Inc.

STATEMENT | **Wendy's Mission Statement**
Deliver Total Quality

| **Wendy's Vision Statement**
To Be The Customer's Restaurant Of Choice And The Employer of Choice

CORPORATE DESCRIPTION

Wendy's International, Inc. is the third largest quick-service hamburger chain in the world with close to 4,200 restaurants worldwide, serving a wide variety of fresh, high-quality and nutritious products. Founded nearly 25 years ago, systemwide sales have grown to over $3.9 billion. The Wendy's system is made up of 1,224 company-operated and 2,944 franchised restaurants.

ADDRESS   4288 W. Dublin Granville Rd.
Dublin, OH 43017

INDUSTRY CATEGORY   Food/Beverage

◆ ◆ ◆ ◆ ◆ ◆ ◆

Westin Hotels & Resorts

STATEMENT | **Westin Hotels & Resorts North America**

Vision

Year after year, Westin and its people will be regarded as the best and most sought after hotel and resort management group in North America.

Mission

In order to realize our Vision, our Mission must be to exceed the expectations of our customers, whom we define as guests, partners, and fellow employees.

We will accomplish this mission by committing to our shared values and by achieving the highest levels of customer satisfaction, with extraordinary emphasis on the creation of value. In this way we will ensure that our profit, quality and growth goals are met.

CORPORATE DESCRIPTION

Westin Hotels and Resorts is the oldest hotel management company in North America.

ADDRESS   The Westin Building
2001 Sixth Ave.
Seattle, WA 98121

INDUSTRY CATEGORY   Hotel, Hospitality, and Entertainment

♦ ♦ ♦ ♦ ♦ ♦ ♦

Weyerhaeuser

STATEMENT | **Our Vision**

The best forest products company in the world.

Strategies

We shall achieve our vision by:

- Making Total Quality the Weyerhaeuser Way of doing business.
- Relentless pursuit of full customer satisfaction.
- Empowering Weyerhaeuser people.
- Leading the industry in forest management and manufacturing excellence.
- Producing superior returns for our shareholders.

Our Values

CUSTOMERS: We listen to our customers and improve our products and services to meet their present and future needs.

PEOPLE: Our success depends upon high-performing people working together in a safe and healthy workplace where diversity, development and teamwork are valued and recognized.

ACCOUNTABILITY: We expect superior performance and are accountable for our actions and results. Our leaders set clear goals and expectations, are supportive, and provide and seek frequent feedback.

CITIZENSHIP: We support the communities where we do business, hold ourselves to the highest standards of ethical conduct and environmental responsibility, and communicate openly with Weyerhaeuser people and the public.

FINANCIAL RESPONSIBILITY: We are prudent and effective in the use of the resources entrusted to us.

Our Behaviors

- Operate as one company
- Safe from the start
- Speed, simplicity and decisiveness

CORPORATE DESCRIPTION

Weyerhaeuser Company (NYSE: WY), one of the world's largest integrated forest products companies, was incorporated in 1900. It has offices or operations in 12 countries, with customers worldwide. Weyerhaeuser is principally engaged in the growing and harvesting of timber; the manufacture, distribution and sale of forest products; and real estate construction, development and related activities. Additional information about Weyerhaeuser's businesses, products or practices is available at www.weyerhaeuser.com.

ADDRESS   P.O. Box 2999
Tacoma, WA 98477-2999

INDUSTRY CATEGORY   Forest Products, Wood Processing, Paper

◆ ◆ ◆ ◆ ◆ ◆ ◆

WICOR, Inc.

STATEMENT | **The WICOR Strategy**

Where we're going is toward creating long-term value for shareholders by capitalizing on changes in the energy industry and pursuing global markets through our manufacturing subsidiaries. How we're growing is through strategic diversification in utility and non-utility businesses. Our companies are united by four common growth objectives: Develop new products and services, make value-adding acquisitions, expand geographically, increase market share.

CORPORATE DESCRIPTION

WICOR, Inc. is a diversified company formed in 1980 to provide shareholders opportunities for financial return through investment in utility and non-utility businesses. WICOR operates six subsidiaries in two industries: energy and utility services and pump manufacturing. The energy subsidiaries are Wisconsin Gas Company, WICOR Energy and FieldTech. The manufacturing subsidiaries are Sta-Rite

Industries, Inc., SHURflo Pump Manufacturing Co., and Hypro Corporation. They manufacture and market pumps and fluid-handling and filtration equipment for a variety of global markets.

ADDRESS   625 E. Wisconsin Ave.
Milwaukee, WI 53202

INDUSTRY CATEGORY   Diversified

◆ ◆ ◆ ◆ ◆ ◆ ◆

Winnebago Industries, Inc.

STATEMENT | **Mission Statement**

Winnebago Industries, Inc. is a leading international manufacturer of recreational vehicles (RVs) and related products and services. Our mission is to continually improve our products and services to meet or exceed the expectations of our customers. We emphasize employee teamwork and involvement in identifying and implementing programs to save time and lower production costs while maintaining the highest quality values. These strategies allow us to prosper as a business with a high degree of integrity and to provide a reasonable return for our shareholders, the ultimate owners of our business.

| **Values**

How we accomplish our mission is as important as the mission itself. Fundamental to the success of the Company are these basic values we describe as the four P's:

People—Our employees are the source of our vast strength. They provide our corporate intelligence and determine our reputation and vitality. Involvement and teamwork are our core human values.

Products—Our products are the end result of our teamwork's combined efforts, and they should be the best in meeting or exceeding our customers' expectations worldwide. As our products are viewed, so are we viewed.

Plant—Our facilities are the most technologically advanced in the RV industry. We continue to review facility improvements that will increase the utilization of our plant capacity and enable us to build the best quality product for the investment.

Profitability—Profitability is the ultimate measure of how efficiently we provide our customers with the best products for their need. Profitability is required to survive and grow. As our respect and position within the marketplace grows, so will our profit.

Guiding Principles

Quality comes first—To achieve customer satisfaction, the quality of our products and services must be our number one priority.

Customers are central to our existence—Our work must be done with our customers in mind, providing products and services that meet or exceed the expectations of our customers. We must not only satisfy customers, we must also surprise and delight them.

Continuous improvement is essential to our success—We must strive for excellence in everything we do: in our products, in their safety and value, as well as in our services, our human relations, our competitiveness, and our profitability.

Employee involvement is our way of life—We are a team. We must treat each other with trust and respect.

Dealers and suppliers are our partners—The Company must maintain mutually beneficial relationships with dealers, suppliers and our other business associates.

Integrity is never compromised—The Company must pursue conduct worldwide in a manner that is socially responsible and that commands respect for its integrity and for its positive contributions to society. Our doors are open to all men and women alike without discrimination and without regard to ethnic origin or personal beliefs.

CORPORATE DESCRIPTION

Winnebago Industries, Inc., headquartered in Forest City, Iowa, is a leading United States manufacturer of motor homes, self-contained recreation vehicles used primarily in leisure travel and outdoor recreation activities.

ADDRESS   P.O. Box 152
605 W. Crystal Lake Rd.
Forest City, IA 50436

INDUSTRY CATEGORY   Motor Vehicles and Related

◆   ◆   ◆   ◆   ◆   ◆   ◆

Wisconsin Energy Corporation

STATEMENT | **Wisconsin Energy Corporation
Mission and Goals Statement**

Our Mission:

To be the premier provider of energy and energy related services in the North Central United States.

Our Goals:

- ◆ To establish a position as the low-cost provider of energy in the region.
- ◆ To focus on customer addition, retention and expansion through the development of value-added products and services.
- ◆ To grow through expansion of the area we serve, and through partnerships and alliances that complement our strengths.

CORPORATE DESCRIPTION

Wisconsin Energy Corp. is a holding company with subsidiaries in utility and nonutility businesses. Its principal subsidiaries are Wisconsin Electric Power Co. and Wisconsin Natural Gas Co.

Wisconsin Electric is engaged principally in the generation, transmission, distribution and sale of electric energy in a territory of approximately 12,600 square miles in southeastern Wisconsin, the east central and northern portions of Wisconsin and the Upper

Peninsula of Michigan. The operating area includes metropolitan Milwaukee and has an estimated population of more than 2 million.

Wisconsin Natural purchases gas from various supply areas, transports gas to Wisconsin through pipeline companies and then distributes and sells it in three areas in Wisconsin. The gas service territory has an estimated population of more than 1 million, mainly within the electric service area of Wisconsin Electric.

ADDRESS   231 W. Michigan St.
P.O. Box 2046
Milwaukee, WI 53201

INDUSTRY CATEGORY   Utility

◆　◆　◆　◆　◆　◆　◆

Wisconsin Public Service Corporation

STATEMENT | **Our Vision**

People Creating The World's Premier Energy Company

Behind the Words of the Vision

A vision is a mental image of the company we want to be. It's intended to give all employees, as well as everyone else the company works with and serves, a consistent picture of the company we are creating.

"People"

All employees sharing a commitment to work together, and with customers and suppliers, to become the World's Premier Energy Company.

"Creating"

Employees immersing themselves in the excitement of continuously inventing and improving products and services in a world of ever-changing needs, expectations, and demands.

"World's Premier Energy Company"

An organization that, in the eyes of customers and all others, creates best-value services and products for customers, constantly improves, and respects all people. Its employees share common beliefs, are committed to a common purpose and quality, and are highly skilled.

| Our Mission

Provide Customers with the Best Value in Energy and Related Services

Behind the Words of the Mission

A mission describes the aim of our current business practices. It offers us direction.

"Provide Customers"

Employees working with customers, suppliers, and others to ensure that products and services exceed customers' expectations.

"Best Value"

What customers recognize as the most desirable combination of service, quality, reliability and price.

"Energy and Related Services"

Employees providing products primarily associated with electricity and natural gas, as well as expertise, assistance and programs associated with customers' energy use.

| The Beliefs We Share

To be the company we have described in our Vision, we need to create a new culture for ourselves—one that encourages and allows us to act in harmony with the following central beliefs.

It is important that each of us explore our understanding of these beliefs and decide whether we can share them with others in the company, because these beliefs will direct our company actions and decisions for the future.

- ◆ Our customers are the primary focus of our effort.
- ◆ Our actions must always be rooted in honesty and integrity; we should always foster truth, faith in others, fairness and respect.

- Our learning through study, review, dialogue and experimentation benefits our customers, ourselves and our company.
- We must continuously work together to create and improve processes, and eliminate those that are not longer valuable.
- We cannot tolerate actions that crush people's self-esteem, aspirations, individuality or dignity.
- We must recognize that every employee adds value to the company; therefore, we must not allow job titles or positions to stand in the way of an employee's ability or willingness to contribute.
- We must acknowledge and use the experiences and insights brought to the company through people's diverse backgrounds, choices, life situations and perspectives, and ensure the freedom to express our diversity.
- We must be flexible as individuals and as a company.
- We must share information, ideas and knowledge freely, quickly, candidly and unencumbered by organizational structures or individuals.
- We must responsibly act as faithful stewards of the resources entrusted to us by others.
- Work should enrich and bring joy to every employee.

CORPORATE DESCRIPTION

Wisconsin Public Service Corporation is an investor-owned electric and gas utility providing services to a 10,000 square mile area of Northeastern Wisconsin and an adjacent part of Upper Michigan.

ADDRESS   700 North Adams
P.O. Box 19001
Green Bay, WI 54307-9001

INDUSTRY CATEGORY   Utility

♦   ♦   ♦   ♦   ♦   ♦   ♦

WMX Technologies, Inc.

STATEMENT

The mission of WMX Technologies, Inc. is to be the acknowledged worldwide leader in providing comprehensive environmental, waste management and related services of the highest quality to industry, government and consumers using state-of-the-art systems responsive to customer need, sound environmental policy and the highest standards of corporate citizenship.

In fulfilling this mission, we shall provide a rewarding work environment for our people, cooperate with all relevant government agencies, and promote a spirit of partnership with the communities and enterprises we serve as we strive to be a responsible neighbor, while increasing shareholder value.

CORPORATE DESCRIPTION

The WMX Technologies is a family of environmental service companies.

The WMX Technologies family of companies includes five subsidiaries: Waste Management, Inc., Chemical Waste Management, Inc., Wheelabator Technologies, Inc., Rust International Inc. and Waste Management International plc.

These companies offer clear, comprehensive and lasting environmental solutions.

ADDRESS   3003 Butterfield Rd.
Oak Brook, IL 60521-1100

INDUSTRY CATEGORY   Diversified

◆   ◆   ◆   ◆   ◆   ◆   ◆

York International

STATEMENT | **Mission Statement**

Build on the York International tradition of innovative technology to become the worldwide leader of environmentally responsive heating, ventilation, air conditioning and refrigeration systems designed to improve the quality of life.

CORPORATE DESCRIPTION

York International is the largest independent supplier of heating, ventilating, air conditioning and refrigeration products in the United States and a leading competitor worldwide. York designs, manufactures, sells and services heating, ventilation and air conditioning systems, and compressors for residential and commercial markets, gas compression equipment for industrial processing, industrial and commercial refrigeration equipment, and compressors for air conditioning and refrigeration applications.

ADDRESS   P.O. Box 1592-364B
York, PA 17405-1592

INDUSTRY CATEGORY   Manufacturing

◆ ◆ ◆ ◆ ◆ ◆ ◆

A TAXING MISSION: THE MISSION OF THE INTERNAL REVENUE SERVICE

In real life, following close on the heels of the nation's top companies, is another organization dedicated to its own singular purpose: the U.S. Internal Revenue Service.

So it seems fitting to close this survey of corporate mission statements with the official mission of the I.R.S.

THE IRS MISSION

Provide America's taxpayers top quality service by helping them understand and meet their tax responsibilities and by applying the tax law with integrity and fairness to all.

Source: I.R.S. Document 6897 (Rev. 9-98)

PART III

INDEX 1 | COMPANIES ARRANGED BY INDUSTRY CATEGORY

Communications and Telecommunications

Ameritech
AT&T Corp.
Comptek Research, Inc.
Lucent Technologies Inc.
MCI Communications Corporation
Sprint

Construction

Butler Manufacturing Company
Caterpillar Inc.
Kaufman and Broad Home Corporation
Lafarge Corporation
Perini Corporation
Ply Gem Industries, Inc.
Turner Corporation, The

Consumer Goods and Services

Avon Products, Inc.
Blockbuster Inc.
Clorox Company, The
Fortune Brands, Inc.
Gillette Company, The
Johnson Wax (S.C. Johnson & Sons, Inc.)
Jostens, Inc.
Kellwood Company
Levi Strauss & Co.
Nike
Rubbermaid Incorporated
Shaklee U.S., Inc.
Stride Rite Corporation
TravelSmith
Tultex Corporation
VF Corporation

Diversified

Eastern Enterprises
General Electric Company
Rollins Inc.
TRW Inc.

United Dominion Industries
United Vision Group
WICOR, Inc.
WMX Technologies, Inc.

Electronics

AMP Incorporated
Kent Electronics Corporation
Litton Industries
Rockwell International Corporation
Sensormatic

Environmental Engineering

Geraghty & Miller, Inc.

Financial Investment Services

Advest, Inc.
American Express
Edwards (A.G. Edwards & Sons, Inc.)
General Motors Acceptance Corporation (GMAC)
Household International, Inc.
MBIA Inc.
Merrill Lynch & Co., Inc.
Schwab (The Charles Schwab Corporation)

Food/Beverage

Anheuser-Busch Companies, Inc.
Ben & Jerry's Homemade, Inc.
Bruno's, Inc.
Coca-Cola
ConAgra
Dreyer's Grand Ice Cream, Inc.
Flagstar Companies, Inc.
Fleming Companies, Inc.
Foremost Farms USA
General Mills, Inc.
Hershey Foods Corporation
Hormel Foods Corporation
Kellogg's (Kellogg Company)
Kroger Co., The

Mid-America Dairymen, Inc.
Mondavi (Robert Mondavi Winery)
PepsiCo, Inc.
Pillsbury Company, The
Rich Products Corporation
Rykoff-Sexton, Inc.
Savannah Foods & Industries, Inc.
Stroh Brewery Company, The
SYSCO Corporation
Tootsie Roll Industries, Inc.
Universal Foods Corporation
Vons Companies, Inc., The
Wendy's International, Inc.

Forest Products, Wood Processing, Paper
Potlatch Corporation
Weyerhaeuser

Health Care
Bard (C.R. Bard, Inc.)
Columbia/HCA Healthcare Corp.
Continental Medical Systems, Inc.
Johnson & Johnson
Warner-Lambert Company

High Technology
Apple Computer
Autodesk, Inc.
Computer Sciences Corporation
Computervision Corporation
Conner Peripherals, Inc.
Cray Research, Inc.
Hewlett-Packard Company
IBM (International Business Machines Corporation)
LSI Logic Corporation
Microsoft Corporation
National Semiconductor
SAS Institute Inc.
Texas Instruments

Hotel, Hospitality, and Entertainment
Harrah's Entertainment, Inc.
International Game Technology
Marriott International, Inc.
Westin Hotels & Resorts

Industrial, Specialized
Alliant Techsystems, Inc.
AlliedSignal Inc.
Carpenter Technology Corporation
CBI Industries, Inc.
Ferro Corporation
Flowserve Corporation
Safety-Kleen Corporation
UTILX Corporation
Vulcan Materials Company

Insurance
American Family Insurance Group
American United Life Insurance
    Company
Ameritas Life Insurance Corp.
CNA Insurance Companies
CUNA Mutual Insurance Group
General American Life Insurance
    Company
Kansas City Life Insurance Company
Kemper Corporation
Keyport Life Insurance Company
Lincoln National Corporation
New York Life
Northwestern Mutual Life
Principal Financial Group
Protective Life Corporation
State Auto Insurance Companies
United States Fidelity and Guaranty
    Corporation
UNUM Corporation

Manufacturing

Aeroquip-Vickers, Inc.
AMETEK Inc.
Armstrong World Industries, Inc.
Baldor Electric Company
Ball Corporation
Bethlehem Steel
Chemfab Corporation
Copperweld Corporation
Corning Incorporated
Deere & Company (John Deere)
Eaton Corporation
Federal-Mogul Corporation
Fuller (H.B. Fuller Company)
Harsco Corporation
Haworth Inc.
Ingersoll-Rand Company
Inland Paperboard & Packaging, Inc.
Inland Steel Industries
Kaydon Corporation
Oneida Ltd.
Reynolds Metals Company
Sonoco Products Company
Sta-Rite Industries
Varlen Corporation
Weirton Steel Corporation
Wellman, Inc.
York International

Media

Banta Corporation
Gannett Company, Inc.
Knight-Ridder, Inc.
Scripps (The E.W. Scripps Company)
Time Warner
Times Mirror Company
Tribune Company
Valassis Communications, Inc.

Medical Products and Services

Baxter Healthcare Corporation
Haemonetics Corporation
Owens & Minor
SpaceLabs Medical, Inc.

Motor Vehicles and Related

Coachmen Industries, Inc.
Cooper Tire & Rubber Company
Dana Corporation
Donnelly Corporation
Ford Motor Company
General Motors Corporation
Goodyear Tire & Rubber Company
Saturn Corporation
Winnebago Industries, Inc.

Oil and Gas

Chevron Corporation
Diamond Shamrock, Inc.
Energen Corporation
Exxon
Forest Oil Corporation
Maxus Energy Corporation
Shell Chemical Company
Sun Company
Unocal Corporation

Package Delivery Service

Airborne Express
FDX Corporation (FedEx)
United Parcel Service

Pharmaceutical/Biotechnology

Amgen
ICN Pharmaceuticals, Inc.
Merck & Co., Inc.
Pfizer
Research Industries Corporation
Rhône-Poulenc Rorer Inc.

Retail

Ace Hardware Corporation
Federated Department Stores, Inc.
Gibson Greetings, Inc.
Kmart
Lowe's Companies, Inc.
Meyer (Fred Meyer, Inc.)
Penney (J.C. Penney Company, Inc.)
Tandy Corporation (RadioShack)
United States Shoe Corporation, The

**Scientific, Photo, and Control
Equipment**

Bausch & Lomb Incorporated
Becton Dickinson and Company
Honeywell
Medtronic, Inc.
Minnesota Mining and Manufacturing
    Company (3M)

Security

American Protective Services, Inc.
Borg-Warner Security Corporation

Transportation

AMR Corporation (American Airlines)
Avis Rent A Car
Burlington Northern Santa Fe
    Corporation
Consolidated Freightways, Inc.
Continental Airlines
CSX Corporation

Delta Air Lines, Inc.
Landstar Systems, Inc.
Norfolk Southern Corporation
Ryder System, Inc.
SkyWest Airlines, Inc.
Southwest Airlines Co.

Utility

Atlanta Gas Light Company
CMS Energy
Duke Power Company
FPL Group, Inc.
General Public Utilities Corporation
Houston Industries Incorporated
Illinova Corporation
Kansas City Power & Light Company
Montana Power Company
Niagara Mohawk Power Corp.
Northeast Utilities
Northern States Power Company
Oklahoma Natural Gas Company
PacifiCorp
Pennsylvania Power & Light Company
Public Service Enterprise Group
    Incorporated
Southern California Edison Company
Southern Company
Union Electric
Washington Gas
Wisconsin Energy Corporation
Wisconsin Public Service Corporation

Haworth Inc.
Kaydon Corporation
Kellogg's (Kellogg Company)
Kelly Services, Inc.
Kmart
Old Kent Financial Corporation
Stroh Brewery Company, The
Valassis Communications, Inc.

Minnesota

Alliant Techsystems, Inc.
Cenex, Inc.
Cray Research, Inc.
Deluxe Corporation
Ecolab Inc.
Fuller (H.B. Fuller Company)
General Mills, Inc.
Honeywell
Hormel Foods Corporation
Jostens, Inc.
Medtronic, Inc.
Minnesota Mining and Manufacturing
    Company (3M)
Northern States Power Company
Pillsbury Company, The
TCF Financial Corporation
U.S. Bancorp

Mississippi

Deposit Guaranty Corp.

Missouri

Anheuser-Busch Companies, Inc.
Butler Manufacturing Company
Edwards (A.G. Edwards & Sons, Inc.)
General American Life Insurance
    Company
Kansas City Life Insurance Company
Kansas City Power & Light Company
Kellwood Company
Maritz Inc.

Mid-America Dairyman, Inc.
Union Electric

Montana

Montana Power Company

Nebraska

Ameritas Life Insurance Corp.
Commercial Federal Corporation
ConAgra

Nevada

International Game Technology

New Hampshire

Chemfab Corporation

New Jersey

AlliedSignal Inc.
Bard (C.R. Bard, Inc.)
Becton Dickinson and Company
General Public Utilities Corporation
Hoechst Celanese Corporation
Ingersoll-Rand Company
Johnson & Johnson
Lucent Technologies Inc.
Merck & Co., Inc.
Public Service Enterprise Group
    Incorporated
Warner-Lambert Company
Wellman, Inc.

New York

American Express
AT&T Corp.
Avis Rent A Car
Avon Products, Inc.
Bausch & Lomb Incorporated
Chase Manhattan Corporation
Chemical Banking Corporation
Citicorp
Comptek Research, Inc.
Corning Incorporated

IBM (International Business Machines
    Corporation)
MBIA Inc.
Merrill Lynch & Co., Inc.
New York Life
Niagara Mohawk Power Corp.
Oneida Ltd.
PepsiCo, Inc.
Pfizer
Ply Gem Industries, Inc.
Rich Products Corporation
Time Warner
Turner Corporation, The
United Vision Group

North Carolina
Centura Banks, Inc.
Duke Power Company
Lowe's Companies, Inc.
SAS Institute Inc.
United Dominion Industries
VF Corporation

Ohio
Aeroquip-Vickers, Inc.
Cooper Tire & Rubber Company
Dana Corporation
Eaton Corporation
Federated Department Stores, Inc.
Ferro Corporation
Gibson Greetings, Inc.
Goodyear Tire & Rubber Company
Hanna (M.A. Hanna Company)
Huntington Bancshares Incorporated
Kroger Co., The
OfficeMax, Inc.
Rubbermaid Incorporated
Scripps (The E.W. Scripps Company)
Standard Register Company, The
State Auto Insurance Companies
TRW Inc.

United States Shoe Corporation, The
Wendy's International, Inc.

Oklahoma
Fleming Companies, Inc.
Oklahoma Natural Gas Company

Oregon
Meyer (Fred Meyer, Inc.)
Nike
PacifiCorp

Pennsylvania
AMETEK Inc.
AMP Incorporated
Aristech Chemical Corporation
Armstrong World Industries, Inc.
Bethlehem Steel
Betz Laboratories, Inc.
Carpenter Technology Corporation
Continental Medical Systems, Inc.
Copperweld Corporation
Harsco Corporation
Hershey Foods Corporation
Meridian Bancorp, Inc.
Pennsylvania Power & Light Company
Rhône-Poulenc Rorer Inc.
Sun Company
Unisys Corporation
York International

South Carolina
Flagstar Companies, Inc.
Sonoco Products Company

Tennessee
Columbia/HCA Healthcare Corp.
FDX Corporation (FedEx)
First American Corporation
First Tennessee National Corporation
Harrah's Entertainment, Inc.
Saturn Corporation

Texas

AMR Corporation (American Airlines)
Blockbuster Inc.
Burlington Northern Santa Fe
   Corporation
Continental Airlines
Diamond Shamrock, Inc.
Exxon
Flowserve Corporation
Houston Industries Incorporated
Kent Electronics Corporation
Lyondell Petrochemical Company
Maxus Energy Corporation
Penney (J.C. Penney Company, Inc.)
Shell Chemical Company
Southwest Airlines Co.
SYSCO Corporation
Tandy Corporation (RadioShack)
Texas Instruments

Utah

Research Industries Corporation
SkyWest Airlines, Inc.

Vermont

Ben & Jerry's Homemade, Inc.

Virginia

CSX Corporation
Ethyl Corporation
First Virginia Banks, Inc.
Gannett Company, Inc.
Lafarge Corporation

Norfolk Southern Corporation
Owens & Minor
Reynolds Metals Company
Tultex Corporation

Washington

Airborne Express
Microsoft Corporatio
Potlatch Corporation
SpaceLabs Medical, Inc.
UTILX Corporation
Washington Mutual Inc.
Westin Hotels & Resorts
Weyerhaeuser

West Virginia

Weirton Steel Corporation

Wisconsin

American Family Insurance Group
Banta Corporation
CUNA Mutual Insurance Group
Foremost Farms USA
Johnson Controls, Inc.
Johnson Wax (S.C. Johnson & Sons,
   Inc.)
Northwestern Mutual Life
Sta-Rite Industries
Universal Foods Corporation
WICOR, Inc.
Wisconsin Energy Corporation
Wisconsin Public Service Corporation